A BRAND-NEW YEAR—
A PROMISING NEW START

With expert readings and forecasts, you can chart a course to romance, adventure, good health, or career opportunities while gaining valuable insight into yourself and others. Offering a daily outlook for 18 full months, this fascinating guide shows you:

- The important dates in your life
- What to expect from an astrological reading
- How the stars can help you stay healthy and fit
  And more!

Let this sound advice guide you through a year of heavenly possibilities—for today and for every day of 2008!

SYDNEY OMARR'S® DAY-BY-DAY
ASTROLOGICAL GUIDE FOR

ARIES—March 21–April 19
TAURUS—April 20–May 20
GEMINI—May 21–June 20
CANCER—June 21–July 22
LEO—July 23–August 22
VIRGO—August 23–September 22
LIBRA—September 23–October 22
SCORPIO—October 23–November 21
SAGITTARIUS—November 22–December 21
CAPRICORN—December 22–January 19
AQUARIUS—January 20–February 18
PISCES—February 19–March 20

IN 2008

SYDNEY OMARR'S®

DAY-BY-DAY ASTROLOGICAL GUIDE FOR

LIBRA

SEPTEMBER 23–OCTOBER 22

2008

By Trish MacGregor
with Carol Tonsing

A SIGNET BOOK

SIGNET
Published by New American Library, a division of
Penguin Group (USA) Inc., 375 Hudson Street,
New York, New York 10014, USA
Penguin Group (Canada), 90 Eglinton Avenue East, Suite 700, Toronto,
Ontario M4P 2Y3, Canada (a division of Pearson Penguin Canada Inc.)
Penguin Books Ltd., 80 Strand, London WC2R 0RL, England
Penguin Ireland, 25 St. Stephen's Green, Dublin 2,
Ireland (a division of Penguin Books Ltd.)
Penguin Group (Australia), 250 Camberwell Road, Camberwell, Victoria 3124,
Australia (a division of Pearson Australia Group Pty. Ltd.)
Penguin Books India Pvt. Ltd., 11 Community Centre, Panchsheel Park,
New Delhi - 110 017, India
Penguin Group (NZ), 67 Apollo Drive, Rosedale, North Shore,
Auckland 1311, New Zealand (a division of Pearson New Zealand Ltd.)
Penguin Books (South Africa) (Pty.) Ltd., 24 Sturdee Avenue,
Rosebank, Johannesburg 2196, South Africa

Penguin Books Ltd., Registered Offices:
80 Strand, London WC2R 0RL, England

First published by Signet, an imprint of New American Library,
a division of Penguin Group (USA) Inc.

First Printing, June 2007
10 9 8 7 6 5 4 3 2 1

PUBLISHER'S NOTE
While the author has made every effort to provide accurate telephone numbers
and Internet addresses at the time of publication, neither the publisher nor the
author assumes any responsibility for errors, or for changes that occur after publication. Further, publisher does not have any control over and does not assume
any responsibility for author or third-party Web sites or their content.

If you purchased this book without a cover you should be aware that this book
is stolen property. It was reported as "unsold and destroyed" to the publisher
and neither the author nor the publisher has received any payment for this
"stripped book."

The scanning, uploading and distribution of this book via the Internet or via any
other means without the permission of the publisher is illegal and punishable by
law. Please purchase only authorized electronic editions, and do not participate
in or encourage electronic piracy of copyrighted materials. Your support of the
author's rights is appreciated.

CONTENTS

♎ INTRODUCTION

Put Astrology in Your Life

This year marks a time of transition as our personal universe opens up with possibilities we never imagined. Thanks to the Internet, we have a command-control center from which we can travel the globe at warp speed. We can meet friends and lovers in cyberspace, gather information from remote sources in moments, and manage the details of our daily lives online. But, as the saying goes, the more things change, the more they stay the same. In our personal lives, we are still searching for the same things that have always made life worth living: love, meaningful work, and fulfilling personal relationships.

Astrology is an age-old tool that can guide us in our search, one that works as well today as it has for several millennia. It can be a support system, career coach, and guide through difficult times. It can help you find your own strengths or assess your marketable talents to land the perfect job. Like links in the Internet, astrological clues can speed you from where you are now to where you'd like to be. But just like many of the newest high-tech laptops, there's a learning curve before you can use it to best advantage. It will take some practice and familiarity to operate effectively in your life. Fortunately a little knowledge can get you up and running quickly.

In this year's guide, we give you basic information to help you get hands-on with astrology. We tell you what you need to know about your sun sign and how to decipher the mysterious symbols on a horoscope chart. Then you can look up other planets in your horoscope to find out how each contributes to your total personality.

Many readers are fascinated by astrology's insights into

relationships. This leap year, find out who you're most likely to get along with and why, then how to attract the right sign. You'll see the celebrity combinations with your sign that made romantic history—and some that didn't.

Whether it's wealth-building advice, fashion tips, or help finding the perfect gift for a hard-to-please relative, astrology has something to say. Astrology can even guide you to the best place to take your vacation. For those who like to surf the Web, we recommend astrology-savvy sites where you can get your chart calculated free. Connecting with other astrology fans is a breeze with the reputable conferences, clubs, and even an accredited college that we list.

There are so many ways to put astrology into your life. Redecorating your home? Follow your sun sign's colors and styles to create the perfect environment. Share your birthday with a celebrity. Design a fitness program according to your sign's preferences.

So here are the year's picks and predictions, along with eighteen months of on-target daily horoscopes to make 2008 your best year ever.

CHAPTER 1

It's A Year of Change: What This Means for You

Astrologers judge the trends of a year by following the slow-moving planets, from Jupiter through Pluto. A change in sign indicates a new cycle, with new emphasis. The farthest planets (Uranus, Neptune, and Pluto), which stay in a sign for at least seven years, cause a very significant change in the atmosphere when they change signs. Shifts in Jupiter, which changes every year, and Saturn, which changes every two years, are more obvious in current events and daily lives. Jupiter generally brings a fortunate, expansive emphasis to its new sign, while Saturn's two-year cycle is a reality check, bringing tests of maturity, discipline, and responsibility.

Does Pluto Still Count?

At this writing, astronomers have demoted tiny Pluto from being a full-fledged planet to a dwarf planet, outranked by its celestial siblings. However, astrologers have been tracking its influence since Pluto was discovered in 1930 and have witnessed that this minuscule celestial body has a powerful effect on both a personal and a global level. So Pluto, which moves into the sign of Capricorn this year, will still be called a planet by astrologers and will be given just as much importance as before.

Capricorn Is the Sign to Watch

This year, we will be moving from a fire-sign emphasis to an earth-sign emphasis as Jupiter, Saturn, and Pluto all take up residence in earth signs. Until January 2008, Pluto had been emphasizing everything associated with Sagittarius to prepare us philosphically and spiritually for things to come. Perhaps the most pervasive sign of Pluto in Sagittarius over the past few years has been globalization in all its forms, re-forming boundaries, creating new forms of travel, interacting with exotic cultures and religions as never before.

As it passed through truth-telling Sagittarius, Pluto shifted our emphasis away from acquiring wealth to a quest for the meaning of it all, as upward strivers discover that money and power are not enough and religious extremists assert themselves. We search the cosmos for something to believe in when many lies and scandals are exposed to public view, exposing leaders in the corporate, political, and religious domains. When ideals and idols are shattered, it becomes time to reevaluate our goals and ask ourselves what is really important in our lives.

Sagittarius is the sign of linking everything together; therefore, the trend has been to find ways to interconnect on spiritual, philosophical, and intellectual levels. The spiritual emphasis of Pluto in Sagittarius has filtered down to our home lives, as religion—and religious controversy—has entered local communities. Vast church complexes are being built to combine religious activities with sports centers, health clubs, malls, and theme parks. Religious education and book publishing have expanded as well.

Sagittarius is known for love of animals, especially horses. It's no surprise that horse racing has become popular again and that America has never been more pet happy. Look for extremes related to animal welfare, such as vegetarianism as a lifestyle. As habitats are destroyed, the care, feeding, and control of wild animals will become a larger issue, especially when deer, bears, and coyotes invade our backyard.

The Sagittarius love of the outdoors combined with

Pluto's power has already promoted extreme sports, especially those that require strong legs, like rock climbing, trekking, or snowboarding. Expect the trend toward more adventurous travel to continue, as well as fitness or sports-oriented vacations. Exotic hiking trips to unexplored territories, mountain-climbing expeditions, spa vacations, and sports-associated resorts are part of this trend.

Publishing, which is associated with Sagittarius, has been transformed by global conglomerates and the Internet. It is fascinating that the online bookstore Amazon.com took the Sagittarius-influenced name of the fierce female tribe of archer warriors.

Capricorn Brings Us Down to Earth

This year, both Pluto and Jupiter will meet in Capricorn, which marks a major shift in emphasis to Capricorn-related themes. Until 2024, Pluto will exert its influence in this practical, building, healing earth sign. Capricorn relates to structures, institutions, order, mountains and mountain countries, mineral rights, and issues involving the elderly and growing older—all of which will be emphasized in the coming years. It is the sign of established order, corporations, big business—all of which will be accented. Possibly, it will fall to business structures to create a new sense of order in the world.

Starting this year, you should feel the rumblings of change in the Capricorn area of your horoscope and in the world at large. The last time Pluto was in Capricorn was the years up to and during the American Revolutionary War. Therefore this should be an important time on the United States political scene, as well as a reflection of the aging and maturing of American society in general. Both the rise and fall of the Ottoman Empire happened under Pluto in Capricorn.

Jupiter in Capricorn

During the year that Jupiter remains in a sign, the fields associated with that sign are the ones that arouse excitement and enthusiasm, usually providing excellent opportunities for expansion, fame, and fortune.

One place we notice the Jupiter influence is in fashion, which should veer away from the flamboyance and sexuality of recent years to a more conservative look. Capricorn is concerned with quality, status, and prestige, and should elevate our collective taste level.

Those born under Capricorn should have many opportunities during the year. However, the key is to keep your feet on the ground. The flip side of Jupiter is that there are no limits. You can expand off the planet under a Jupiter transit, which is why the planet is often called the Gateway to Heaven. If something is going to burst (such as an artery) or overextend or go over the top in some way, it could happen under a supposedly lucky Jupiter transit. So beware.

Those born under Cancer may find their best opportunities working with partners this year, as Jupiter will be transiting their seventh house of relationships.

Saturn in Virgo: The Maturing of the Baby Boomers, Reforms in Care and Maintenance

Saturn, the planet of limitation, testing, and restriction, is now transiting Virgo. This is a time when Virgo issues— health care and maintenance and moral standards and controls—will come to the fore. For the next two years, we will be adjusting the structures of our lives, making changes so that we can function at an optimal efficient level. We'll be challenged with a reality check in areas where we have been too optimistic or expansive.

Continuing Trends

Uranus and Neptune continue to do a kind of astrological dance called a mutual reception. This is a supportive relationship where Uranus is in Pisces, the sign ruled by Neptune, while Neptune is in Aquarius, the sign ruled by Uranus. When this dance is over in 2011, it is likely that we will be living under very different political and social circumstances.

Uranus in Pisces

Uranus, known as the Great Awakener, tends to cause both upheaval and innovation in the sign it transits. During previous episodes of Uranus in Pisces, great religions and spiritual movements have come into being, most recently Mormonism and Christian Fundamentalism. In its most positive mode, Pisces promotes imagination and creativity, the art of illusion in theater and film, the inspiration of great artists. A water sign, Pisces is naturally associated with all things liquid—oceans, oil, alcohol—and with those creatures that live in the water—fish, the fishing industry, fish habitats, and fish farming. Currently there is a great debate going on about overfishing, contamination of fish, and fish farming. The underdog, the enslaved, and the disenfranchised should also benefit from Uranus in Pisces.

Since Uranus is a disruptive influence that aims to challenge the status quo, the forces of nature that manifest will most likely be in the Pisces area: oceans, seas, and rivers. We have seen unprecedented rainy seasons, floods, mud slides, and disastrous hurricanes. Note that 2005's devastating Hurricane Katrina hit an area known for both the oil and fishing industries.

Pisces is associated with the prenatal phase of life, which is related to regenerative medicine. The controversy over embryonic stem cell research should continue to be debated. Petroleum issues, both in the oil-producing countries and offshore oil drilling, will come to a head. Uranus in

Pisces suggests that development of new hydroelectric sources may provide the power we need to continue our current power-thirsty lifestyle.

As in previous eras, there should continue to be a flourishing of the arts. We are seeing many new artistic forms developing now, such as computer-created actors and special effects. The sky's the limit on this influence.

Those who have problems with Uranus are those who resist change, so the key is to embrace the future.

Neptune in Aquarius

Neptune is a planet of imagination and creativity, but also of deception and illusion. Neptune is associated with hospitals, which have been the subject of much controversy. On the positive side, hospitals are acquiring cutting-edge technology. The atmosphere of many hospitals is already changing from the intimidating and sterile environment of the past to that of a health-promoting spa. Alternative therapies, such as massage, diet counseling, and aromatherapy, are becoming commonplace, which expresses this Neptune trend. New procedures in plastic surgery, also a Neptune glamour field, and anti-aging therapies are restoring the illusion of youth.

However, issues involving the expense and quality of health care and the evolving relationship between doctors, drug companies, and HMOs reflect a darker side of this trend.

What About the New Planets?

Our solar system is very crowded; astronomers continue to discover new objects circling the sun. In addition to the familiar planets, there are dwarf planets, comets, cometoids, asteroids, and strange icy bodies in the Kuiper Belt beyond Neptune. The newest object at this writing is a planetlike orb slightly larger than Pluto, discovered in 2005, which was tentatively named Xena, after the TV series heroine. Recently this dwarf planet was christened with a permanent name by its dicoverer, Dr. Michael E. Brown of the California Institute of Technology. He dubbed the new planet Eris, after a goddess of discord and strife. In mythology, Eris was a troublemaker who made men think their opinions were right and others wrong. What an appropriate name for a planet discovered during a time of discord in the Middle East and elsewhere! Eris has a companion moon named Dysnomia for her daughter, described as a demon spirit of lawlessness. With mythological associations like these, we wonder what the effect of this mother-daughter duo will be. Once Eris's orbit is established, astrologers will track the impact of this planet on our horoscopes. Eris takes about 560 years to orbit the sun, which means its emphasis in a given astrological sign will affect several generations.

♎ CHAPTER 2

Put Time on Your Side

"Do not squander time, for that is the stuff that life is made of," said Benjamin Franklin, our practical Founding Father. Yet many times your best-laid plans run amuck, your schedule is upset by sudden events, or your projects stall. On the other hand, there are days when projects get done effortlessly, people respond to you favorably, and perhaps you have some extra sex appeal.

Astrology offers many explanations why this might happen. For instance, when mischievous Mercury creates havoc with communications, it's time to back up your vital computer files, read between the lines of contracts, and be extra patient with coworkers. When Venus passes through your sign you've got extra sex appeal, time to try a knockout new outfit or hairstyle, and the nerve to ask someone you'd like to know better to dinner. Venus timing can also help you charm clients with a stunning sales pitch or make an offer they won't refuse.

In this chapter, you will learn how to manage your time by working with natural astrological cycles. You can find your best times to do specific projects as well as which times to avoid them. You will also learn how to read the moods of the moon and make them work for you. Use the information in this chapter and the planet tables in this book and also use the moon sign listings in your daily forecasts.

Here are the happenings to note on your agenda:

- Dates of your sun sign (high-energy period)
- The month previous to your sun sign (low-energy period)

- Dates of planets in your sign this year
- Full and new moons (Pay special attention when these fall in your sun sign!)
- Eclipses
- Moon in your sun sign every month, as well as moon in the opposite sign (listed in daily forecast)
- Mercury retrogrades
- Other retrograde periods

Your High-Power Time

Every birthday starts off a new cycle of solar energy for you. You should feel a new surge of vitality as the powerful sun enters your sign. This is the time when predominant energies are most favorable to you. So go for it! Start new projects, make your big moves (especially when the new moon is in your sign, doubling your charisma). You'll get the recognition you deserve now, when everyone is attuned to your sun sign. Look in the tables in this book to see if other planets will also be passing through your sun sign at this time. Venus (love, beauty), Mars (energy, drive), and Mercury (communication, mental sharpness) reinforce the sun and give an extra boost to your life in the areas they affect. Venus will rev up your social and love life, making you seem especially attractive. Mars amplifies your energy and drive. Mercury fuels your brainpower and helps you communicate. Jupiter signals an especially lucky period of expansion.

There are two downtimes related to the sun. During the month before your birthday period, when you are winding up your annual cycle, you could be feeling especially vulnerable and depleted. So at that time get extra rest, watch your diet, and take it easy. Don't overstress yourself. Use this time to gear up for a big "push" when the sun enters your sign.

Another downtime is when the sun is in a sign opposite your sun sign (six months from your birthday). That's when the prevailing energies are very different from yours. You may feel at odds with the world. You'll have to work harder for recognition because people are not on your wavelength. However, this could be a good time to work on a team, in cooperation with others, or behind the scenes.

Plan Your Day with the Moon

The moon is a powerful tool to divine the mood of the moment. You can work with the moon in two ways. Plan by the *sign* the moon is in; plan by the *phase* of the moon. The sign will tell you the kind of activities that suit the moon's mood. The phase will tell you the best time to start or finish a certain activity.

Working with the phases of the moon is as easy as looking up at the night sky. During the new moon, when both the sun and moon are in the same sign, begin new ventures—especially activities that are favored by that sign. Then you'll utilize the powerful energies pulling you in the same direction. You'll be focused outward, toward action, and in a doing mode. Postpone breaking off, terminating, deliberating, or reflecting—activities that require introspection and passive work. These are better suited to a later moon phase.

Get your project under way during the first quarter. Then go public at the full moon, a time of high intensity, when feelings come out into the open. This is your time to shine—to express yourself. Be aware, however, that because pressures are being released, other people will also be letting off steam. Since confrontations are possible, take advantage of this time either to air grievances or to avoid arguments.

About three days after the full moon comes the disseminating phase, a time when the energy of the cycle begins to wind down. From the last quarter of the moon to the next new moon, it's a time to cut off unproductive relationships, do serious thinking, and focus on inward-directed activities.

You'll feel some new and full moons more strongly than others, especially those new moons that fall in your sun sign and full moons in your opposite sign. Because that full moon happens at your low-energy time of year, it is likely to be an especially stressful time in a relationship, when any hidden problems or unexpressed emotions could surface.

Full and New Moons in 2008

All dates are calculated for eastern standard time and eastern daylight time.

New Moon—January 8 in Capricorn
Full Moon—January 22 in Leo

New Moon—February 6 in Aquarius (solar eclipse)
Full Moon—February 20 in Virgo (lunar eclipse)

New Moon—March 7 in Pisces
Full Moon—March 21 in Libra

New Moon—April 5 in Aries
Full Moon—April 20 in Scorpio

New Moon—May 5 in Taurus
Full Moon—May 19 in Scorpio (second full moon in Scorpio)

New Moon—June 3 in Gemini
Full Moon—June 18 in Sagittarius

New Moon—July 2 in Cancer
Full Moon—July 18 in Capricorn

New Moon—August 1 in Leo (solar eclipse)
Full Moon—August 16 in Aquarius (lunar eclipse)
New Moon—August 30 in Virgo

Full Moon—September 15 in Pisces
New Moon—September 29 in Libra

Full Moon—October 14 in Aries

New Moon—October 28 in Scorpio

Full Moon—November 13 in Taurus
New Moon—November 27 in Sagittarius

New Moon—December 12 in Gemini
Full Moon—December 27 in Capricorn

How to Schedule Activities by the Moon Sign

To forecast the daily emotional "weather," to determine your monthly high and low days, or to synchronize your activities with the cycles of the moon, take note of the moon sign under your daily forecast at the end of the book. Here are some of the activities favored and the moods you are likely to encounter under each moon sign.

Moon in Aries: Get Moving!

The new moon in Aries is an ideal time to start new projects. Everyone is pushy, raring to go, rather impatient, and short-tempered. Leave details and follow-up for later. Competitive sports or martial arts are great ways to let off steam. Quiet types could use some assertiveness, but it's a great day for dynamos. Be careful not to step on too many toes.

Moon in Taurus: Lay the Foundations for Success

Do solid, methodical tasks like follow-through or backup work. Make investments, buy real estate, do appraisals, do some hard bargaining. Attend to your property. Get out in the country or spend some time in your garden. Enjoy creature comforts, music, a good dinner, sensual lovemaking. Forget starting a diet—this is a day when you'll feel self-indulgent.

14

Moon in Gemini: Communicate

Talk means action today. Telephone, write letters, fax! Make new contacts, stay in touch with steady customers. You can juggle lots of tasks today. It's a great time for mental activity of any kind. Don't try to pin people down— they, too, are feeling restless. Keep it light. Flirtations and socializing are good. Watch gossip—and don't give away secrets.

Moon in Cancer: Pay Attention to Loved Ones

This is a moody, sensitive, emotional time. People respond to personal attention, to mothering. Stay at home, have a family dinner, call your mother. Nostalgia, memories, and psychic powers are heightened. You'll want to hang on to people and things (don't clean out your closets now). You could have shrewd insights into what others really need and want. Pay attention to dreams, intuition, and gut reactions.

Moon in Leo: Be Confident

Everybody is in a much more confident, warm, generous mood. It's a good day to ask for a raise, show what you can do, dress like a star. People will respond to flattery, enjoy a bit of drama and theater. You may be extravagant, treat yourself royally, and show off a bit—but don't break the bank! Be careful you don't promise more than you can deliver.

Moon in Virgo: Be Practical

Do practical down-to-earth chores. Review your budget, make repairs, be an efficiency expert. Not a day to ask for a raise. Tend to personal care and maintenance. Have a health checkup, go on a diet, buy vitamins or health food. Make your home spotless. Take care of details and piled-up chores. Reorganize your work and life so they run more smoothly and efficiently. Save money. Be prepared for others to be in a critical, faultfinding mood.

Moon in Libra: Be Diplomatic

Attend to legal matters. Negotiate contracts. Arbitrate. Do things with your favorite partner. Socialize. Be romantic. Buy a special gift, a beautiful object. Decorate yourself or your surroundings. Buy new clothes. Throw a party. Have an elegant, romantic evening. Smooth over any ruffled feathers. Avoid confrontations. Stick to civilized discussions.

Moon in Scorpio: Solve Problems

This is a day to do things with passion. You'll have excellent concentration and focus. Try not to get too intense emotionally. Avoid sharp exchanges with loved ones. Others may tend to go to extremes, get jealous, overreact. Great for troubleshooting, problem solving, research, scientific work—and making love. Pay attention to those psychic vibes.

Moon in Sagittarius: Sell and Motivate

A great time for travel, philosophical discussions, setting long-range career goals. Work out, do sports, buy athletic equipment. Others will be feeling upbeat, exuberant, and adventurous. Risk taking is favored. You may feel like taking a gamble, betting on the horses, visiting a local casino, buying a lottery ticket. Teaching, writing, and spiritual activities also get the green light. Relax outdoors. Take care of animals.

Moon in Capricorn: Get Organized

You can accomplish a lot now, so get on the ball! Attend to business. Issues concerning your basic responsibilities, duties, family, and elderly parents could crop up. You'll be expected to deliver on promises. Weed out the deadwood from your life. Get a dental checkup. Not a good day for gambling or taking risks.

Moon in Aquarius: Join the Group

A great day for doing things with groups—clubs, meetings, outings, politics, parties. Campaign for your candidate. Work for a worthy cause. Deal with larger issues that affect humanity—the environment and metaphysical questions. Buy a computer or electronic gadget. Watch TV. Wear something outrageous. Try something you've never done before. Present an original idea. Don't stick to a rigid schedule—go with the flow. Take a class in meditation, mind control, yoga.

Moon in Pisces: Be Creative

This can be a very creative day, so let your imagination work overtime. Film, theater, music, ballet could inspire you. Spend some time alone, resting and reflecting, reading or writing poetry. Daydreams can also be profitable. Help those less fortunate. Lend a listening ear to someone who may be feeling blue. Don't overindulge in self-pity or escapism, however. People are especially vulnerable to substance abuse now. Turn your thoughts to romance and someone special.

Retrogrades: When the Planets Seem to Backstep

All the planets, except for the sun and moon, have times when they appear to move backward—or retrograde—as it seems from our point of view on earth. At these times, planets do not work as they normally do. So it's best to "take a break" from that planet's energies in our life and to do some work on an inner level.

Mercury Retrograde: The Key Is in "Re"

Mercury goes retrograde most often, and its effects can be especially irritating. When it reaches a short distance ahead of the sun several times a year, it seems to move backward from our point of view. Astrologers often compare retrograde motion to the optical illusion that occurs when we ride on a train that passes another train traveling at a different speed—the second train appears to be moving in reverse.

What this means to you is that the Mercury-ruled areas of your life—analytical thought processes, communications, scheduling—are subject to all kinds of confusion. Be prepared. Communications equipment can break down. Schedules may be changed on short notice. People are late for appointments or don't show up at all. Traffic is terrible. Major purchases malfunction, don't work out, or get delivered in the wrong color. Letters don't arrive or are delivered to the wrong address. Employees will make errors that have to be corrected later. Contracts don't work out or must be renegotiated.

Since most of us can't put our lives on "hold" during Mercury retrogrades, we should learn to tame the trickster and make it work for us. The key is in the prefix *re-*. This is the time to go back over things in your life, *re*flect on what you've done during the previous months. Now you can get deeper insights, spot errors you've missed. So take time to *re*view and *re*evaluate what has happened. *Re*st and *re*ward yourself—it's a good time to take a vacation, especially if you *re*visit a favorite place. *Re*organize your work and finish up projects that are backed up. Clean out your desk and closets. Throw away what you can't *re*cycle. If you must sign contracts or agreements, do so with a contingency clause that lets you *re*evaluate the terms later.

Postpone major purchases or commitments for the time being. Don't get married (unless you're *re*marrying the same person). Try not to *re*ly on other people keeping appointments, contracts, or agreements to the letter; have several alternatives. Double-check and *re*ad between the lines.

Don't buy anything connected with communications or transportation (if you must, be sure to cover yourself).

Mercury retrograding through your sun sign will intensify its effect on your life.

If Mercury was retrograde when you were born, you may be one of the lucky people who don't suffer the frustrations of this period. If so, your mind probably works in a very intuitive, insightful way.

The sign in which Mercury is retrograding can give you an idea of what's in store—as well as the sun signs that will be especially challenged.

Mercury Retrogrades in 2008

Mercury has three retrograde periods, which fall in the air signs (Aquarius, Gemini, Libra) this year. This means it will be especially important to watch all activities which involve mental processes and communication.

January 28 to February 18 in Aquarius
May 26 to June 19 in Gemini
September 24 to October 15 in Libra

Venus Retrograde: Relationships Move Backward

Retrograding Venus can cause your relationships to take a backward step, or it can make you extravagant and impractical. Shopping till you drop and buying what you cannot afford are problems at this time. It's *not* a good time to redecorate—you'll hate the color of the walls later. Postpone getting a new hairstyle. Try not to fall in love either. But if you wish to make amends in an already troubled relationship, make peaceful overtures at this time.

Venus Retrogrades in 2008

There are no Venus retrograde periods in 2008.

Use the Go Power of Mars

Mars shows how and when to get where you want to go. Timing your moves with Mars on your side can give you a big push. On the other hand, pushing Mars the wrong way can guarantee that you'll run into frustrations in every corner. Your best times to forge ahead are during the weeks when Mars is traveling through your sun sign or your Mars sign (look these up in the tables in this book). Also consider times when Mars is in a compatible sign (fire with air signs, or earth with water signs). You'll be sure to have planetary power on your side.

Mars Retrogrades in 2008

Mars is retrograde in Gemini until January 30, 2008.

When Other Planets Retrograde

The slower-moving planets stay retrograde for months at a time (Jupiter, Saturn, Neptune, Uranus, and Pluto).

When Saturn is retrograde, it's an uphill battle with self-discipline. You may not be in the mood for work. You may feel more like hanging out at the beach than getting things done.

Neptune retrograde promotes a dreamy escapism from reality, when you may feel you're in a fog (Pisces will feel this, especially).

Uranus retrograde may mean setbacks in areas where there have been sudden changes, when you may be forced to regroup or reevaluate the situation.

Pluto retrograde is a time to work on establishing proportion and balance in areas where there have been recent dramatic transformations.

When the planets move forward again, there's a shift in the atmosphere. Activities connected with each planet start moving ahead, plans that were stalled get rolling. Make a special note of those days on your calendar and proceed accordingly.

Other Retrogrades in 2008

The five slower-moving planets all go retrograde in 2008.

Jupiter retrogrades from May 9 to September 7 in Capricorn.

Saturn retrogrades from December 19, 2007, until May 2, 2008, in Virgo. It turns retrograde again on December 31.

Uranus retrogrades from June 26 to November 27 in Pisces.

Neptune retrogrades from May 26 to November 1 in Aquarius.

Pluto turns retrograde from April 2 in Capricorn, then returns to Sagittarius on June 13. It turns direct in Sagittarius on September 8 and reenters Capricorn on November 26.

♎ CHAPTER 3

Planetary Shake-Ups This Year

When the planetary weather is stormy, it's best to be prepared. Fortunately we can predict certain times when there are more likely to be shake-ups in your world, such as eclipses and Saturn transits, two events that could slow you down or make you change direction. With some basic astrological knowledge, you can find out where these events are likely to impact your life and what to expect when they happen.

Eclipses Clear the Air

Eclipses can bring on milestones in your life, if they aspect a key point in your horoscope. In general, they shake up the status quo, bringing hidden areas out into the open. During this time, problems you've been avoiding or have brushed aside can surface to demand your attention. A good coping strategy is to accept whatever comes up as a challenge that could make a positive difference in your life. And don't forget the power of your sense of humor. If you can laugh at something, you'll never be afraid of it.

What Is the Best Thing to Do During an Eclipse?

When the natural rhythms of the sun and moon are disturbed, it's best to postpone important activities. Be sure to mark eclipse days on your calendar, especially if the eclipse falls in your birth sign. This year, those born under Aquarius, Leo, and Virgo should take special note of the feelings that arise. With lunar eclipses, some possibilities could be a break from attachments or the healing of an illness or substance abuse, which had been triggered by the subconscious. The temporary event could be a healing time, when you gain perspective. During solar eclipses, when you might be in a highly subjective state, pay attention to the hidden subconscious patterns that surface, the emotional truth that is revealed at this time.

The effect of the eclipse can reverberate for some time, often months after the event. But it is especially important to stay cool and make no major moves during the period known as the shadow of the eclipse, which begins about a week before and lasts until at least three days after the eclipse. After three days, the daily rhythms should return to normal, and you can proceed with business as usual.

This Year's Eclipse Dates

February 6: Solar eclipse in Aquarius
February 20: Lunar eclipse in Virgo
August 1: Solar eclipse in Leo
August 16: Lunar eclipse in Aquarius

Saturn Gives You a Reality Check

When Saturn hits a critical point in your horoscope, you can count on an experience that will make you slow up, pull back, and reexamine your life. It is a call to eliminate what is not working, to shape up, to set priorities, to examine the boundaries and structures in your life (or lack of them) and set new ones. During this process, you may feel restricted, frustrated, or inhibited—not a fun time, but one that will serve you well in the long run. You may need to take on more responsibilities that will test your limits.

By the end of its twenty-eight-year trip around the zodiac, Saturn will have tested you in all areas of your life. The major tests happen in seven-year cycles, when Saturn passes over the angles of your chart, which means your rising sign, the top of your chart or midheaven, your descendant, and the nadir or bottom of your chart. This is when the real life-changing experiences happen. But you are also in for a testing period whenever Saturn passes a planet in your chart or stresses that planet from a distance. It is useful to check your planetary positions with the timetable of Saturn or prepare in advance, or at least to brace yourself.

When Saturn returns to its location at the time of your birth, at approximately age twenty-eight, you'll have your first Saturn return. At this time, a person usually takes stock or settles down to find his mission in life and assume full adult duties and responsibilities.

Another way Saturn helps us is to reveal the karmic lessons from previous lives and give us the chance to overcome them. So look at Saturn's challenges as much-needed opportunities for self-improvement.

Outwitting the Planets

Second-guessing Saturn and the eclipses this year is easy if you have a copy of your horoscope calculated by a computer. This enables you to pinpoint the area of your life that will be affected. However, you can make an educated guess, by setting up a rough diagram on your own. If you'd like to find out which area of your life this year's Saturn change is most likely to affect, follow these easy steps.

First, you must know the time of day you were born and look up your rising sign listed on the tables in this book (see chapter 7). Set up an estimated horoscope by drawing a circle, then dividing it into four parts by making a cross directly through the center. Continue to divide each of the parts into thirds, as if you were dividing a cake, until you have twelve slices. Write your rising sign on the middle left-hand slice, which would be the nine o'clock point, if you were looking at your watch. Then write the following signs on the dividing line of each slice, working counterclockwise, until you have listed all twelve signs of the zodiac.

You should now have a basic diagram of your horoscope

chart (minus the planets, of course). Starting with your rising-sign slice, number each portion consecutively, again working counterclockwise.

Since this year's eclipses will fall in Aquarius, Leo, and Virgo, find the number of these slices, or houses, on the chart and read the following descriptions for the kinds of issues that are likely to be emphasized. Saturn is now traveling through Virgo, so check this house in your chart for Saturn-related events.

If an eclipse or Saturn falls in your FIRST HOUSE:
Events cause you to examine the ways you are acting independently and push you to become more visible, to assert yourself. This is a time when you feel compelled to make your own decisions. You may want to change your physical appearance, body image, or style of dress in some way. Under affliction, there might be illness or physical harm.

If an eclipse or Saturn falls in your SECOND HOUSE:
This is the place where you consider all matters of security. You consolidate your resources, earn money, acquire property, and decide what you value and what you want to own. On a deeper level, this house reveals your sense of self-worth.

If an eclipse or Saturn falls in your THIRD HOUSE:
Here you reach out to others, express your ideas, and explore different courses of action. You may feel especially restless or have confrontations with neighbors or siblings. In your search for more knowledge, you may decide to improve your skills, get more education, or sign up for a course that interests you. Local transportation, especially your car, might be affected by an eclipse here.

If an eclipse or Saturn falls in your FOURTH HOUSE:
Here is where you put down roots and establish a base. You'll consider what home really means to you. Issues involving parents, the physical setup or location of your home, and your immediate family demand your attention. You may be especially concerned with parenting or relationships with your own mother. You may consider moving your home to a new location or leaving home.

If an eclipse or Saturn falls in your FIFTH HOUSE:

Here is where you express yourself, either through your personal talents or through procreating children. You are interested in making your special talents visible. This is also the house of love affairs and the romantic aspect of life, where you flirt, have fun, and enjoy the excitement of love. Hobbies and crafts fall in this area.

If an eclipse or Saturn falls in your SIXTH HOUSE:

How well are you doing your job? This is your maintenance department, where you take care of your health, organize your life, and set up a daily routine. It is also the place where you perfect your skills and add polish to your life. The chores you do every day, the skills you learn, and the techniques you use fall here. If something doesn't work in your life, an eclipse is sure to bring this to light. If you've been neglecting your health, diet, and fitness, you'll probably pay the consequences during an eclipse. Or you may be faced with work that requires much routine organization and steady effort, rather than creative ability. Or you may be required to perform services for others.

If an eclipse or Saturn falls in your SEVENTH HOUSE:

This is the area of committed relationships, of those which involve legal agreements, of working in a close relationship with another. Here you'll be dealing with how you relate, what you'll be willing to give up for the sake of a marriage or partnership. Eclipses here can put extra pressure on a relationship and, if it's not working, precipitate a breakup. Lawsuits and open enemies also reside here.

If an eclipse or Saturn falls in your EIGHTH HOUSE:

This area is concerned with power and control. Consider what you are willing to give up in order that something might happen. Power struggles, intense relationships, and desires to penetrate deeper mysteries belong here. Debts, loans, financial matters that involve another party, and wheeling and dealing also come into focus. So does sex, where you surrender your individual power to create a new life together. Matters involving birth and death are also involved here.

If an eclipse or Saturn falls in your NINTH HOUSE:

Here is where you look at the big picture. You'll seek information that helps you find meaning in life: higher education, religion, travel, global issues. Eclipses here can push you to get out of your rut, to explore something you've never done before, and to expand your horizons.

If an eclipse or Saturn falls in your TENTH HOUSE:

This is the high-profile point in your chart. Here is where you consider how society looks at you and your position in the outside world. You'll be concerned about whether you receive proper credit for your work and if you're recognized by higher-ups. Promotions, raises, and other forms of recognition can be given or denied. If you have worked hard, Saturn can give you well-deserved rewards here. Either your standing in your career or in your community can be challenged, or you'll be publicly acknowledged for achieving a goal. An eclipse here can make you famous or burst your balloon if you've been too ambitious or neglecting other areas of your life.

If an eclipse or Saturn falls in your ELEVENTH HOUSE:

Your relationship with groups of people comes under scrutiny during an eclipse: whom you are identified with, whom you socialize with, and how well you are accepted by other members of your team. Activities of clubs and political parties, networking, and other social interactions become important. You'll be concerned about what other people think.

If an eclipse or Saturn falls in your TWELFTH HOUSE:

This is the time when the focus turns to your inner life. An especially favorable eclipse here might bring you great insight and inspiration. On the other hand, events may happen that cause you to retreat from public life. Here is where we go to be alone or to work in retreats, hospitals, or religious institutions, or to explore psychotherapy. Here is where you deliver selfless service, through charitable acts. Good aspects from an eclipse could promote an ability to go with the flow or to rise above the competition to find an inner, almost mystical strength that enables you to connect with the deepest needs of others.

♎ CHAPTER 4

Blame It on Moon Glow:
The Moon's Effect on Emotions

In some astrological systems, the moon sign is considered just as important as the sun sign. It adds many levels of meaning to a horoscope, because it reveals how a person reacts to life's problems, what makes the person feel comfortable, secure, romantic. The moon reveals secrets like what you really care about. It's the emotional factor in the horoscope, representing the receptive, reflective, female, nurturing self. It also reflects who you were nurtured by—the mother or mother figure in your chart. In a man's chart, the moon position describes his receptive, emotional, yin side, as well as the woman in his life who will have the deepest effect, usually his mother. (Venus reveals the kind of woman who will attract him physically.)

The moon is more at home in some signs than others. It rules maternal Cancer and is exalted in Taurus—both comforting, home-loving signs where the natural emotional energies of the moon are easily and productively expressed. But when the moon is in the opposite signs—Capricorn and Scorpio—it leaves the comfortable nest and deals with emotional issues of power and achievement in the outside world. Those of you with the moon in these signs are likely to find your emotional role more challenging in life.

Since detailed moon tables are too extensive for this book, check through the following listing to find the moon sign that feels most familiar.

Moon in Aries

This placement makes you both independent and ardent. An idealist, you tend to fall in and out of love easily. You love a challenge but could cool once your quarry is captured. Your emotional reactions are fast and fiery, quickly expressed and quickly forgotten. You may not think before expressing your feelings. It's not easy to hide how you feel. Channeling all your emotional energy could be one of your big challenges.

Moon in Taurus

A sentimental soul, you are very fond of the good life, and you gravitate toward solid, secure relationships. You like displays of affection and creature comforts—all the tangible trappings of a cozy, safe, calm atmosphere. You are sensual and steady emotionally, but very stubborn, possessive, and determined. You can't be pushed, and you tend to dislike changes. You should make an effort to broaden your horizons and to take a risk sometimes. You may become very attached to your home turf. You may also be a collector of objects that are meaningful to you.

Moon in Gemini

You crave mental stimulation and variety in life, which you usually get through either an ever-varied social life, the excitement of flirtation and/or multiple professional involvements. You may marry more than once and have a rather chaotic emotional life due to your difficulty with commitment and settling down, as well as your need to be constantly on the go. (Be sure to find a partner who is as outgoing as you are.) You will have to learn at some point to focus your energies because you tend to be somewhat fragmented—to do two things at once, to have two homes or even two lovers. If you can find a creative way to express your many-faceted nature, you'll be ahead of the game.

Moon in Cancer

This is the most powerful lunar position, which is sure to make a deep imprint on your character. Your needs are very much associated with your reaction to the needs of others. You are very sensitive, caring, and self-protective, though some of you may mask this with a hard shell, like the moon-sensitive crab. This placement also gives an excellent memory, keen intuition, and an uncanny ability to perceive the needs of others. All of the lunar phases will affect you, especially full moons and eclipses, so you would do well to mark them on your calendar. Because you're happiest at home, you may work at home or turn your office into a second home, where you can nurture and comfort people. (You may tend to mother the world.) With natural psychic, intuitive ability, you might be drawn to occult work in some way. Or you may get professionally involved with providing food and shelter to others.

Moon in Leo

This warm, passionate moon takes everything to heart. You are attracted to all that is noble, generous, and aristocratic in life (and may be a bit of a snob). You have an innate ability to take command emotionally, but you do need strong support, loyalty, and loud applause from those you love. You are possessive of your loved ones and your turf and will roar if anyone threatens to take over your territory.

Moon in Virgo

You are rather cool until you decide if others measure up. But once someone or something meets your ideal standards, you hold up your end of the arrangement perfectly. You may, in fact, drive yourself too hard to attain some notion of perfection. Try to be a bit easier on yourself and others. Don't always act the censor! You love to be the teacher and are drawn to situations where you can change others for the better, but sometimes you must learn to accept others for what they are—enjoy what you have!

Moon in Libra

Like other air-sign moons, you think before you feel. Therefore, you may not immediately recognize the emotional needs of others. However, you are relationship oriented and may find it difficult to be alone or to do things alone. After you have learned emotional balance by leaning on yourself first, you can have excellent partnerships. It is best for you to avoid extremes, which set your scales swinging and can make your love life precarious. You thrive in a rather conservative, traditional, romantic relationship, where you receive attention and flattery—but not possessiveness—from your partner. You'll be your most charming in an elegant, harmonious atmosphere.

Moon in Scorpio

This is a moon that enjoys and responds to intense, passionate feelings. You may go to extremes and have a very dramatic emotional life, full of ardor, suspicion, jealousy, and obsession. It would be much healthier to channel your need for power and control into meaningful work. This is a good position for anyone in the fields of medicine, police work, research, the occult, psychoanalysis, or intuitive work, because life-and-death situations don't faze you. However, you do take personal disappointments very hard.

Moon in Sagittarius

You take life's ups and downs with good humor and the proverbial grain of salt. You'll love 'em and leave 'em—take off on a great adventure at a moment's notice. Born free could be your slogan. Attracted by the exotic, you have wanderlust mentally and physically. You may be too much in search of new mental and spiritual stimulation to ever settle down.

31

Moon in Capricorn

Are you ever accused of being too cool and calculating? You have an earthy side, but you take prestige and position very seriously. Your strong drive to succeed extends to your romantic life, where you will be devoted to improving your lifestyle, rising to the top. A structured situation where you can advance methodically makes you feel wonderfully secure. You may be attracted to someone older or very much younger or from a different social world. It may be difficult to look at the lighter side of emotional relationships. Though this moon is placed in the sign of its detriment, the good news is that you tend to be very dutiful and responsible to those you care for.

Moon in Aquarius

You are a people collector with many friends of all backgrounds. You are happiest surrounded by people and may feel uneasy when left alone. Though you usually stay friends with lovers, intense emotions and demanding one-on-one relationships turn you off. You don't like anything to be too rigid or scheduled. Though tolerant and understanding, you can be emotionally unpredictable and may opt for an unconventional love life. With plenty of space, you will be able to sustain relationships with liberal, freedom-loving types.

Moon in Pisces

You are very responsive and empathetic to others, especially if they have problems or are the underdog. (Be on guard against attracting too many people with sob stories.) You'll be happiest if you can express your creative imagination in the arts or in the spiritual or healing professions. Because you may tend to escape in fantasies or overreact to the moods of others, you need an emotional anchor to help you keep a firm foothold in reality. Steer clear of too much escapism (especially in alcohol) or reclusiveness. Places near water soothe your moods. Working in a field that gives you emotional variety will also help you be productive.

CHAPTER 5

Hands-On Astrology for Beginners

After you learn all about your zodiac sign (and those of your friends), you may be ready to delve more deeply into astrology. This chapter can get you up and running. It's a quick owner's manual, your fast track to getting hands-on with astrology. You'll learn the difference between a sign and a constellation (they're not the same). And what happens in a house. You'll be able to define a sign and figure out why astrologers say what they do about each one. When you look at your astrological chart, you'll have a good idea of what's going on in each portion of the horoscope. Here's your key to understanding the basic principles of this fascinating, but often confusing subject.

Signs and Constellations: What's the Difference?

Most readers know their signs, but many often confuse them with constellations. Signs are actually a type of celestial real estate, located on the zodiac, an imaginary 360-degree belt circling the earth. This belt is divided into twelve equal thirty-degree portions, which are the signs. There's a lot of confusion about the difference between the signs and the constellations of the zodiac. The latter are patterns of stars that originally marked the twelve divisions, like signposts. Though a sign is named after the constellation that once marked the same area, the constellations are no longer in the same place relative to the earth that they were many centuries ago. Over hundreds of years, the earth's orbit has shifted, so that from our point of view here on earth, the constellations seem to have moved. However, the signs remain in place. (Most Western astrology uses the twelve-equal-part division of the zodiac, though there are some other methods of astrology that still use the constellations instead of the signs.)

Most people think of themselves in terms of their sun sign. A sun sign refers to the sign the sun is orbiting through at a given moment (from our point of view here on earth). For instance, "I'm an Aries" means that the sun was passing through Aries when that person was born. However, there are nine other planets (plus asteroids, fixed stars, and sensitive points) that also form our total astrological personality, and some or many of these will be located in other signs. No one is completely Aries, with all astrological components in one sign! (Please note that, in astrology, the sun and moon are usually referred to as planets, though of course they're not.) Pluto is also still called a planet by astrologers.

As we mentioned before, the sun signs are places on the zodiac. They do not do anything (the planets are the doers). However, they are associated with many things, depending on their location.

How We Define the Signs

The definitions of the signs evolved systematically from four components that interrelate. These four different criteria are a sign's element: its quality, its polarity or sex, and its order in the progression of the zodiac. All these factors work together to tell us what the sign is like.

The system is magically mathematical. The number 12—as in the twelve signs of the zodiac—is divisible by 4, by 3, and by 2. There are four elements, three qualities, and two polarities, which follow each other in sequence around the zodiac.

The four elements (earth, air, fire, and water) are the building blocks of astrology. The use of an element to describe a sign probably dates from man's first attempts to categorize what he saw. Ancient sages believed that all things were composed of combinations of these basic elements—earth, air, fire, and water. This included the human character, which was fiery/choleric, earthy/melancholy, airy/sanguine, or watery/phlegmatic. The elements also correspond to our emotional (water), physical (earth), mental (air) and spiritual (fire) natures. The energies of each of the elements were then observed to be related to the time of year when the sun was passing through a certain segment of the zodiac.

Those born with the sun in fire signs—Aries, Leo, Sagittarius—embody the characteristic of that element. Optimism, warmth, hot tempers, enthusiasm, and spirit are typical of these signs. Taurus, Virgo, and Capricorn are earthy—more grounded, physical, materialistic, organized and deliberate than fire-sign people. Air-sign people—Gemini, Libra, and Aquarius—are mentally oriented communicators. Water signs—Cancer, Scorpio, and Pisces—are emotional, sensitive, and creative.

Think of what each element does to the others. Water puts out fire or evaporates under heat. Air fans the flames or blows them out. Earth smothers fire, drifts and erodes with too much wind, becomes mud or fertile soil with water. Those are often perfect analogies for the relationships between people of different sun-sign elements. This astrochemistry was one of the first ways man described his relationships. Fortunately, no one is entirely air or fire. We all have a bit, or a lot, of each element in our horoscopes. It is this unique mix that defines each astrological personality.

Within each element, there are three qualities that describe types of behavior associated with the sign. Those of cardinal signs are activists, go-getters. These four signs—Aries, Cancer, Libra, and Capricorn—begin each season. Fixed signs, which happen in the middle of the season, are associated with builders, stabilizers. You'll find that sun signs Taurus, Leo, Scorpio, and Aquarius are usually gifted with concentration, stamina, and focus. Mutable signs—Gemini, Virgo, Sagittarius, and Pisces—fall at the end of each season and thus are considered catalysts for change. People born under mutable signs are flexible, adaptable.

The polarity of a sign is either its positive or negative charge. It can be masculine, active, positive, and yang like air or fire signs. Or feminine, reactive, negative, and yin like the water and earth signs.

Finally, we consider the sign's place in the order of the zodiac. This is vital to the balance of all the forces and the transmission of energy moving through the signs. You may have noticed that your sign is quite different from your neighboring sign on either side. Yet each seems to grow out of its predecessor like links in a chain and transmits a synthesis of energy gathered along the chain to the following sign, beginning with the fire-powered, active, positive charge of Aries.

How the Signs Add Up

SIGN	ELEMENT	QUALITY	POLARITY	PLACE
Aries	fire	cardinal	masculine	first
Taurus	earth	fixed	feminine	second
Gemini	air	mutable	masculine	third
Cancer	water	cardinal	feminine	fourth
Leo	fire	fixed	masculine	fifth
Virgo	earth	mutable	feminine	sixth
Libra	air	cardinal	masculine	seventh
Scorpio	water	fixed	feminine	eighth
Sagittarius	fire	mutable	masculine	ninth
Capricorn	earth	cardinal	feminine	tenth
Aquarius	air	fixed	masculine	eleventh
Pisces	water	mutable	feminine	twelfth

Your Sign's Special Planet

Each sign has a ruling planet that is most compatible with its energies. Mars adds its fiery assertive characteristics to Aries. The sensual beauty and comfort-loving side of Venus rules Taurus, whereas the idealistic side of Venus rules Libra. Quick-moving Mercury rules two mutable signs, Gemini and Virgo. Its mental agility belongs to Gemini while its analytical, critical side is best expressed in Virgo. The changeable emotional moon is associated with Cancer, while the outgoing Leo personality is ruled by the sun. Scorpio originally shared Mars, but when Pluto was discovered in this century, its powerful magnetic energies were deemed more suitable to the intense vibrations of the fixed water sign Scorpio. Though Pluto has, as of this writing, been downgraded, it is still considered by astrologers to be a powerful force in the horoscope. Disciplined Capricorn is ruled by Saturn, and expansive Sagittarius by Jupiter. Unpredictable Aquarius is ruled by Uranus and creative, imaginative Pisces by Neptune. In a horoscope, if a planet is placed in the sign it rules, it is sure to be especially powerful.

The Layout of a Horoscope Chart

A horoscope chart is a map of the heavens at a given moment in time. It looks like a wheel divided with twelve spokes. In between each of the spokes is a section called a house.

Each house deals with a different area of life and is influenced by a special sign and a planet. Astrologers look at the house to tell in what area of life an event is happening or about to happen.

The house is governed by the sign passing over the spoke (or cusp of the house) at that particular moment. Though the first house is naturally associated with Aries and Mars, it would also have an additional Capricorn influence if that sign was passing over the house cusp at the time the chart was cast. The sequence of the houses starts with the first house located at the left center spoke (or the number 9 position, if you were reading a clock). The houses are then read counterclockwise around the chart, with the fourth house at the bottom of the chart, and the tenth house at the top or twelve o'clock position.

Where do the planets belong? Around the horoscope, planets are placed within the houses according to their location at the time of the chart. That is why it is so important to have an accurate time; with no specific time, the planets have no specific location in the houses and one cannot determine which area of life they will apply to. Since the signs move across the houses as the earth turns, planets in a house will naturally intensify the importance of that house. The house that contains the sun is naturally one of the most prominent.

The First House: Home of Aries and Mars

The sign passing over the first house at the time of your birth is known as your *ascendant,* or *rising sign.* The first house is the house of "firsts"—the first impression you make, how you initiate matters, the image you choose to project. This is where you advertise yourself, where you project your personality. Planets that fall here will intensify the way you come across to others.

The Second House: Home of Taurus and Venus

This house is where you experience the material world— what you value. Here are your attitudes about money, possessions, finances, whatever belongs to you, and what you own, as well as your earning and spending capacity. On a deeper level, this house reveals your sense of self-worth, the inner values that draw wealth in various forms.

The Third House: Home of Gemini and Mercury

This house describes how you communicate with others, how you reach out to others nearby, and how you interact with the immediate environment. It shows how your thinking process works and the way you express your thoughts. Are you articulate or tongue-tied? Can you think on your feet? This house also shows your first relationships, your experiences with brothers and sisters, and how you deal with people close to you such as your neighbors or pals. It's where you take short trips, write letters, or use the telephone. It shows how your mind works in terms of left-brain logical and analytical functions.

The Fourth House: Home of Cancer and the Moon

The fourth house shows the foundation of life, the psychological underpinnings. At the bottom of the chart, this house shows how you are nurtured and made to feel secure—your roots! It shows your early home environment and the circumstances at the end of your life (your final "home") as well as the place you call home now. Astrologers look here for information about the parental nurturers in your life.

The Fifth House: Home of Leo and the Sun

The fifth house is where the creative potential develops. Here you express yourself and procreate in the sense that children are outgrowths of your creative ability. But this house most represents your inner childlike self who delights in play. If your inner security has been established by the time you reach this house, you are now free to have fun, romance, and love affairs and to give of yourself. This is also the place astrologers look for playful love affairs, flirtations, and brief romantic encounters (rather than long-term commitments).

The Sixth House: Home of Virgo and Mercury

The sixth house has been called the "care and maintenance" department. This house shows how you take care of your body and organize yourself to perform efficiently in the world. Here is where you get things done, look after others, and fulfill service duties such as taking care of pets. Here is what you do to survive on a day-to-day basis. The sixth house demands order in your life; otherwise there would be chaos. This house is your "job" (as opposed to your career, which is the domain of the tenth house), your diet, and your health and fitness regimens.

The Seventh House: Home of Libra and Venus

This house shows your attitude toward partners and those with whom you enter into commitments, contracts, or agreements. Here is the way you relate to others, as well as your close, intimate, one-on-one relationships (including open enemies—those you "face off" with). Open hostilities, lawsuits, divorces, and marriages happen here. If the first house represents the "I," the seventh or opposite house is the "not-I"—the complementary partner you attract by the way you come across. If you are having trouble with partnerships, consider what you are attracting by the energies of your first and seventh houses.

The Eighth House: Home of Scorpio and Pluto (also Mars)

The eighth house refers to how you merge with something or someone, and how you handle power and control. This is one of the most mysterious and powerful houses, where your energy transforms itself from "I" to "we." As you give up power and control by uniting with something or someone, two kinds of energies merge and become something greater, leading to a regeneration of the self on a higher level. Here are your attitudes toward sex, shared resources, taxes (what you share with the government). Because this house involves what belongs to others, you face issues of control and power struggles, or undergo a deep psychological transformation as you bond with another. Here you transcend yourself with dreams, drugs, and occult or psychic experiences that reflect the collective unconscious.

The Ninth House: Home of Sagittarius and Jupiter

The ninth house shows your search for wisdom and higher knowledge—your belief system. As the third house represents the "lower mind," its opposite on the wheel, the ninth house, is the "higher mind"—the abstract, intuitive, spiritual mind that asks "big" questions like "Why are we here?" After the third house has explored what was close at hand, the ninth stretches out to broaden you mentally with higher education and travel. Here you stretch spiritually with religious activity. Since you are concerned with how everything is related, you tend to push boundaries, take risks. Here is where you express your ideas in a book or thesis, where you pontificate, philosophize, or preach.

The Tenth House: Home of Capricorn and Saturn

The tenth house is associated with your public life and high-profile activities. Located directly overhead at the "high noon" position on the horoscope wheel, this is the most "visible" house in the chart, the one where the world sees you. It deals with your career (but not your routine "job") and your reputation. Here is where you go public, take on responsibilities (as opposed to the fourth house, where you stay home). This will affect the career you choose and your "public relations." This house is also associated with your father figure or the main authority figure in your life.

The Eleventh House: Home of Aquarius and Uranus

The eleventh house is where you extend yourself to a group, a goal, or a belief system. This house is where you define what you really want, the kinds of friends you have, your political affiliations, and the kind of groups you identify with as an equal. Here is where you become concerned with "what other people think" or where you rebel against social conventions. Here is where you could become a socially conscious humanitarian or a partygoing social butterfly. It's where you look to others to stimulate you and discover your kinship to the rest of humanity. The sign on this house can help you understand what you gain and lose from friendships.

The Twelfth House: Home of Pisces and Neptune

Old-fashioned astrologers used to put a rather negative spin on this house, calling it the house of self-undoing. When we undo ourselves, we surrender control, boundaries, limits, and rules. The twelfth house is where the boundaries between yourself and others become blurred and you become selfless. But instead of being self-undoing, the twelfth house can be a place of great creativity and talent. It is the place where you can tap into the collective unconscious, where your imagination is limitless.

In your trip around the zodiac, you've gone from the I of self-assertion in the first house to the final house, which symbolizes the dissolution that happens before rebirth. The twelfth house is where accumulated experiences are processed in the unconscious. Spiritually oriented astrologers look to this house for evidence of past lives and karma. Places where we go for solitude or to do spiritual or reparatory work belong here, such as retreats, religious institutions, or hospitals. Here is also where we withdraw from society voluntarily or involuntarily or are put in prison because of antisocial activity. Selfless giving through charitable acts is part of this house, as is dependence on charity.

In your daily life, the twelfth house reveals your deepest intimacies, your best-kept secrets, especially those you hide from yourself and keep repressed deep in the unconscious. It is where we surrender a sense of a separate self to a deep feeling of wholeness, such as selfless service in religion or any activity that involves merging with the greater whole. Many sports stars have important planets in the twelfth house that enable them to play in the zone, finding an inner, almost mystical, strength that transcends their limits.

Who's Home in Your Houses?

Houses are stronger or weaker depending on how many planets are inhabiting them. If there are many planets in a given house, it follows that the activities of that house will be especially important in your life. If the planet that rules the house is also located there, this too adds power to the house.

CHAPTER 6

Getting to Know All Your Planets

When you know a person's sun sign, you already know some very useful generic qualities about that person. But when you know the placement of all ten planets, that person becomes an astrological individual, with a unique horoscope. The horoscope chart lights up with colorations from many different signs and planets. Therefore, you'll have a much more accurate profile, and with the full planetary picture of the horoscope, you'll be more capable of predicting how that individual will act in a given situation.

The planets are the actors of the chart, each representing a basic force in life. The sign and house where the planet is located represent how and where this force will manifest. The importance of a planet in your horoscope depends on its position. A planet that's close to your rising sign will be highlighted in your chart. If two or more planets are grouped together in one sign, they usually operate like a team, playing off each other rather than expressing their energy singularly. A lone planet that stands far away from the others is usually outstanding and often calls the shots.

The sign of each planet also has a powerful influence. In some signs, the planetary energies are very much at home and can easily express themselves. In others, the planet has to work harder and is slightly out of sorts. The sign that most corresponds to the energies of a planet is said to be ruled by that planet and obviously is the best place for it to be. The next best place is in a sign where it is exalted, or especially harmonious. On the other hand, there are places in the horoscope where a planet has to work harder to play its role, such as the sign opposite a planet's rulership, which embodies the opposite area of life, and the sign opposite its exaltation. However, a planet that must work harder can actually be more complete, because it must stretch itself to meet the challenges of living in a more difficult sign. Like world leaders who've had to struggle for greatness, this planet may actually develop great strength and character.

Here's a list of the best places for each planet to be. Note that, as new planets were discovered, they replaced the traditional rulers of signs which best complemented their energies.

ARIES—Mars
TAURUS—Venus, in its most sensual form
GEMINI—Mercury, in its communicative role
CANCER—the moon
LEO—the sun
VIRGO—also Mercury, this time in its more critical capacity
LIBRA—also Venus, in its more aesthetic, judgmental form
SCORPIO—Pluto, replacing Mars, the sign's original ruler
SAGITTARIUS—Jupiter
CAPRICORN—Saturn
AQUARIUS—Uranus, replacing Saturn, its original ruler
PISCES—Neptune, replacing Jupiter, its original ruler

A person who has many planets in exalted signs is lucky indeed, for here is where the planet can accomplish the most and be its most influential and creative.

SUN—exalted in Aries, where its energy creates action
MOON—exalted in Taurus, where instincts and reactions operate on a highly creative level
MERCURY—exalted in Aquarius, where it can reach analytical heights
VENUS—exalted in Pisces, a sign whose sensitivity encourages love and creativity
MARS—exalted in Capricorn, a sign that puts energy to work productively
JUPITER—exalted in Cancer, where it encourages nurturing and growth

SATURN—at home in Libra, where it steadies the scales of
    justice and promotes balanced, responsible judgment
URANUS—powerful in Scorpio, where it promotes trans-
    formation
NEPTUNE—especially favored in Cancer, where it gains
    the security to transcend to a higher state
PLUTO—exalted in Pisces, where it dissolves the old cycle
    to make way for transition to the new

The Personal Planets: Mercury, Venus, and Mars

These planets work in your immediate personal life.

Mercury affects how you communicate and how your mental processes work. Are you a quick study who grasps information rapidly? Or do you learn more slowly and thoroughly? How is your concentration? Can you express yourself easily? Are you a good writer? All these questions can be answered by your Mercury placement.

Venus shows what you react to. What turns you on? What appeals to you aesthetically? Are you charming to others? Are you attractive to look at? Your taste, your refinement, your sense of balance and proportion are all Venus-ruled.

Mars is your outgoing energy, your drive and ambition. Do you reach out for new adventures? Are you assertive? Are you motivated? Self-confident? Hot-tempered? How you channel your energy and drive is revealed by your Mars placement.

Mercury Shows How Your Mind Works

Mercury shows how you think and speak, how logical you are. Since it stays close to the sun, read the description for Mercury in your sun sign, then the sign preceding and following it. Then decide which reflects the way you think.

Mercury in Aries

Your mind is very active and assertive. It approaches a plan aggressively. You never hesitate to say what you think, never shy away from a battle. In fact, you may relish a verbal confrontation. Tact is not your strong point, so you may have to learn not to trip over your tongue.

Mercury in Taurus

This is a cautious Mercury. Though you may be a slow learner, you have good concentration and mental stamina. You want to make your ideas really happen. You'll attack a problem methodically and consider every angle thoroughly, never jumping to conclusions. You'll stick with a subject until you master it.

Mercury in Gemini

You are a wonderful communicator with great facility for expressing yourself both verbally and in writing. You love gathering all kinds of information. You probably finish other people's sentences, and express yourself with eloquent hand gestures. You can talk to anybody anytime . . . and probably have phone and e-mail bills to prove it. You read anything from sci-fi to Shakespeare, and might need an extra room just for your book collection. Though you learn fast, you may lack focus and discipline. Watch a tendency to jump from subject to subject.

Mercury in Cancer

You rely on intuition more than logic. Your mental processes are usually colored by your emotions, so you may seem shy or hesitant to voice your opinions. However, this placement gives you the advantage of great imagination and empathy in the way you communicate with others.

Mercury in Leo

You are enthusiastic and very dramatic in the way you express yourself. You like to hold the attention of groups, and could be a great public speaker. Your mind thinks big, so you prefer to deal with the overall picture rather than with the details.

Mercury in Virgo

This is one of the best places for Mercury. It should give you critical ability, attention to details, and thorough analysis. Your mind focuses on the practical side of things. This type of thinking is very well suited to being a teacher or editor.

Mercury in Libra

You're either a born diplomat who smoothes over ruffled feathers or a talented debater. Many lawyers have this placement. However, since you're forever weighing the pros and cons of a situation, you may vacillate when making decisions.

Mercury in Scorpio

This is an investigative mind that stops at nothing to get the answers. You may have a sarcastic, stinging wit or a gift for the cutting remark. There's always a grain of truth to your verbal sallies, thanks to your penetrating insight.

Mercury in Sagittarius

You are a supersalesman with a tendency to expound. Though you are very broad-minded, you can be dogmatic when it comes to telling others what's good for them. You won't hesitate to tell the truth as you see it, so watch a tendency toward tactlessness. On the plus side, you have a great sense of humor. This position of Mercury is often considered by astrologers to be at a disadvantage because

Sagittarius opposes Gemini, the sign Mercury rules, and squares off with Virgo, another Mercury-ruled sign. What often happens is that Mercury in Sagittarius oversteps its bounds and loses sight of the facts in a situation. Do a reality check before making promises you may not be able to deliver.

Mercury in Capricorn

This placement endows good mental discipline. You have a love of learning and a very orderly approach to your subjects. You will patiently plod through the facts and figures until you have mastered the tasks. You grasp structured situations easily, but may be short on creativity.

Mercury in Aquarius

An independent, original thinker, you'll have more cutting-edge ideas than the average person. You will be quick to check out any unusual opportunities. Your opinions are so well-researched and grounded that once your mind is made up, it is difficult to change.

Mercury in Pisces

You have the psychic and intuitive mind of a natural poet. Learn to make use of your creative imagination. You may think in terms of helping others, but check a tendency to be vague and forgetful of details.

Venus Relates

Venus shows where you receive pleasure, what you love to do. Find your Venus placement from the charts at the end of this chapter by looking for the year of your birth in the left-hand column. Then follow the line of that year across the page until you reach the time period of your birthday. The sign heading that column will be your Venus. If you were born on a day when Venus was changing signs, check the signs preceding or following that day to determine if that sign feels more like your Venus nature.

Venus in Aries

You can't stand to be bored, confined, or ordered around. But a good challenge, maybe even a rousing row, turns you on. Confess—don't you pick a fight now and then just to get someone stirred up? You're attracted by the chase, not the catch, which could cause some problems in your love life if the object of your affection becomes too attainable. You like to wear red, and you can spot a trend before anyone else.

Venus in Taurus

All your senses work in high gear. You love to be surrounded by glorious tastes, smells, textures, sounds, and visuals. Austerity is not for you! Neither is being rushed. You like time to enjoy your pleasures. Soothing surroundings with plenty of creature comforts are your cup of tea. You like to feel secure in your nest, with no sudden jolts or surprises. You like familiar objects—in fact, you may hate to let anything or anyone go.

Venus in Gemini

You are a lively, sparkling personality who thrives in a situation that affords a constant variety and a frequent change of scenery. A varied social life is important to you, with plenty of stimulation and a chance to engage in some light flirtation. Commitment may be difficult, because playing the field is so much fun.

Venus in Cancer

An atmosphere where you feel protected, coddled, and mothered is best for you. You love to be surrounded by children in a cozy, homelike situation. You are attracted to those who are tender and nurturing, who make you feel secure and well provided for. You may be quite secretive about your emotional life, or attracted to clandestine relationships.

Venus in Leo

First-class attention in large doses turns you on, and so does the glitter of real gold and the flash of mirrors. You like to feel like a star at all times, surrounded by your admiring audience. The side effect is that you may be attracted to flatterers and tinsel, while the real gold requires some digging.

Venus in Virgo

Everything neatly in its place? On the surface, you are attracted to an atmosphere where everything is in perfect order, but underneath are some basic, earthy urges. You are attracted to those who appeal to your need to teach, to be of service, or to play out a Pygmalion fantasy. You are at your best when you are busy doing something useful.

Venus in Libra

Elegance and harmony are your key words. You can't abide an atmosphere of contention. Your taste tends toward the classic, with light harmonies of color—nothing clashing, trendy, or outrageous. You love doing things with a partner, and should be careful to pick one who is decisive but patient enough to let you weigh the pros and cons. And steer clear of argumentative types!

Venus in Scorpio

Hidden mysteries intrigue you. In fact, anything that is too open and aboveboard is a bit of a bore. You surely have a stack of whodunits by the bed, along with an erotic magazine or two. You like to solve puzzles, and may also be fascinated with the occult, crime, or scientific research. Intense, all-or-nothing situations add spice to your life, and you love to ferret out the secrets of others. But you could get burned by your flair for living dangerously. The color black, spicy food, dark wood furniture, and heady perfume all get you in the right mood.

Venus in Sagittarius

If you are not actually a world traveler, your surroundings are sure to reflect your love of faraway places. You like a casual outdoor atmosphere and a dog or two to pet. There should be plenty of room for athletic equipment and suitcases. You're attracted to kindred souls who love to travel and who share your freedom-loving philosophy of life. Athletics and spiritual or New Age pursuits could be other interests.

Venus in Capricorn

No fly-by-night relationships for you! You want substance in life, and you are attracted to whatever will help you get where you are going. Status objects turn you on. And so do those who have a serious, responsible, businesslike approach as well as those who remind you of a beloved parent. It is characteristic of this placement to be attracted to someone of a different generation. Antiques, traditional clothing, and dignified behavior are becoming to you.

Venus in Aquarius

This Venus wants to make friends, to be "cool." You like to be in a group, particularly one pushing a worthy cause. You feel quite at home surrounded by people, and could even court fame. Yet all the while you remain detached from any intense commitment. Original ideas and unpredictable people fascinate you. You don't like everything to be planned out in advance, preferring spontaneity and delightful surprises.

Venus in Pisces

This Venus loves to give of yourself, and you find plenty of takers. Stray animals and people appeal to your heart and your pocketbook, but be careful to look at their motives realistically once in a while. You are extremely vulnerable to sob stories of all kinds. Fantasy, the arts (especially film, dance, and theater), and psychic or spiritual activities also speak to you.

Mars Creates Action

Mars is the mover and shaker in your life. It shows how you pursue your goals, whether you have energy to burn or proceed at a slow, steady pace. It will also show how you get angry. Do you explode or do a slow burn or hold everything inside, then get revenge later?

To find your Mars, turn to the charts on pages 88–97. Then find your birth year in the left-hand column and trace the line across horizontally until you come to the column headed by the month of your birth. There you will find an abbreviation of your Mars sign. If the description of your Mars sign doesn't ring true, read the description of the signs preceding and following it. You may have been born on a day when Mars was changing signs, in which case your Mars might be in the adjacent sign.

Mars in Aries

In the sign it rules, Mars shows its brilliant fiery nature. You have an explosive temper and can be quite impatient. On the other hand, you have tremendous courage, energy, and drive. You'll let nothing stand in your way as you race to be first! Obstacles are met head-on and broken through by force. However, those that require patience and persistence can have you exploding in rage. You're a great starter, but not necessarily around for the finish.

Mars in Taurus

Slow, steady, concentrated energy gives you staying power to last until the finish line. You have great stamina, and you never give up. Your tactic is to wear away obstacles with your persistence. Often you come out a winner because you've had the patience to hang in there. When angered, you do a slow burn.

Mars in Gemini

You can't sit still for long. This Mars craves variety. You often have two or more things going on at once—it's all an amusing game to you. Your life can get very complicated, but that only adds spice and stimulation. What drives you into a nervous, hyper state? Boredom, sameness, routine, and confinement. You can do wonderful things with your hands, and you have a way with words.

Mars in Cancer

You rarely attack head-on. Instead, you'll keep things to yourself, make plans in secret, and always cover your actions. This might be interpreted by some as manipulative, but you are only being self-protective. You get furious when anyone knows too much about you. But you do like to know all about others. Your mothering and feeding instincts can be put to good use if you work in the food, hotel, or child-care business. You may have to overcome your fragile sense of security, which prompts you not to take risks and to get physically upset when criticized. Don't take things so personally!

Mars in Leo

You have a very dominant personality that takes center stage. Modesty is not one of your traits, nor is taking a backseat. You prefer giving the orders, and have been known to make a dramatic scene if they are not obeyed.

Properly used, this Mars confers leadership ability, endurance, and courage.

Mars in Virgo

You are the faultfinder of the zodiac. You notice every detail. Mistakes of any kind make you very nervous. You may worry, even if everything is going smoothly. You may not express your anger directly, but you sure can nag. You have definite likes and dislikes, and you are sure you can do the job better than anyone else. You are certainly more industrious and detail-oriented than other signs. Your Mars energy is often most positively expressed in some kind of teaching role.

Mars in Libra

This Mars will have a passion for beauty, justice, and art. Generally, you will avoid confrontations at all costs. You prefer to spend your energy finding diplomatic solutions or weighing pros and cons. Your other techniques are passive aggression or exercising your well-known charm to get people to do what you want.

Mars in Scorpio

This is a powerful placement, so intense that it demands careful channeling into worthwhile activities. Otherwise, you could become obsessed with your sexuality or might use your need for power and control to manipulate others. You are strong-willed, shrewd, and very private about your affairs, and you'll usually have a secret agenda behind your actions. Your great stamina, focus, and discipline would be excellent assets for careers in the military or medical fields, especially research or surgery. When angry, you don't get mad—you get even!

Mars in Sagittarius

This expansive Mars often propels people into sales, travel, athletics, or philosophy. Your energies function well when you are on the move. You have a hot temper, and are inclined to say what you think before you consider the consequences. You shoot for high goals—and talk endlessly about them—but you may be weak on groundwork. This Mars needs a solid foundation. Watch a tendency to take unnecessary risks.

Mars in Capricorn

This is an ambitious Mars with an excellent sense of timing. You have an eye for those who can be of use to you, and you may dismiss people ruthlessly when you're angry, but you drive yourself hard and deliver full value. This is a good placement for an executive. You'll aim for status and a high material position in life, and you'll keep climbing despite the odds. A great Mars to have!

Mars in Aquarius

This is the most rebellious Mars. You seem to have a drive to assert yourself against the status quo. You may enjoy provoking people, shocking them out of traditional views. Or this placement could express itself in an offbeat sex life. Somehow you often find yourself in unconventional situations. You enjoy being a leader of an active group, which pursues forward-looking studies, politics, or goals.

Mars in Pisces

This Mars is a good actor who knows just how to appeal to the sympathies of others. You create and project wonderful fantasies, or you use your sensitive antennae to crusade for those less fortunate. You get what you want through creating a veil of illusion and glamour. This is a good Mars for someone in the creative and imaginative fields—a dancer, performer, photographer, actor. Many famous film stars have this placement. Watch a tendency to manipulate by making others feel sorry for you.

Jupiter Expands Your Life

This big, bright, swirling mass of gases is associated with abundance, prosperity, and the kind of windfall you get without too much hard work. You're optimistic under Jupiter's influence, when anything seems possible. You'll travel, expand your mind with higher education, and publish to share your knowledge widely. On the other hand, Jupiter's influence is neither discriminating nor disciplined. It represents the principle of growth without judgment, and therefore could result in extravagance, weight gain, laziness, and carelessness, if not kept in check.

Be sure to look up your Jupiter in the tables in this book. When the current position of Jupiter is favorable, you may get that lucky break. This is a great time to try new things, take risks, travel, or get more education. Opportunities seem to open up easily, so take advantage of them.

Once a year, Jupiter changes signs. That means you are due for an expansive time every twelve years, when Jupiter travels through your sun sign. You'll also have up periods every four years, when Jupiter is in the same element as your sun sign.

Jupiter in Aries

You are the soul of enthusiasm and optimism. Your luckiest times are when you are getting started on an exciting project or selling an idea that you really believe in. You may have to watch a tendency to be arrogant with those who do not share your enthusiasm. You follow your impulses, often ignoring budget or other commonsense limitations. To produce real, solid benefits, you'll need patience and follow-through wherever this Jupiter falls in your horoscope.

Jupiter in Taurus

You'll spend on beautiful material things, especially those that come from nature—items made of rare woods, natural fabrics, or precious gems, for instance. You can't have too much comfort or too many sensual pleasures. Watch a tendency to overindulge in good food, or to overpamper yourself with nothing but the best. Spartan living is not for you! You may be especially lucky in matters of real estate.

Jupiter in Gemini

You are the great talker of the zodiac, and you may be a great writer, too. But restlessness could be your weak point. You jump around, talk too much, and could be a jack-of-all-trades. Keeping a secret is especially difficult, so you'll have to watch a tendency to spill the beans. Since you love to be at the center of a beehive of activity, you'll have a vibrant social life. Your best opportunities will come through your talent for language—speaking, writing, communicating, and selling.

Jupiter in Cancer

You are luckiest in situations where you can find emotional closeness or deal with basic security needs such as food, nurturing, or shelter. You may be a great collector. Or you may simply love to accumulate things—you are the one who stashes things away for a rainy day. You probably have a very good memory and love children. In fact, you may have many children to care for. The food, hotel, child-care, and shipping businesses hold good opportunities for you.

Jupiter in Leo

You are a natural showman who loves to live in a larger-than-life way. Yours is a personality full of color that always finds its way into the limelight. You can't have too much attention or applause. Showbiz is a natural place for you, and so is any area where you can play to a crowd.

Exercising your flair for drama, your natural playfulness, and your romantic nature brings you good fortune. But watch a tendency to be overly extravagant or to monopolize center stage.

Jupiter in Virgo

You actually love those minute details others find boring. To you, they make all the difference between the perfect and the ordinary. You are the fine craftsman who spots every flaw. You expand your awareness by finding the most efficient methods and by being of service to others. Many of you will be drawn to medical or teaching fields. You'll also have luck in publishing, crafts, nutrition, and service professions. Watch out for a tendency to overwork.

Jupiter in Libra

This is an other-directed Jupiter that develops best with a partner. The stimulation of others helps you grow. You are also most comfortable in harmonious, beautiful situations and you work well with artistic people. You have a great sense of fair play and an ability to evaluate the pros and cons of a situation. You usually prefer to play the role of diplomat rather than adversary.

Jupiter in Scorpio

You love the feeling of power and control, of taking things to their limit. You can't resist a mystery. Your shrewd, penetrating mind sees right through to the heart of most situations and people. You have luck in work that provides for solutions to matters of life and death. You may be drawn to undercover work, behind-the-scenes intrigue, psychotherapy, the occult, and sex-related ventures. Your challenge will be to develop a sense of moderation and tolerance for other beliefs. You may have luck in handling other people's money—insurance, taxes, and inheritance can bring you a windfall.

Jupiter in Sagittarius

Independent, outgoing, and idealistic, you'll shoot for the stars. This Jupiter compels you to travel far and wide, both physically and mentally, via higher education. You may have luck while traveling in an exotic place. You also have luck with outdoor ventures, exercise, and animals, particularly horses. Since you tend to be very open about your opinions, watch a tendency to be tactless and to exaggerate. Instead, use your wonderful sense of humor to make your point.

Jupiter in Capricorn

Jupiter is much more restrained in Capricorn, the sign of rules and authority. Here, Jupiter can make you overwork and heighten any ambition or sense of duty you may have. You'll expand in areas that advance your position, putting you farther up the social or corporate ladder. You are lucky working within the establishment in a very structured situation where you can show off your ability to organize and reap rewards for your hard work.

Jupiter in Aquarius

This is another freedom-loving Jupiter, with great tolerance and originality. You are at your best when you are working for a humanitarian cause and in the company of many supporters. This is a good Jupiter for a political career. You'll relate to all kinds of people on all social levels. You have an abundance of original ideas, but you are best off away from routine and any situation that imposes rigid rules. You need mental stimulation!

Jupiter in Pisces

You are a giver whose feelings and pocketbook are easily touched by others, so choose your companions with care. You could be the original sucker for a hard-luck story. Better find a worthy hospital or a charity that will appreciate your selfless support. You have a great creative imagination. You may attract good fortune in fields related to oil, perfume, pharmaceuticals, petroleum, dance, footwear, and alcohol. But beware of overindulgence in alcohol—focus on a creative outlet instead.

Saturn Puts on the Brakes

Jupiter speeds you up with *lucky breaks* and quick energy. Then along comes Saturn to slow you down with the *disciplinary brakes*. Saturn has unfairly been called a malefic planet, one of the bad guys of the zodiac. On the contrary, Saturn is one of our best friends, the kind who tells you what you need to hear even if it's not good news. Under a Saturn transit, we grow up, take responsibility for our lives, and emerge from whatever test this planet has in store as far wiser, more capable and mature human beings. It is when we are under pressure that we grow stronger.

When Saturn hits a critical point in your horoscope, you can count on an experience that will make you slow up, pull back, and reexamine your life. It is a call to eliminate what is not working and to shape up. By the end of its twenty-eight-year trip around the zodiac, Saturn will have tested you in all areas of your life. The major tests happen in seven-year cycles, when Saturn passes over the angles of your chart—your rising sign, the top of your chart or midheaven, your descendant, and the nadir, or bottom, of your chart. This is when the real life-changing experiences happen. But you are also in for a testing period whenever Saturn passes a planet in your chart or stresses that planet from a distance. Therefore, it is useful to check your planetary positions with the timetable of Saturn to prepare in advance, or at least to brace yourself.

When Saturn returns to its location at the time of your birth, at approximately age twenty-eight, you'll have your first Saturn return. At this time, a person usually takes stock or settles down to find his mission in life and assumes full adult duties and responsibilities.

Another way Saturn helps us is to reveal the karmic les-

sons from previous lives and give us the chance to overcome them. So look at Saturn's challenges as much-needed
opportunities for self-improvement. Under a Jupiter influence, you'll have more fun, but Saturn gives you solid, long-
lasting results.

Look up your natal Saturn in the tables in this book for
clues on where you need work.

Saturn in Aries

Saturn here puts the brakes on Aries' natural drive and
enthusiasm. There is often an angry side to this placement.
You don't let anyone push you around, and you know
what's best for yourself. Following orders is not your strong
point, and neither is diplomacy. You tend to be quick to
go on the offensive in relationships, attacking first, before
anyone attacks you. Because no one quite lives up to your
standards, you often wind up doing everything yourself.
You'll have to learn to cooperate and tone down self-
centeredness. Both Pat Buchanan and Saddam Hussein
have this Saturn.

Saturn in Taurus

A big issue is getting control of the cash flow. There will
be lean periods that can be frightening, but you have the
patience and endurance to stick them out and the methodical drive to prosper in the end. Learn to take a philosophical attitude, like Ben Franklin, who also had this placement
and who said, "A penny saved is a penny earned."

Saturn in Gemini

You are a serious student of life, but you may have difficulty communicating or sharing your knowledge. You may
be shy, speak slowly, or have fears about communicating,
like Eleanor Roosevelt. You dwell in the realms of science,
theory, or abstract analysis—even when you are dealing
with the emotions, like Sigmund Freud, who also had this
placement.

Saturn in Cancer

Your tests come with establishing a secure emotional base. In doing so, you may have to deal with some very basic fears centering on your early home environment. Most of your Saturn tests will have emotional roots in those early childhood experiences. You may have difficulty remaining objective in terms of what you try to achieve. So it will be especially important for you to deal with negative feelings such as guilt, paranoia, jealousy, resentment, and suspicion. Galileo and Michelangelo also navigated these murky waters.

Saturn in Leo

This is an authoritarian Saturn—a strict, demanding parent who may deny the pleasure principle in your zeal to see that rules are followed. Though you may feel guilty about taking the spotlight, you are very ambitious and loyal. You have to watch a tendency toward rigidity, also toward over-work and holding back affection. Joseph Kennedy and Billy Graham share this placement.

Saturn in Virgo

This is a cautious, exacting Saturn. You are intensely hard on yourself. Most of all, you give yourself the roughest time with your constant worries about every little detail, often making yourself sick. You may have difficulties setting priorities and getting the job done. Your tests will come in learning tolerance and understanding of others. Charles de Gaulle, Mae West, and Nathaniel Hawthorne had this meticulous Saturn.

Saturn in Libra

Saturn is exalted here, which makes this planet an ally. You may choose very serious, older partners in life, perhaps stemming from a fear of dependency. You need to learn to stand solidly on your own before you commit to another.

You are extremely cautious as you deliberate every involvement—with good reason. It is best that you find an occupation that makes good use of your sense of duty and honor. Steer clear of fly-by-night situations. Both Khrushchev and Mao Tse-tung had this placement.

Saturn in Scorpio

You have great staying power. This Saturn tests you in situations involving the control of others. You may feel drawn to some kind of intrigue or undercover work, like J. Edgar Hoover. Or there may be an air of mystery surrounding your life and death, like Marilyn Monroe and Robert Kennedy, who both had this placement. There are lessons to be learned from your sexual involvements. Often sex is used for manipulation or is somehow out of the ordinary. The Roman emperor Caligula and the transsexual Christine Jorgensen are extreme cases.

Saturn in Sagittarius

Your challenges and lessons will come from tests of your spiritual and philosophical values, as happened to Martin Luther King and Gandhi. You are high-minded and sincere with this reflective, moral placement. Uncompromising in your ethical standards, you could become a benevolent despot.

Saturn in Capricorn

With the help of Saturn at maximum strength, your judgment will improve with age. And like Spencer Tracy's screen image, you'll be the gray-haired hero with a strong sense of responsibility. You advance in life slowly but steadily, always with a strong hand at the helm and an eye for the advantageous situation. Like Pat Robertson, you're likely to stand for conservative values. Negatively, you may be a loner, prone to periods of melancholy.

Saturn in Aquarius

Your tests come from relationships with groups. Do you care too much about what others think? Do you feel like an outsider, like Greta Garbo? You may fear being different from others and therefore slight your own unique, forward-looking gifts. Or like Lord Byron and Howard Hughes, you may take the opposite tack and rebel in the extreme. You can apply discipline to accomplish great humanitarian goals, as Albert Schweitzer did.

Saturn in Pisces

Your fear of the unknown and the irrational may lead you to the safety and protection of an institution. You may go on the run like Jesse James, who had this placement, to avoid looking too deeply inside. Or you might go in the opposite, more positive direction and develop a disciplined psychoanalytic approach, which puts you more in control of your feelings. Some of you will take refuge in work with hospitals, charities, or religious institutions. Queen Victoria, who had this placement, symbolized an era when institutions of all kinds were sustained. Discipline applied to artistic work, especially poetry and dance, or to spiritual work, such as yoga or meditation, might be helpful.

How Uranus, Neptune, and Pluto Influence a Whole Generation

These three planets remain in signs such a long time that a whole generation bears the imprint of the sign. Mass movements, great sweeping changes, fads that characterize a generation, even the issues of the conflicts and wars of the time are influenced by these "outer three" planets. When one of those distant planets changes signs, there is a definite shift in the atmosphere, the feeling of the end of an era.

Since these planets are so far away from the sun—too distant to be seen by the naked eye—they pick up signals from the universe at large. These planetary receivers literally link the sun with distant energies, and then perform a similar function in your horoscope by linking your central character with intuitive, spiritual, transformative forces from the cosmos. Each planet has a special domain, and will reflect this in the area of your chart where it falls.

Uranus Is the Surprise Ingredient

Uranus is the unexpected ingredient that sets you and your generation apart. There is nothing ordinary about this quirky green planet that seems to be traveling on its side, surrounded by a swarm of moons. Is it any wonder that astrologers assigned it to Aquarius, the most eccentric and gregarious sign? Uranus seems to wend its way around the sun, marching to its own tune.

Significantly, Uranus follows Saturn, the planet of limitations and structures. Often we get caught up in the structures we have created to give ourselves a sense of security. However, if we lose contact with our spiritual roots, then Uranus is likely to jolt us out of our comfortable rut and wake us up.

Uranus energy is electrical, happening in sudden flashes. It is not influenced by karma or past events, nor does it regard tradition, sex, or sentiment. The Uranus key words are surprise and awakening. Suddenly, there's that flash of inspiration, that bright idea, that totally new approach to revolutionize whatever scheme you were undertaking. A Uranus event takes you by surprise; it happens from out of the blue, for better or for worse. The Uranus place in your life is where you awaken and become your own person, leaving the structures of Saturn behind. And it is probably the most unconventional place in your chart.

Look up the sign of Uranus at the time of your birth and see where you follow your own tune.

Uranus in Aries

Birth Dates:
    March 31, 1927–November 4, 1927

January 13, 1928–June 6, 1934
October 10, 1934–March 28, 1935
   Your generation is original, creative, pioneering. It developed the computer, the airplane, and the cyclotron. You let nothing hold you back from exploring the unknown, and you have a powerful mixture of fire and electricity behind you. Women of your generation were among the first to be liberated. You were the unforgettable style setters. You have a surprise in store for everyone. Like Yoko Ono, Grace Kelly, and Jacqueline Onassis, your life may be jolted by sudden and violent changes.

Uranus in Taurus

Birth Dates:
   June 6, 1934–October 10, 1934
   March 28, 1935–August 7, 1941
   October 5, 1941–May 15, 1942
   The great territorial shake-ups of World War II began during your generation. You are independent, probably self-employed or would like to be. You have original ideas about making money, and you brace yourself for sudden changes of fortune. This Uranus can cause shake-ups, particularly in finances, but it can also make you a born entrepreneur, like Martha Stewart.

Uranus in Gemini

Birth Dates:
   August 7, 1941–October 5, 1941
   May 15, 1942–August 30, 1948
   November 12, 1948–June 10, 1949
   You were the first children to be influenced by television. Now, in your adult years, your generation stocks up on answering machines, cell phones, computers, and fax machines—any new way you can communicate. You have an inquiring mind, but your interests may be rather short-lived. This Uranus can be easily fragmented if there is no structure and focus.

Uranus in Cancer

Birth Dates:
   August 30, 1948–November 12, 1948
   June 10, 1949–August 24, 1955
   January 28, 1956–June 10, 1956

This generation came at a time when divorce was becoming commonplace, so your home image is unconventional. You may have an unusual relationship with your parents; you may have come from a broken home or an unconventional one. You'll have unorthodox ideas about parenting, intimacy, food, and shelter. You may also be interested in dreams, psychic phenomena, and memory work.

Uranus in Leo

Birth Dates:
   August 24, 1955–January 28, 1956
   June 10, 1956–November 1, 1961
   January 10, 1962–August 10, 1962

This generation understood how to use electronic media. Many of your group are now leaders in the high-tech industries, and you also understand how to use the new media to promote yourself. Like Isadora Duncan, you may have a very eccentric kind of charisma and a life that is sparked by unusual love affairs. Your children, too, may have traits that are out of the ordinary. Where this planet falls in your chart, you'll have a love of freedom, be a bit of an egomaniac, and show the full force of your personality in a unique way, like tennis great Martina Navratilova.

Uranus in Virgo

Birth Dates:
   November 1, 1961–January 10, 1962
   August 10, 1962–September 28, 1968
   May 20, 1969–June 24, 1969

You'll have highly individual work methods. Many of you will be finding newer, more practical ways to use computers. Like Einstein, who had this placement, you'll break the rules brilliantly. Your generation came at a time of student rebellions, the civil rights movement, and the general acceptance of health foods. Chances are, you're concerned about pollution and cleaning up the environment. You may also be involved with nontraditional healing methods.

Uranus in Libra

Birth Dates:
    September 28, 1968–May 20, 1969
    June 24, 1969–November 21, 1974
    May 1, 1975–September 8, 1975
Your generation will be always changing partners. Born during the era of women's liberation, you may have come from a broken home and may have no clear image of what a marriage entails. There will be many sudden splits and experiments before you settle down. Your generation will be much involved in legal and political reforms and in changing artistic and fashion looks.

Uranus in Scorpio

Birth Dates:
    November 21, 1974–May 1, 1975
    September 8, 1975–February 17, 1981
    March 20, 1981–November 16, 1981
Interest in transformation, meditation, and life after death signaled the beginning of New Age consciousness. Your generation recognizes no boundaries, no limits, and no external controls. You'll have new attitudes toward death and dying, psychic phenomena, and the occult. Like Mae West and Casanova, you'll shock 'em sexually, too.

Uranus in Sagittarius

Birth Dates:
    February 17, 1981–March 20, 1981
    November 16, 1981–February 15, 1988
    May 27, 1988–December 2, 1988
Could this generation be the first to travel in outer

space? An earlier generation with this placement included Charles Lindbergh and a time when the first zeppelins and the Wright Brothers were conquering the skies. Uranus here forecasts great discoveries, mind expansion, and long-distance travel. Like Galileo and Martin Luther, those born in these years will generate new theories about the cosmos and mankind's relation to it.

Uranus in Capricorn

Birth Dates:
    December 20, 1904–January 30, 1912
    September 4, 1912–November 12, 1912
    February 15, 1988–May 27, 1988
    December 2, 1988–April 1, 1995
    June 9, 1995–January 12, 1996
This generation, now growing up, will challenge traditions with the help of electronic gadgets. In these years, we got organized with the help of technology put to practical use. The Internet was born following the great economic boom of the 1990s. Great leaders who were movers and shakers of history, like Julius Caesar and Henry VIII, were born under this placement.

Uranus in Aquarius

Birth Dates:
    January 30, 1912–September 4, 1912
    November 12, 1912–April 1, 1919
    August 16, 1919–January 22, 1920
    April 1, 1995–June 9, 1995
    January 12, 1996–March 10, 2003
    September 15, 2003–December 30, 2003
Uranus in Aquarius is the strongest placement for this planet. Recently we've had the opportunity to witness the full force of its power of innovation, as well as its sudden wake-up calls and insistence on humanitarian values. This was a time of high-tech development, when home computers became as ubiquitous as television. It was a time of globalization, of surprise attacks (9/11), and underdevel-

oped countries demanding attention. The last generation with this placement produced great innovative minds such as Leonard Bernstein and Orson Welles. The next will become another radical breakthrough generation, much concerned with global issues that involve all humanity.

Uranus in Pisces

Birth Dates:
  April 1, 1919–August 16, 1919
  January 22, 1920–March 31, 1927
  November 4, 1927–January 12, 1928
  March 10, 2003–September 15, 2003
  December 20, 2003–May 28, 2010

Uranus is now in Pisces, ushering in a new generation. In the past century, Uranus in Pisces focused attention on the rise of electronic entertainment—radio and the cinema—and the secretiveness of Prohibition. This produced a generation of idealists exemplified by Judy Garland's theme "Somewhere over the Rainbow." Uranus in Pisces also hints at stealth activities, at hospital and prison reform, at high-tech drugs and medical experiments, at shake-ups and reforms in the Pisces-ruled petroleum industry, offshore drilling in new and unusual locations. Issues regarding the water and oil supply, water-related storm damage (Hurricane Katrina), sudden hurricanes, and floods demand our attention.

Neptune Is the Magic Solvent

Neptune is often maligned as the planet of illusions that dissolves reality, enabling you to escape the material world. Under Neptune's influence, you see what you want to see. But Neptune also encourages you to create. It embodies glamour, subtlety, mystery, and mysticism, and it governs anything that takes you beyond the mundane world, including out-of-body experiences.

Neptune acts to transcend your ordinary perceptions to take you to another level, where you experience either confusion or ecstasy. Its force can pull you off course only if you allow this to happen. Those who use Neptune wisely can translate their daydreams into poetry, theater, design, or inspired moves in the business world, avoiding the tricky "con artist" side of this planet.

Find your Neptune listed below.

Neptune in Cancer

Birth Dates:
    July 19, 1901–December 25, 1901
    May 21, 1902–September 23, 1914
    December 14, 1914–July 19, 1915
    March 19, 1916–May 2, 1916
Dreams of the homeland, idealistic patriotism, and glamorization of the nurturing assets of women characterized this time. You who were born here have unusual psychic ability and deep insights into basic needs of others.

Neptune in Leo

Birth Dates:
    September 23, 1914–December 14, 1914
    July 19, 1915–March 19, 1916
    May 2, 1916–September 21, 1928
    February 19, 1929–July 24, 1929
Neptune in Leo brought us the glamour and high living of the 1920s and the big spenders of that time. The Neptune temptations of gambling, seduction, theater, and lavish entertaining distracted from the realities of the age. Those born in that generation also made great advances in the arts.

Neptune in Virgo

Birth Dates:
    September 21, 1928–February 19, 1929
    July 24, 1929–October 3, 1942
    April 17, 1943–August 2, 1943
Neptune in Virgo encompassed the 1930s, the Great De-

pression, and the beginning of World War II, when a new order was born. There was a time of facing "what doesn't work." Many were unemployed and found solace at the movies, watching the great Virgo star Greta Garbo or the escapist dance films of Busby Berkeley. New public services were born. Those with Neptune in Virgo later spread the gospel of health and fitness. This generation's devotion to spending hours at the office inspired the term *workaholic*.

Neptune in Libra

Birth Dates:
  October 3, 1942–April 17, 1943
  August 2, 1943–December 24, 1955
  March 12, 1956–October 19, 1956
  June 15, 1957–August 6, 1957

This was the time of World War II and the postwar period, when the world regained balance and returned to relative stability. Neptune in Libra was the romantic generation who would later be concerned with relating. As this generation matured, there was a new trend toward marriage and commitment. Racial and sexual equality became important issues, as they redesigned traditional roles to suit modern times.

Neptune in Scorpio

Birth Dates:
  December 24, 1955–March 12, 1956
  October 19, 1956–June 15, 1957
  August 6, 1957–January 4, 1970
  May 3, 1970–November 6, 1970

Neptune in Scorpio brought in a generation that would become interested in transformative power. Born in an era that glamorized sex, drugs, rock and roll, and Eastern religion, they matured in a more sobering time of AIDS, cocaine abuse, and New Age spirituality. As they evolve, they will become active in healing the planet from the results of the abuse of power.

Neptune in Sagittarius

Birth Dates:
  January 4, 1970–May 3, 1970
  November 6, 1970–January 19, 1984
  June 23, 1984–November 21, 1984

Neptune in Sagittarius was the time when space and astronaut travel became a reality. The Neptune influence glamorized new approaches to mysticism, religion, and mind expansion. This generation will take a new approach to spiritual life, with emphasis on visions, mysticism, and clairvoyance.

Neptune in Capricorn

Birth Dates:
  January 19, 1984–June 23, 1984
  November 21, 1984–January 29, 1998

Neptune in Capricorn brought a time when delusions about material power were glamorized in the mid–1980s and 1990s. There was a boom in the stock market, and the Internet era spawned young tycoons who later lost it all. It was also a time when the psychic and occult worlds spawned a new category of business enterprise, and sold services on television.

Neptune in Aquarius

Birth Dates:
  January 29, 1998–April 4, 2011

This should continue to be a time of breakthroughs. Here the creative influence of Neptune reaches a universal audience. This is a time of dissolving barriers, of globalization—when we truly become one world. During this transit of high-tech Aquarius, new kinds of entertainment media reach across cultural differences. However, the transit of Neptune has also raised boundary issues between cultures, especially in Middle Eastern countries with Neptune-ruled oil fields. As Neptune raises issues of social and political structures not being as solid as they seem, this could continue to produce rebellion and chaos in the environment. However, by using imagination (Neptune) in partnership with a global view (Aquarius) we could reach creative solutions.

Those born with this placement should be true citizens of the world with a remarkable creative ability to transcend social and cultural barriers.

Pluto Can Transform You

Though Pluto is a tiny, mysterious body in space, its influence is great. When Pluto zaps a strategic point in your horoscope, your life changes dramatically.

Little Pluto is the power behind the scenes; it affects you at deep levels of consciousness, causing events to come to the surface that will transform you and your generation. Nothing escapes, or is sacred, with this probing planet. Its purpose is to wipe out the past so something new can happen.

The Pluto place in your horoscope is where you have invisible power (Mars governs the visible power), where you can transform, heal, and affect the unconscious needs of the masses. Pluto tells lots about how your generation projects power, what makes it seem cool to others. And when Pluto changes signs, there is a whole new concept of what's cool. Pluto's strange elliptical orbit occasionally runs inside the orbit of neighboring Neptune. Because of its eccentric path, the length of time Pluto stays in any given sign can vary from thirteen to thirty-two years. It covered only seven signs in the last century.

Pluto in Gemini

Birth Dates:
  Late 1800s–May 26, 1914
  This was a time of mass suggestion and breakthroughs in communications, a time when many brilliant writers such as Ernest Hemingway and F. Scott Fitzgerald were born. Henry Miller, D. H. Lawrence, and James Joyce scandalized society by using explicit sexual images and language

in their literature. "Muckraking" journalists exposed corruption. Pluto-ruled Scorpio President Theodore Roosevelt said, "Speak softly, but carry a big stick." This generation had an intense need to communicate and made major breakthroughs in knowledge. A compulsive restlessness and a thirst for a variety of experiences characterized many of this generation.

Pluto in Cancer

Birth Dates:
  May 26, 1914–June 14, 1939
  Dictators and mass media arose to wield emotional power over the masses. Women's rights was a popular issue. Deep sentimental feelings, acquisitiveness, and possessiveness characterized these times and people. Most of the great stars of the Hollywood era that embodied the American image were born during this period: Grace Kelly, Esther Williams, Frank Sinatra, Lana Turner, to name a few.

Pluto in Leo

Birth Dates:
  June 14, 1939–August, 19, 1957
  The performing arts played on the emotions of the masses. Mick Jagger, John Lennon, and rock and roll were born at this time. So were "baby boomers" like Bill and Hillary Clinton. Those born here tend to be self-centered, powerful, and boisterous. This generation does its own thing, for better or for worse.

Pluto in Virgo

Birth Dates:
  August 19, 1957–October 5, 1971
  April 17, 1972–July 30, 1972
  This is the "yuppie" generation that sparked a mass movement toward fitness, health, and career. It is a much more sober, serious, driven generation than the fun-loving Pluto in Leo. During this time, machines were invented to

process detail work efficiently. Inventions took a practical turn with answering machines, fax machines, car phones, and home office equipment—all making the workplace far more efficient.

Pluto in Libra

Birth Dates:
  October 5, 1971–April 17, 1972
  July 30, 1972–November 5, 1983
  May 18, 1984–August 27, 1984

A mellower generation, people born at this time are concerned with partnerships, working together, and finding diplomatic solutions to problems. Marriage is important to this generation, and they will define it by combining traditional values with equal partnership. This was a time of women's liberation, gay rights, ERA, and legal battles over abortion, all of which transformed our ideas about relationships.

Pluto in Scorpio

Birth Dates:
  November 5, 1983–May 18, 1984
  August 27, 1984–January 17, 1995

Pluto was in the sign it rules for a comparatively short period of time. However, this was a time of record achievements, destructive sexually transmitted diseases, nuclear power controversies, and explosive political issues. Pluto destroys in order to create new understanding—the phoenix rising from the ashes—which should be some consolation for those of you who felt Pluto's force before 1995. Sexual shockers were par for the course during these intense years when black clothing, transvestites, body piercing, tattoos, and sexually explicit advertising pushed the boundaries of good taste.

Pluto in Sagittarius

Birth Dates:
  January 17, 1995–April 20, 1995

November 10, 1995–January 26, 2008

During the most recent Pluto transit, we were pushed to expand our horizons, to find deeper spiritual meaning in life. Pluto's opposition with Saturn in 2001 brought an enormous conflict between traditional societies and the forces of change. It signals a time when religious convictions exerted more power in our political life as well.

Since Sagittarius is associated with travel, Pluto, the planet of extremes, made space travel a reality for some wealthy adventurers, who paid for the privilege of travel on space shuttles.

New dimensions in electronic publishing, concern with animal rights and the environment, and an increasing emphasis on extreme forms of religion are other signs of these times. Charismatic religious leaders asserted themselves and questions of the boundaries between church and state arose. There were also sexual scandals associated with the church. Because this period ends this year, hopefully we will have developed far-reaching philosphies to elevate our lives with a new sense of purpose.

Pluto in Capricorn

Birth Dates:
  January 25, 2008–June 13, 2008
  November 26, 2008–January 20, 2024

Since Pluto in Jupiter-ruled Sagittarius signaled a time of expansion and globalization, Pluto's entry into Saturn-ruled Capricorn this year will signal a time of adjustment, of facing reality and limitations, then finding pragmatic solutions. It will be a time when a new structure is imposed, when we become concerned with what actually works. Because Capricorn is associated with corporations and also with responsibility and duty, look for dramatic changes in business practices, hopefully with more attention paid to ethical and social responsibility as well as the bottom line. Big business will have enormous power during this transit, perhaps handling what governments have been unable to accomplish. There will be an emphasis on trimming down, perhaps a new belt-tightening regime. And since Capricorn is the sign of Father Time, there will be a new emphasis on the aging of the population. The generation born now is sure to be a more practical and realistic one than that of their older Pluto-in-Sagittarius siblings.

VENUS SIGNS 1901–2008

	Aries	Taurus	Gemini	Cancer	Leo	Virgo
1901	3/29–4/22	4/22–5/17	5/17–6/10	6/10–7/5	7/5–7/29	7/29–8/23
1902	5/7–6/3	6/3–6/30	6/30–7/25	7/25–8/19	8/19–9/13	9/13–10/7
1903	2/28–3/24	3/24–4/18	4/18–5/13	5/13–6/9	6/9–7/7	7/7–8/17
						9/6–11/8
1904	3/13–5/7	5/7–6/1	6/1–6/25	6/25–7/19	7/19–8/13	8/13–9/6
1905	2/3–3/6	3/6–4/9	7/8–8/6	8/6–9/1	9/1–9/27	9/27–10/21
	4/9–5/28	5/28–7/8				
1906	3/1–4/7	4/7–5/2	5/2–5/26	5/26–6/20	6/20–7/16	7/16–8/11
1907	4/27–5/22	5/22–6/16	6/16–7/11	7/11–8/4	8/4–8/29	8/29–9/22
1908	2/14–3/10	3/10–4/5	4/5–5/5	5/5–9/8	9/8–10/8	10/8–11/3
1909	3/29–4/22	4/22–5/16	5/16–6/10	6/10–7/4	7/4–7/29	7/29–8/23
1910	5/7–6/3	6/4–6/29	6/30–7/24	7/25–8/18	8/19–9/12	9/13–10/6
1911	2/28–3/23	3/24–4/17	4/18–5/12	5/13–6/8	6/9–7/7	7/8–11/18
1912	4/13–5/6	5/7–5/31	6/1–6/24	6/24–7/18	7/19–8/12	8/13–9/5
1913	2/3–3/6	3/7–5/1	7/8–8/5	8/6–8/31	9/1–9/26	9/27–10/20
	5/2–5/30	5/31–7/7				
1914	3/14–4/6	4/7–5/1	5/2–5/25	5/26–6/19	6/20–7/15	7/16–8/10
1915	4/27–5/21	5/22–6/15	6/16–7/10	7/11–8/3	8/4–8/28	8/29–9/21
1916	2/14–3/9	3/10–4/5	4/6–5/5	5/6–9/8	9/9–10/7	10/8–11/2
1917	3/29–4/21	4/22–5/15	5/16–6/9	6/10–7/3	7/4–7/28	7/29–8/21
1918	5/7–6/2	6/3–6/28	6/29–7/24	7/25–8/18	8/19–9/11	9/12–10/5
1919	2/27–3/22	3/23–4/16	4/17–5/12	5/13–6/7	6/8–7/7	7/8–11/8
1920	4/12–5/6	5/7–5/30	5/31–6/23	6/24–7/18	7/19–8/11	8/12–9/4
1921	2/3–3/6	3/7–4/25	7/8–8/5	8/6–8/31	9/1–9/25	9/26–10/20
	4/26–6/1	6/2–7/7				
1922	3/13–4/6	4/7–4/30	5/1–5/25	5/26–6/19	6/20–7/14	7/15–8/9
1923	4/27–5/21	5/22–6/14	6/15–7/9	7/10–8/3	8/4–8/27	8/28–9/20
1924	2/13–3/8	3/9–4/4	4/5–5/5	5/6–9/8	9/9–10/7	10/8–11/12
1925	3/28–4/20	4/21–5/15	5/16–6/8	6/9–7/3	7/4–7/27	7/28–8/21

Libra	Scorpio	Sagittarius	Capricorn	Aquarius	Pisces
8/23–9/17	9/17–10/12	10/12–1/16	1/16–2/9 11/7–12/5	2/9–3/5 12/5–1/11	3/5–3/29
10/7–10/31	10/31–11/24	11/24–12/18	12/18–1/11	2/6–4/4	1/11–2/6 4/4–5/7
8/17–9/6 11/8–12/9	12/9–1/5			1/11–2/4	2/4–2/28
9/6–9/30	9/30–10/25	1/5–1/30 10/25–11/18	1/30–2/24 11/18–12/13	2/24–3/19 12/13–1/7	3/19–4/13
10/21–11/14	11/14–12/8	12/8–1/1/06			1/7–2/3
8/11–9/7	9/7–10/9 12/15–12/25	10/9–12/15 12/25–2/6	1/1–1/25	1/25–2/18	2/18–3/14
9/22–10/16	10/16–11/9	11/9–12/3	2/6–3/6 12/3–12/27	3/6–4/2 12/27–1/20	4/2–4/27
11/3–11/28	11/28–12/22	12/22–1/15			1/20–2/4
8/23–9/17	9/17–10/12	10/12–11/17	1/15–2/9 11/17–12/5	2/9–3/5 12/5–1/15	3/5–3/29
10/7–10/30	10/31–11/23	11/24–12/17	12/18–12/31	1/1–1/15 1/29–4/4	1/16–1/28 4/5–5/6
11/19–12/8	12/9–12/31		1/1–1/10	1/11–2/2	2/3–2/27
9/6–9/30	1/1–1/4 10/1–10/24	1/5–1/29 10/25–11/17	1/30–2/23 11/18–12/12	2/24–3/18 12/13–12/31	3/19–4/12
10/21–11/13	11/14–12/7	12/8–12/31		1/1–1/6	1/7–2/2
8/11–9/6	9/7–10/9 12/6–12/30	10/10–12/5 12/31	1/1–1/24	1/25–2/17	2/18–3/13
9/22–10/15	10/16–11/8	1/1–1/26 11/9–12/2	2/7–3/6 12/3–12/26	3/7–4/1 12/27–12/31	4/2–4/26
11/3–11/27	11/28–12/21	12/22–12/31		1/1–1/19	1/20–2/13
8/22–9/16	9/17–10/11	1/1–1/14 10/12–11/6	1/15–2/7 11/17–12/5	2/8–3/4 12/6–12/31	3/5–3/28
10/6–10/29	10/30–11/22	11/23–12/16	12/17–12/31	1/1–4/5	4/6–5/6
11/9–12/8	12/9–12/31		1/1–1/9	1/10–2/2	2/3–2/26
9/5–9/30	1/1–1/3 9/31–10/23	1/4–1/28 10/24–11/17	1/29–2/22 11/18–12/11	2/23–3/18 12/12–12/31	3/19–4/11
10/21–11/13	11/14–12/7	12/8–12/31		1/1–1/6	1/7–2/2
8/10–9/6	9/7–10/10 11/29–12/31	10/11–11/28	1/1–1/24	1/25–2/16	2/17–3/12
9/21–10/14	1/1 10/15–11/7	1/2–2/6 11/8–12/1	2/7–3/5 12/2–12/25	3/6–3/31 12/26–12/31	4/1–4/26
11/13–11/26	11/27–12/21	12/22–12/31		1/1–1/19	1/20–2/12
8/22–9/15	9/16–10/11	1/1–1/14 10/12–11/6	1/15–2/7 11/7–12/5	2/8–3/3 12/6–12/31	3/4–3/27

VENUS SIGNS 1901–2008

	Aries	Taurus	Gemini	Cancer	Leo	Virgo
1926	5/7–6/2	6/3–6/28	6/29–7/23	7/24–8/17	8/18–9/11	9/12–10/5
1927	2/27–3/22	3/23–4/16	4/17–5/11	5/12–6/7	6/8–7/7	7/8–11/9
1928	4/12–5/5	5/6–5/29	5/30–6/23	6/24–7/17	7/18–8/11	8/12–9/4
1929	2/3–3/7	3/8–4/19	7/8–8/4	8/5–8/30	8/31–9/25	9/26–10/19
	4/20–6/2	6/3–7/7				
1930	3/13–4/5	4/6–4/30	5/1–5/24	5/25–6/18	6/19–7/14	7/15–8/9
1931	4/26–5/20	5/21–6/13	6/14–7/8	7/9–8/2	8/3–8/26	8/27–9/19
1932	2/12–3/8	3/9–4/3	4/4–5/5	5/6–7/12	9/9–10/6	10/7–11/1
			7/13–7/27	7/28–9/8		
1933	3/27–4/19	4/20–5/28	5/29–6/8	6/9–7/2	7/3–7/26	7/27–8/20
1934	5/6–6/1	6/2–6/27	6/28–7/22	7/23–8/16	8/17–9/10	9/11–10/4
1935	2/26–3/21	3/22–4/15	4/16–5/10	5/11–6/6	6/7–7/6	7/7–11/8
1936	4/11–5/4	5/5–5/28	5/29–6/22	6/23–7/16	7/17–8/10	8/11–9/4
1937	2/2–3/8	3/9–4/13	7/7–8/3	8/4–8/29	8/30–9/24	9/25–10/18
	4/14–6/3	6/4–7/6				
1938	3/12–4/4	4/5–4/28	4/29–5/23	5/24–6/18	6/19–7/13	7/14–8/8
1939	4/25–5/19	5/20–6/13	6/14–7/8	7/9–8/1	8/2–8/25	8/26–9/19
1940	2/12–3/7	3/8–4/3	4/4–5/5	5/6–7/4	9/9–10/5	10/6–10/31
			7/5–7/31	8/1–9/8		
1941	3/27–4/19	4/20–5/13	5/14–6/6	6/7–7/1	7/2–7/26	7/27–8/20
1942	5/6–6/1	6/2–6/26	6/27–7/22	7/23–8/16	8/17–9/9	9/10–10/3
1943	2/25–3/20	3/21–4/14	4/15–5/10	5/11–6/6	6/7–7/6	7/7–11/8
1944	4/10–5/3	5/4–5/28	5/29–6/21	6/22–7/16	7/17–8/9	8/10–9/2
1945	2/2–3/10	3/11–4/6	7/7–8/3	8/4–8/29	8/30–9/23	9/24–10/18
	4/7–6/3	6/4–7/6				
1946	3/11–4/4	4/5–4/28	4/29–5/23	5/24–6/17	6/18–7/12	7/13–8/8
1947	4/25–5/19	5/20–6/12	6/13–7/7	7/8–8/1	8/2–8/25	8/26–9/18
1948	2/11–3/7	3/8–4/3	4/4–5/6	5/7–6/28	9/8–10/5	10/6–10/31
			6/29–8/2	8/3–9/7		
1949	3/26–4/19	4/20–5/13	5/14–6/6	6/7–6/30	7/1–7/25	7/26–8/19
1950	5/5–5/31	6/1–6/26	6/27–7/21	7/22–8/15	8/16–9/9	9/10–10/3
1951	2/25–3/21	3/22–4/15	4/16–5/10	5/11–6/6	6/7–7/7	7/8–11/9

Libra	Scorpio	Sagittarius	Capricorn	Aquarius	Pisces
10/6–10/29	10/30–11/22	11/23–12/16	12/17–12/31	1/1–4/5	4/6–5/6
11/10–12/8	12/9–12/31	1/1–1/7	1/8	1/9–2/1	2/2–2/26
9/5–9/28	1/1–1/3	1/4–1/28	1/29–2/22	2/23–3/17	3/18–4/11
	9/29–10/23	10/24–11/16	11/17–12/11	12/12–12/31	
10/20–11/12	11/13–12/6	12/7–12/30	12/31	1/1–1/5	1/6–2/2
8/10–9/6	9/7–10/11	10/12–11/21	1/1–1/23	1/24–2/16	2/17–3/12
	11/22–12/31				
9/20–10/13	1/1–1/3	1/4–2/6	2/7–3/4	3/5–3/31	4/1–4/25
	10/14–11/6	11/7–11/30	12/1–12/24	12/25–12/31	
11/2–11/25	11/26–12/20	12/21–12/31		1/1–1/18	1/19–2/11
8/21–9/14	9/15–10/10	1/1–1/13	1/14–2/6	2/7–3/2	3/3–3/26
		10/11–11/5	11/6–12/4	12/5–12/31	
10/5–10/28	10/29–11/21	11/22–12/15	12/16–12/31	1/1–4/5	4/6–5/5
11/9–12/7	12/8–12/31		1/1–1/7	1/8–1/31	2/1–2/25
9/5–9/27	1/1–1/2	1/3–1/27	1/28–2/21	2/22–3/16	3/17–4/10
	9/28–10/22	10/23–11/15	11/16–12/10	12/11–12/31	
10/19–11/11	11/12–12/5	12/6–12/29	12/30–12/31	1/1–1/5	1/6–2/1
8/9–9/6	9/7–10/13	10/14–11/14	1/1–1/22	1/23–2/15	2/16–3/11
	11/15–12/31				
9/20–10/13	1/1–1/3	1/4–2/5	2/6–3/4	3/5–3/30	3/31–4/24
	10/14–11/6	11/7–11/30	12/1–12/24	12/25–12/31	
11/1–11/25	11/26–12/19	12/20–12/31		1/1–1/18	1/19–2/11
8/21–9/14	9/15–10/9	1/1–1/12	1/13–2/5	2/6–3/1	3/2–3/26
		10/10–11/5	11/6–12/4	12/5–12/31	
10/4–10/27	10/28–11/20	11/21–12/14	12/15–12/31	1/1–4/5	4/6–5/5
11/9–12/7	12/8–12/31		1/1–1/7	1/8–1/31	2/1–2/24
9/3–9/27	1/1–1/2	1/3–1/27	1/28–2/20	2/21–3/16	3/17–4/9
	9/28–10/21	10/22–11/15	11/16–12/10	12/11–12/31	
10/19–11/11	11/12–12/5	12/6–12/29	12/30–12/31	1/1–1/4	1/5–2/1
8/9–9/6	9/7–10/15	10/16–11/7	1/1–1/21	1/22–2/14	2/15–3/10
	11/8–12/31				
9/19–10/12	1/1–1/4	1/5–2/5	2/6–3/4	3/5–3/29	3/30–4/24
	10/13–11/5	11/6–11/29	11/30–12/23	12/24–12/31	
11/1–11/25	11/26–12/19	12/20–12/31		1/1–1/17	1/18–2/10
8/20–9/14	9/15–10/9	1/1–1/12	1/13–2/5	2/6–3/1	3/2–3/25
		10/10–11/5	11/6–12/5	12/6–12/31	
10/4–10/27	10/28–11/20	11/21–12/13	12/14–12/31	1/1–4/5	4/6–5/4
11/10–12/7	12/8–12/31		1/1–1/7	1/8–1/31	2/1–2/24

VENUS SIGNS 1901–2008

	Aries	Taurus	Gemini	Cancer	Leo	Virgo
1952	4/10–5/4	5/5–5/28	5/29–6/21	6/22–7/16	7/17–8/9	8/10–9/3
1953	2/2–3/3	3/4–3/31	7/8–8/3	8/4–8/29	8/30–9/24	9/25–10/18
	4/1–6/5	6/6–7/7				
1954	3/12–4/4	4/5–4/28	4/29–5/23	5/24–6/17	6/18–7/13	7/14–8/8
1955	4/25–5/19	5/20–6/13	6/14–7/7	7/8–8/1	8/2–8/25	8/26–9/18
1956	2/12–3/7	3/8–4/4	4/5–5/7	5/8–6/23	9/9–10/5	10/6–10/31
			6/24–8/4	8/5–9/8		
1957	3/26–4/19	4/20–5/13	5/14–6/6	6/7–7/1	7/2–7/26	7/27–8/19
1958	5/6–5/31	6/1–6/26	6/27–7/22	7/23–8/15	8/16–9/9	9/10–10/3
1959	2/25–3/20	3/21–4/14	4/15–5/10	5/11–6/6	6/7–7/8	7/9–9/20
					9/21–9/24	9/25–11/9
1960	4/10–5/3	5/4–5/28	5/29–6/21	6/22–7/15	7/16–8/9	8/10–9/2
1961	2/3–6/5	6/6–7/7	7/8–8/3	8/4–8/29	8/30–9/23	9/24–10/17
1962	3/11–4/3	4/4–4/28	4/29–5/22	5/23–6/17	6/18–7/12	7/13–8/8
1963	4/24–5/18	5/19–6/12	6/13–7/7	7/8–7/31	8/1–8/25	8/26–9/18
1964	2/11–3/7	3/8–4/4	4/5–5/9	5/10–6/17	9/9–10/5	10/6–10/31
			6/18–8/5	8/6–9/8		
1965	3/26–4/18	4/19–5/12	5/13–6/6	6/7–6/30	7/1–7/25	7/26–8/19
1966	5/6–5/31	6/1–6/26	6/27–7/21	7/22–8/15	8/16–9/8	9/9–10/2
1967	2/24–3/20	3/21–4/14	4/15–5/10	5/11–6/6	6/7–7/8	7/9–9/9
					9/10–10/1	10/2–11/9
1968	4/9–5/3	5/4–5/27	5/28–6/20	6/21–7/15	7/16–8/8	8/9–9/2
1969	2/3–6/6	6/7–7/6	7/7–8/3	8/4–8/28	8/29–9/22	9/23–10/17
1970	3/11–4/3	4/4–4/27	4/28–5/22	5/23–6/16	6/17–7/12	7/13–8/8
1971	4/24–5/18	5/19–6/12	6/13–7/6	7/7–7/31	8/1–8/24	8/25–9/17
1972	2/11–3/7	3/8–4/3	4/4–5/10	5/11–6/11		
			6/12–8/6	8/7–9/8	9/9–10/5	10/6–10/30
1973	3/25–4/18	4/18–5/12	5/13–6/5	6/6–6/29	7/1–7/25	7/26–8/19
1974	5/5–5/31	6/1–6/25	6/26–7/21	7/22–8/14	8/15–9/8	9/9–10/2
1975	2/24–3/20	3/21–4/13	4/14–5/9	5/10–6/6	6/7–7/9	7/10–9/2
					9/3–10/4	10/5–11/9

Libra	Scorpio	Sagittarius	Capricorn	Aquarius	Pisces
9/4–9/27	1/1–1/2	1/3–1/27	1/28–2/20	2/21–3/16	3/17–4/9
	9/28–10/21	10/22–11/15	11/16–12/10	12/11–12/31	
10/19–11/11	11/12–12/5	12/6–12/29	12/30–12/31	1/1–1/5	1/6–2/1
8/9–9/6	9/7–10/22	10/23–10/27	1/1–1/22	1/23–2/15	2/16–3/11
	10/28–12/31				
9/19–10/13	1/1–1/6	1/7–2/5	2/6–3/4	3/5–3/30	3/31–4/24
	10/14–11/5	11/6–11/30	12/1–12/24	12/25–12/31	
11/1–11/25	11/26–12/19	12/20–12/31		1/1–1/17	1/18–2/11
8/20–9/14	9/15–10/9	1/1–1/12	1/13–2/5	2/6–3/1	3/2–3/25
		10/10–11/5	11/6–12/6	12/7–12/31	
10/4–10/27	10/28–11/20	11/21–12/14	12/15–12/31	1/1–4/6	4/7–5/5
11/10–12/7	12/8–12/31		1/1–1/7	1/8–1/31	2/1–2/24
9/3–9/26	1/1–1/2	1/3–1/27	1/28–2/20	2/21–3/15	3/16–4/9
	9/27–10/21	10/22–11/15	11/16–12/10	12/11–12/31	
10/18–11/11	11/12–12/4	12/5–12/28	12/29–12/31	1/1–1/5	1/6–2/2
8/9–9/6	9/7–12/31		1/1–1/21	1/22–2/14	2/15–3/10
9/19–10/12	1/1–1/6	1/7–2/5	2/6–3/4	3/5–3/29	3/30–4/23
	10/13–11/5	11/6–11/29	11/30–12/23	12/24–12/31	
11/1–11/24	11/25–12/19	12/20–12/31		1/1–1/16	1/17–2/10
8/20–9/13	9/14–10/9	1/1–1/12	1/13–2/5	2/6–3/1	3/2–3/25
		10/10–11/5	11/6–12/7	12/8–12/31	
10/3–10/26	10/27–11/19	11/20–12/13	2/7–2/25	1/1–2/6	4/7–5/5
			12/14–12/31	2/26–4/6	
11/10–12/7	12/8–12/31		1/1–1/6	1/7–1/30	1/31–2/23
9/3–9/26	1/1	1/2–1/26	1/27–2/20	2/21–3/15	3/16–4/8
	9/27–10/21	10/22–11/14	11/15–12/9	12/10–12/31	
10/18–11/10	11/11–12/4	12/5–12/28	12/29–12/31	1/1–1/4	1/5–2/2
8/9–9/7	9/8–12/31		1/1–1/21	1/22–2/14	2/15–3/10
9/18–10/11	1/1–1/7	1/8–2/5	2/6–3/4	3/5–3/29	3/30–4/23
	10/12–11/5	11/6–11/29	11/30–12/23	12/24–12/31	
10/31–11/24	11/25–12/18	12/19–12/31		1/1–1/16	1/17–2/10
8/20–9/13	9/14–10/8	1/1–1/12	1/13–2/4	2/5–2/28	3/1–3/24
		10/9–11/5	11/6–12/7	12/8–12/31	
10/3–10/26	10/27–11/19	11/20–12/13	12/14–12/31	3/1–4/6	4/7–5/4
			1/30–2/28	1/1–1/29	
11/10–12/7	12/8–12/31		1/1–1/6	1/7–1/30	1/31–2/23

VENUS SIGNS 1901–2008

	Aries	Taurus	Gemini	Cancer	Leo	Virgo
1976	4/8–5/2	5/2–5/27	5/27—6/20	6/20–7/14	7/14–8/8	8/8–9/1
1977	2/2–6/6	6/6–7/6	7/6–8/2	8/2–8/28	8/28–9/22	9/22–10/17
1978	3/9–4/2	4/2–4/27	4/27–5/22	5/22–6/16	6/16–7/12	7/12–8/6
1979	4/23–5/18	5/18–6/11	6/11–7/6	7/6–7/30	7/30–8/24	8/24–9/17
1980	2/9–3/6	3/6–4/3	4/3–5/12 6/5–8/6	5/12–6/5 8/6–9/7	9/7–10/4	10/4–10/30
1981	3/24–4/17	4/17–5/11	5/11–6/5	6/5–6/29	6/29–7/24	7/24–8/18
1982	5/4–5/30	5/30–6/25	6/25–7/20	7/20–8/14	8/14–9/7	9/7–10/2
1983	2/22–3/19	3/19–4/13	4/13–5/9	5/9–6/6	6/6–7/10 8/27–10/5	7/10–8/27 10/5–11/9
1984	4/7–5/2	5/2–5/26	5/26–6/20	6/20–7/14	7/14–8/7	8/7–9/1
1985	2/2–6/6	6/7–7/6	7/6–8/2	8/2–8/28	8/28–9/22	9/22–10/16
1986	3/9–4/2	4/2–4/26	4/26–5/21	5/21–6/15	6/15–7/11	7/11–8/7
1987	4/22–5/17	5/17–6/11	6/11–7/5	7/5–7/30	7/30–8/23	8/23–9/16
1988	2/9–3/6	3/6–4/3	4/3–5/17 5/27–8/6	5/17–5/27 8/28–9/22	9/7–10/4 9/22–10/16	10/4–10/29
1989	3/23–4/16	4/16–5/11	5/11–6/4	6/4–6/29	6/29–7/24	7/24–8/18
1990	5/4–5/30	5/30–6/25	6/25–7/20	7/20–8/13	8/13–9/7	9/7–10/1
1991	2/22–3/18	3/18–4/13	4/13–5/9	5/9–6/6	6/6–7/11 8/21–10/6	7/11–8/21 10/6–11/9
1992	4/7–5/1	5/1–5/26	5/26–6/19	6/19–7/13	7/13–8/7	8/7–8/31
1993	2/2–6/6	6/6–7/6	7/6–8/1	8/1–8/27	8/27–9/21	9/21–10/16
1994	3/8–4/1	4/1–4/26	4/26–5/21	5/21–6/15	6/15–7/11	7/11–8/7
1995	4/22–5/16	5/16–6/10	6/10–7/5	7/5–7/29	7/29–8/23	8/23–9/16
1996	2/9–3/6	3/6–4/3	4/3–8/7	8/7–9/7	9/7–10/4	10/4–10/29
1997	3/23–4/16	4/16–5/10	5/10–6/4	6/4–6/28	6/28–7/23	7/23–8/17
1998	5/3–5/29	5/29–6/24	6/24–7/19	7/19–8/13	8/13–9/6	9/6–9/30
1999	2/21–3/18	3/18–4/12	4/12–5/8	5/8–6/5	6/5–7/12 8/15–10/7	7/12–8/15 10/7–11/9
2000	4/6–5/1	5/1–5/25	5/25–6/13	6/13–7/13	7/13–8/6	8/6–8/31
2001	2/2–6/6	6/6–7/5	7/5–8/1	8/1–8/26	8/26–9/20	9/20–10/15
2002	3/7–4/1	4/1–4/25	4/25–5/20	5/20–6/14	6/14–7/10	7/10–8/7
2003	4/21–5/16	5/16–6/9	6/9–7/4	7/4–7/29	7/29–8/22	8/22–9/15
2004	2/8–3/5	3/5–4/3	4/3–8/7	8/7–9/6	9/6–10/3	10/3–10/28
2005	3/22–4/15	4/15–5/10	5/10–6/3	6/3–6/28	6/28–7/23	7/23–8/17
2006	5/3–5/29	5/29–6/24	6/24–7/19	7/19–8/12	8/12–9/6	9/6–9/30
2007	2/21–3/16	3/17–4/10	4/11–5/7	5/8–6/4	6/5–7/13 8/8–10/6	7/14–8/7 10/7–11/7
2008	4/6–4/30	5/1–5/24	5/25–6/17	6/18–7/11	7/12–8/4	8/5–8/29

Libra	Scorpio	Sagittarius	Capricorn	Aquarius	Pisces
9/1–9/26	9/26–10/20	1/1–1/26	1/26–2/19	2/19–3/15	3/15–4/8
10/17–11/10	11/10–12/4	12/4–12/27	12/27–1/20/78		1/4–2/2
8/6–9/7	9/7–1/7			1/20–2/13	2/13–3/9
9/17–10/11	10/11–11/4	1/7–2/5	2/5–3/3	3/3–3/29	3/29–4/23
		11/4–11/28	11/28–12/22	12/22–1/16/80	
10/30–11/24	11/24–12/18	12/18–1/11/81			1/16–2/9
8/18–9/12	9/12–10/9	10/9–11/5	1/11–2/4	2/4–2/28	2/28–3/24
			11/5–12/8	12/8–1/23/82	
10/2–10/26	10/26–11/18	11/18–12/12	1/23–3/2	3/2–4/6	4/6–5/4
			12/12–1/5/83		
11/9–12/6	12/6–1/1/84			1/5–1/29	1/29–2/22
9/1–9/25	9/25–10/20	1/1–1/25	1/25–2/19	2/19–3/14	3/14–4/7
		10/20–11/13	11/13–12/9	12/10–1/4	
10/16–11/9	11/9–12/3	12/3–12/27	12/28–1/19		1/4–2/2
8/7–9/7	9/7–1/7			1/20–2/13	2/13–3/9
9/16–10/10	10/10–11/3	1/7–2/5	2/5–3/3	3/3–3/28	3/28–4/22
		11/3–11/28	11/28–12/22	12/22–1/15	
10/29–11/23	11/23–12/17	12/17–1/10			1/15–2/9
8/18–9/12	9/12–10/8	10/8–11/5	1/10–2/3	2/3–2/27	2/27–3/23
			11/5–12/10	12/10–1/16/90	
10/1–10/25	10/25–11/18	11/18–12/12	1/16–3/3	3/3–4/6	4/6–5/4
			12/12–1/5		
11/9–12/6	12/6–12/31	12/31–1/25/92		1/5–1/29	1/29–2/22
8/31–9/25	9/25–10/19	10/19–11/13	1/25–2/18	2/18–3/13	3/13–4/7
			11/13–12/8	12/8–1/3/93	
10/16–11/9	11/9–12/2	12/2–12/26	12/26–1/19		1/3–2/2
8/7–9/7	9/7–1/7			1/19–2/12	2/12–3/8
9/16–10/10	10/10–11/13	1/7–2/4	2/4–3/2	3/2–3/28	3/28–4/22
		11/3–11/27	11/27–12/21	12/21–1/15	
10/29–11/23	11/23–12/17	12/17–1/10/97			1/15–2/9
8/17–9/12	9/12–10/8	10/8–11/5	1/10–2/3	2/3–2/27	2/27–3/23
			11/5–12/12	12/12–1/9	
9/30–10/24	10/24–11/17	11/17–12/11	1/9–3/4	3/4–4/6	4/6–5/3
11/9–12/5	12/5–12/31	12/31–1/24		1/4–1/28	1/28–2/21
8/31–9/24	9/24–10/19	10/19–11/13	1/24–2/18	2/18–3/12	3/13–4/6
			11/13–12/8	12/8	
10/15–11/8	11/8–12/2	12/2–12/26	12/26/01–1/18/02	12/8/00–1/3/01	1/3–2/2
8/7–9/7	9/7–1/7/03		12/26/01–1/18	1/18–2/11	2/11–3/7
9/15–10/9	10/9–11/2	1/7–2/4	2/4–3/2	3/2–3/27	3/27–4/21
		11/2–11/26	11/26–12/21	12/21–1/14/04	
10/28–11/22	11/22–12/16	12/16–1/9/05		1/1–1/14	1/14–2/8
8/17–9/11	9/11–10/8	10/8–11/15	1/9–2/2	2/2–2/26	2/26–3/22
			11/5–12/15	12/15–1/1/06	
9/30–10/24	10/24–11/17	11/17–12/11	1/1–3/5	3/5–4/6	4/6–5/3
11/8–12/4	12/5–12/29	12/30–1/24/08		1/3–1/26	1/27–2/20
8/30–9/22	9/23–10/17	10/18–11/11	1/24–2/16	2/17–3/11	3/12–4/5
			11/12–12/6	12/7–1/2/09	

How to Use the Mars, Jupiter, and Saturn Tables

Find the year of your birth on the left side of each column. The dates when the planet entered each sign are listed on the right side of each column. (Signs are abbreviated to three letters.) Your birthday should fall on or between each date listed, and your planetary placement should correspond to the earlier sign of that period.

All planet changes are calculated for the Greenwich Mean Time zone.

MARS SIGNS 1901–2008

1901	MAR	1	Leo		OCT	1	Vir
	MAY	11	Vir		NOV	20	Lib
	JUL	13	Lib	1905	JAN	13	Scp
	AUG	31	Scp		AUG	21	Sag
	OCT	14	Sag		OCT	8	Cap
	NOV	24	Cap		NOV	18	Aqu
1902	JAN	1	Aqu		DEC	27	Pic
	FEB	8	Pic	1906	FEB	4	Ari
	MAR	19	Ari		MAR	17	Tau
	APR	27	Tau		APR	28	Gem
	JUN	7	Gem		JUN	11	Can
	JUL	20	Can		JUL	27	Leo
	SEP	4	Leo		SEP	12	Vir
	OCT	23	Vir		OCT	30	Lib
	DEC	20	Lib		DEC	17	Scp
1903	APR	19	Vir	1907	FEB	5	Sag
	MAY	30	Lib		APR	1	Cap
	AUG	6	Scp		OCT	13	Aqu
	SEP	22	Sag		NOV	29	Pic
	NOV	3	Cap	1908	JAN	11	Ari
	DEC	12	Aqu		FEB	23	Tau
1904	JAN	19	Pic		APR	7	Gem
	FEB	27	Ari		MAY	22	Can
	APR	6	Tau		JUL	8	Leo
	MAY	18	Gem		AUG	24	Vir
	JUN	30	Can		OCT	10	Lib
	AUG	15	Leo		NOV	25	Scp

1909	JAN	10	Sag		MAR	9	Pic
	FEB	24	Cap		APR	16	Ari
	APR	9	Aqu		MAY	26	Tau
	MAY	25	Pic		JUL	6	Gem
	JUL	21	Ari		AUG	19	Can
	SEP	26	Pic		OCT	7	Leo
	NOV	20	Ari	1916	MAY	28	Vir
1910	JAN	23	Tau		JUL	23	Lib
	MAR	14	Gem		SEP	8	Scp
	MAY	1	Can		OCT	22	Sag
	JUN	19	Leo		DEC	1	Cap
	AUG	6	Vir	1917	JAN	9	Aqu
	SEP	22	Lib		FEB	16	Pic
	NOV	6	Scp		MAR	26	Ari
	DEC	20	Sag		MAY	4	Tau
1911	JAN	31	Cap		JUN	14	Gem
	MAR	14	Aqu		JUL	28	Can
	APR	23	Pic		SEP	12	Leo
	JUN	2	Ari		NOV	2	Vir
	JUL	15	Tau	1918	JAN	11	Lib
	SEP	5	Gem		FEB	25	Vir
	NOV	30	Tau		JUN	23	Lib
1912	JAN	30	Gem		AUG	17	Scp
	APR	5	Can		OCT	1	Sag
	MAY	28	Leo		NOV	11	Cap
	JUL	17	Vir		DEC	20	Aqu
	SEP	2	Lib	1919	JAN	27	Pic
	OCT	18	Scp		MAR	6	Ari
	NOV	30	Sag		APR	15	Tau
1913	JAN	10	Cap		MAY	26	Gem
	FEB	19	Aqu		JUL	8	Can
	MAR	30	Pic		AUG	23	Leo
	MAY	8	Ari		OCT	10	Vir
	JUN	17	Tau		NOV	30	Lib
	JUL	29	Gem	1920	JAN	31	Scp
	SEP	15	Can		APR	23	Lib
1914	MAY	1	Leo		JUL	10	Scp
	JUN	26	Vir		SEP	4	Sag
	AUG	14	Lib		OCT	18	Cap
	SEP	29	Scp		NOV	27	Aqu
	NOV	11	Sag	1921	JAN	5	Pic
	DEC	22	Cap		FEB	13	Ari
1915	JAN	30	Aqu		MAR	25	Tau

	MAY	6	Gem		OCT	26	Scp
	JUN	18	Can		DEC	8	Sag
	AUG	3	Leo	1928	JAN	19	Cap
	SEP	19	Vir		FEB	28	Aqu
	NOV	6	Lib		APR	7	Pic
	DEC	26	Scp		MAY	16	Ari
1922	FEB	18	Sag		JUN	26	Tau
	SEP	13	Cap		AUG	9	Gem
	OCT	30	Aqu		OCT	3	Can
	DEC	11	Pic		DEC	20	Gem
1923	JAN	21	Ari	1929	MAR	10	Can
	MAR	4	Tau		MAY	13	Leo
	APR	16	Gem		JUL	4	Vir
	MAY	30	Can		AUG	21	Lib
	JUL	16	Leo		OCT	6	Scp
	SEP	1	Vir		NOV	18	Sag
	OCT	18	Lib		DEC	29	Cap
	DEC	4	Scp	1930	FEB	6	Aqu
1924	JAN	19	Sag		MAR	17	Pic
	MAR	6	Cap		APR	24	Ari
	APR	24	Aqu		JUN	3	Tau
	JUN	24	Pic		JUL	14	Gem
	AUG	24	Aqu		AUG	28	Can
	OCT	19	Pic		OCT	20	Leo
	DEC	19	Ari	1931	FEB	16	Can
1925	FEB	5	Tau		MAR	30	Leo
	MAR	24	Gem		JUN	10	Vir
	MAY	9	Can		AUG	1	Lib
	JUN	26	Leo		SEP	17	Scp
	AUG	12	Vir		OCT	30	Sag
	SEP	28	Lib		DEC	10	Cap
	NOV	13	Scp	1932	JAN	18	Aqu
	DEC	28	Sag		FEB	25	Pic
1926	FEB	9	Cap		APR	3	Ari
	MAR	23	Aqu		MAY	12	Tau
	MAY	3	Pic		JUN	22	Gem
	JUN	15	Ari		AUG	4	Can
	AUG	1	Tau		SEP	20	Leo
1927	FEB	22	Gem		NOV	13	Vir
	APR	17	Can	1933	JUL	6	Lib
	JUN	6	Leo		AUG	26	Scp
	JUL	25	Vir		OCT	9	Sag
	SEP	10	Lib		NOV	19	Cap

	DEC	28	Aqu		FEB	17	Tau
1934	FEB	4	Pic		APR	1	Gem
	MAR	14	Ari		MAY	17	Can
	APR	22	Tau		JUL	3	Leo
	JUN	2	Gem		AUG	19	Vir
	JUL	15	Can		OCT	5	Lib
	AUG	30	Leo		NOV	20	Scp
	OCT	18	Vir	1941	JAN	4	Sag
	DEC	11	Lib		FEB	17	Cap
1935	JUL	29	Scp		APR	2	Aqu
	SEP	16	Sag		MAY	16	Pic
	OCT	28	Cap		JUL	2	Ari
	DEC	7	Aqu	1942	JAN	11	Tau
1936	JAN	14	Pic		MAR	7	Gem
	FEB	22	Ari		APR	26	Can
	APR	1	Tau		JUN	14	Leo
	MAY	13	Gem		AUG	1	Vir
	JUN	25	Can		SEP	17	Lib
	AUG	10	Leo		NOV	1	Scp
	SEP	26	Vir		DEC	15	Sag
	NOV	14	Lib	1943	JAN	26	Cap
1937	JAN	5	Scp		MAR	8	Aqu
	MAR	13	Sag		APR	17	Pic
	MAY	14	Scp		MAY	27	Ari
	AUG	8	Sag		JUL	7	Tau
	SEP	30	Cap		AUG	23	Gem
	NOV	11	Aqu	1944	MAR	28	Can
	DEC	21	Pic		MAY	22	Leo
1938	JAN	30	Ari		JUL	12	Vir
	MAR	12	Tau		AUG	29	Lib
	APR	23	Gem		OCT	13	Scp
	JUN	7	Can		NOV	25	Sag
	JUL	22	Leo	1945	JAN	5	Cap
	SEP	7	Vir		FEB	14	Aqu
	OCT	25	Lib		MAR	25	Pic
	DEC	11	Scp		MAY	2	Ari
1939	JAN	29	Sag		JUN	11	Tau
	MAR	21	Cap		JUL	23	Gem
	MAY	25	Aqu		SEP	7	Can
	JUL	21	Cap		NOV	11	Leo
	SEP	24	Aqu		DEC	26	Can
	NOV	19	Pic	1946	APR	22	Leo
1940	JAN	4	Ari		JUN	20	Vir

	AUG	9	Lib	OCT	12	Cap
	SEP	24	Scp	NOV	21	Aqu
	NOV	6	Sag	DEC	30	Pic
	DEC	17	Cap	1953 FEB	8	Ari
1947	JAN	25	Aqu	MAR	20	Tau
	MAR	4	Pic	MAY	1	Gem
	APR	11	Ari	JUN	14	Can
	MAY	21	Tau	JUL	29	Leo
	JUL	1	Gem	SEP	14	Vir
	AUG	13	Can	NOV	1	Lib
	OCT	1	Leo	DEC	20	Scp
	DEC	1	Vir	1954 FEB	9	Sag
1948	FEB	12	Leo	APR	12	Cap
	MAY	18	Vir	JUL	3	Sag
	JUL	17	Lib	AUG	24	Cap
	SEP	3	Scp	OCT	21	Aqu
	OCT	17	Sag	DEC	4	Pic
	NOV	26	Cap	1955 JAN	15	Ari
1949	JAN	4	Aqu	FEB	26	Tau
	FEB	11	Pic	APR	10	Gem
	MAR	21	Ari	MAY	26	Can
	APR	30	Tau	JUL	11	Leo
	JUN	10	Gem	AUG	27	Vir
	JUL	23	Can	OCT	13	Lib
	SEP	7	Leo	NOV	29	Scp
	OCT	27	Vir	1956 JAN	14	Sag
	DEC	26	Lib	FEB	28	Cap
1950	MAR	28	Vir	APR	14	Aqu
	JUN	11	Lib	JUN	3	Pic
	AUG	10	Scp	DEC	6	Ari
	SEP	25	Sag	1957 JAN	28	Tau
	NOV	6	Cap	MAR	17	Gem
	DEC	15	Aqu	MAY	4	Can
1951	JAN	22	Pic	JUN	21	Leo
	MAR	1	Ari	AUG	8	Vir
	APR	10	Tau	SEP	24	Lib
	MAY	21	Gem	NOV	8	Scp
	JUL	3	Can	DEC	23	Sag
	AUG	18	Leo	1958 FEB	3	Cap
	OCT	5	Vir	MAR	17	Aqu
	NOV	24	Lib	APR	27	Pic
1952	JAN	20	Scp	JUN	7	Ari
	AUG	27	Sag	JUL	21	Tau

	SEP	21	Gem		NOV	6	Vir
	OCT	29	Tau	1965	JUN	29	Lib
1959	FEB	10	Gem		AUG	20	Scp
	APR	10	Can		OCT	4	Sag
	JUN	1	Leo		NOV	14	Cap
	JUL	20	Vir		DEC	23	Aqu
	SEP	5	Lib	1966	JAN	30	Pic
	OCT	21	Scp		MAR	9	Ari
	DEC	3	Sag		APR	17	Tau
1960	JAN	14	Cap		MAY	28	Gem
	FEB	23	Aqu		JUL	11	Can
	APR	2	Pic		AUG	25	Leo
	MAY	11	Ari		OCT	12	Vir
	JUN	20	Tau		DEC	4	Lib
	AUG	2	Gem	1967	FEB	12	Scp
	SEP	21	Can		MAR	31	Lib
1961	FEB	5	Gem		JUL	19	Scp
	FEB	7	Can		SEP	10	Sag
	MAY	6	Leo		OCT	23	Cap
	JUN	28	Vir		DEC	1	Aqu
	AUG	17	Lib	1968	JAN	9	Pic
	OCT	1	Scp		FEB	17	Ari
	NOV	13	Sag		MAR	27	Tau
	DEC	24	Cap		MAY	8	Gem
1962	FEB	1	Aqu		JUN	21	Can
	MAR	12	Pic		AUG	5	Leo
	APR	19	Ari		SEP	21	Vir
	MAY	28	Tau		NOV	9	Lib
	JUL	9	Gem		DEC	29	Scp
	AUG	22	Can	1969	FEB	25	Sag
	OCT	11	Leo		SEP	21	Cap
1963	JUN	3	Vir		NOV	4	Aqu
	JUL	27	Lib		DEC	15	Pic
	SEP	12	Scp	1970	JAN	24	Ari
	OCT	25	Sag		MAR	7	Tau
	DEC	5	Cap		APR	18	Gem
1964	JAN	13	Aqu		JUN	2	Can
	FEB	20	Pic		JUL	18	Leo
	MAR	29	Ari		SEP	3	Vir
	MAY	7	Tau		OCT	20	Lib
	JUN	17	Gem		DEC	6	Scp
	JUL	30	Can	1971	JAN	23	Sag
	SEP	15	Leo		MAR	12	Cap

	MAY	3	Aqu		JUN	6	Tau
	NOV	6	Pic		JUL	17	Gem
	DEC	26	Ari		SEP	1	Can
1972	FEB	10	Tau		OCT	26	Leo
	MAR	27	Gem	1978	JAN	26	Can
	MAY	12	Can		APR	10	Leo
	JUN	28	Leo		JUN	14	Vir
	AUG	15	Vir		AUG	4	Lib
	SEP	30	Lib		SEP	19	Scp
	NOV	15	Scp		NOV	2	Sag
	DEC	30	Sag		DEC	12	Cap
1973	FEB	12	Cap	1979	JAN	20	Aqu
	MAR	26	Aqu		FEB	27	Pic
	MAY	8	Pic		APR	7	Ari
	JUN	20	Ari		MAY	16	Tau
	AUG	12	Tau		JUN	26	Gem
	OCT	29	Ari		AUG	8	Can
	DEC	24	Tau		SEP	24	Leo
1974	FEB	27	Gem		NOV	19	Vir
	APR	20	Can	1980	MAR	11	Leo
	JUN	9	Leo		MAY	4	Vir
	JUL	27	Vir		JUL	10	Lib
	SEP	12	Lib		AUG	29	Scp
	OCT	28	Scp		OCT	12	Sag
	DEC	10	Sag		NOV	22	Cap
1975	JAN	21	Cap		DEC	30	Aqu
	MAR	3	Aqu	1981	FEB	6	Pic
	APR	11	Pic		MAR	17	Ari
	MAY	21	Ari		APR	25	Tau
	JUL	1	Tau		JUN	5	Gem
	AUG	14	Gem		JUL	18	Can
	OCT	17	Can		SEP	2	Leo
	NOV	25	Gem		OCT	21	Vir
1976	MAR	18	Can		DEC	16	Lib
	MAY	16	Leo	1982	AUG	3	Scp
	JUL	6	Vir		SEP	20	Sag
	AUG	24	Lib		OCT	31	Cap
	OCT	8	Scp		DEC	10	Aqu
	NOV	20	Sag	1983	JAN	17	Pic
1977	JAN	1	Cap		FEB	25	Ari
	FEB	9	Aqu		APR	5	Tau
	MAR	20	Pic		MAY	16	Gem
	APR	27	Ari		JUN	29	Can

	AUG	13	Leo	1990	JAN	29	Cap
	SEP	30	Vir		MAR	11	Aqu
	NOV	18	Lib		APR	20	Pic
1984	JAN	11	Scp		MAY	31	Ari
	AUG	17	Sag		JUL	12	Tau
	OCT	5	Cap		AUG	31	Gem
	NOV	15	Aqu		DEC	14	Tau
	DEC	25	Pic	1991	JAN	21	Gem
1985	FEB	2	Ari		APR	3	Can
	MAR	15	Tau		MAY	26	Leo
	APR	26	Gem		JUL	15	Vir
	JUN	9	Can		SEP	1	Lib
	JUL	25	Leo		OCT	16	Scp
	SEP	10	Vir		NOV	29	Sag
	OCT	27	Lib	1992	JAN	9	Cap
	DEC	14	Scp		FEB	18	Aqu
1986	FEB	2	Sag		MAR	28	Pic
	MAR	28	Cap		MAY	5	Ari
	OCT	9	Aqu		JUN	14	Tau
	NOV	26	Pic		JUL	26	Gem
1987	JAN	8	Ari		SEP	12	Can
	FEB	20	Tau	1993	APR	27	Leo
	APR	5	Gem		JUN	23	Vir
	MAY	21	Can		AUG	12	Lib
	JUL	6	Leo		SEP	27	Scp
	AUG	22	Vir		NOV	9	Sag
	OCT	8	Lib		DEC	20	Cap
	NOV	24	Scp	1994	JAN	28	Aqu
1988	JAN	8	Sag		MAR	7	Pic
	FEB	22	Cap		APR	14	Ari
	APR	6	Aqu		MAY	23	Tau
	MAY	22	Pic		JUL	3	Gem
	JUL	13	Ari		AUG	16	Can
	OCT	23	Pic		OCT	4	Leo
	NOV	1	Ari		DEC	12	Vir
1989	JAN	19	Tau	1995	JAN	22	Leo
	MAR	11	Gem		MAY	25	Vir
	APR	29	Can		JUL	21	Lib
	JUN	16	Leo		SEP	7	Scp
	AUG	3	Vir		OCT	20	Sag
	SEP	19	Lib		NOV	30	Cap
	NOV	4	Scp	1996	JAN	8	Aqu
	DEC	18	Sag		FEB	15	Pic

	MAR	24	Ari		MAR	1	Tau
	MAY	2	Tau		APR	13	Gem
	JUN	12	Gem		MAY	28	Can
	JUL	25	Can		JUL	13	Leo
	SEP	9	Leo		AUG	29	Vir
	OCT	30	Vir		OCT	15	Lib
1997	JAN	3	Lib		DEC	1	Scp
	MAR	8	Vir	2003	JAN	17	Sag
	JUN	19	Lib		MAR	4	Cap
	AUG	14	Scp		APR	21	Aqu
	SEP	28	Sag		JUN	17	Pic
	NOV	9	Cap		DEC	16	Ari
	DEC	18	Aqu	2004	FEB	3	Tau
1998	JAN	25	Pic		MAR	21	Gem
	MAR	4	Ari		MAY	7	Can
	APR	13	Tau		JUN	23	Leo
	MAY	24	Gem		AUG	10	Vir
	JUL	6	Can		SEP	26	Lib
	AUG	20	Leo		NOV	11	Sep
	OCT	7	Vir		DEC	25	Sag
	NOV	27	Lib	2005	FEB	6	Cap
1999	JAN	26	Scp		MAR	20	Aqu
	MAY	5	Lib		MAY	1	Pic
	JUL	5	Scp		JUN	12	Ari
	SEP	2	Sag		JUL	28	Tau
	OCT	17	Cap	2006	FEB	17	Gem
	NOV	26	Aqu		APR	14	Can
2000	JAN	4	Pic		JUN	3	Leo
	FEB	12	Ari		JUL	22	Vir
	MAR	23	Tau		SEP	8	Lib
	MAY	3	Gem		OCT	23	Scp
	JUN	16	Can		DEC	6	Sag
	AUG	1	Leo	2007	JAN	16	Cap
	SEP	17	Vir		FEB	25	Aqu
	NOV	4	Lib		APR	6	Pic
	DEC	23	Scp		MAY	15	Ari
2001	FEB	14	Sag		JUNE	24	Tau
	SEP	8	Cap		AUG	7	Gem
	OCT	27	Aqu		SEP	28	Can
	DEC	8	Pic		DEC	31	Gem*
2002	JAN	18	Ari				

*Repeat means planet is retrograde.

96

2008	MAR	4	Can		OCT	3	Scp
	MAY	9	Leo		NOV	16	Sag
	JUL	1	Vir		DEC	27	Cap
	AUG	19	Lib				

JUPITER SIGNS 1901–2008

1901	JAN	19	Cap		SEP	11	Pic
1902	FEB	6	Aqu	1928	JAN	23	Ari
1903	FEB	20	Pic		JUN	4	Tau
1904	MAR	1	Ari	1929	JUN	12	Gem
	AUG	8	Tau	1930	JUN	26	Can
	AUG	31	Ari	1931	JUL	17	Leo
1905	MAR	7	Tau	1932	AUG	11	Vir
	JUL	21	Gem	1933	SEP	10	Lib
	DEC	4	Tau	1934	OCT	11	Scp
1906	MAR	9	Gem	1935	NOV	9	Sag
	JUL	30	Can	1936	DEC	2	Cap
1907	AUG	18	Leo	1937	DEC	20	Aqu
1908	SEP	12	Vir	1938	MAY	14	Pic
1909	OCT	11	Lib		JUL	30	Aqu
1910	NOV	11	Scp		DEC	29	Pic
1911	DEC	10	Sag	1939	MAY	11	Ari
1913	JAN	2	Cap		OCT	30	Pic
1914	JAN	21	Aqu		DEC	20	Ari
1915	FEB	4	Pic	1940	MAY	16	Tau
1916	FEB	12	Ari	1941	MAY	26	Gem
	JUN	26	Tau	1942	JUN	10	Can
	OCT	26	Ari	1943	JUN	30	Leo
1917	FEB	12	Tau	1944	JUL	26	Vir
	JUN	29	Gem	1945	AUG	25	Lib
1918	JUL	13	Can	1946	SEP	25	Scp
1919	AUG	2	Leo	1947	OCT	24	Sag
1920	AUG	27	Vir	1948	NOV	15	Cap
1921	SEP	25	Lib	1949	APR	12	Aqu
1922	OCT	26	Scp		JUN	27	Cap
1923	NOV	24	Sag		NOV	30	Aqu
1924	DEC	18	Cap	1950	APR	15	Pic
1926	JAN	6	Aqu		SEP	15	Aqu
1927	JAN	18	Pic		DEC	1	Pic
	JUN	6	Ari	1951	APR	21	Ari

1952	APR	28	Tau
1953	MAY	9	Gem
1954	MAY	24	Can
1955	JUN	13	Leo
	NOV	17	Vir
1956	JAN	18	Leo
	JUL	7	Vir
	DEC	13	Lib
1957	FEB	19	Vir
	AUG	7	Lib
1958	JAN	13	Scp
	MAR	20	Lib
	SEP	7	Scp
1959	FEB	10	Sag
	APR	24	Scp
	OCT	5	Sag
1960	MAR	1	Cap
	JUN	10	Sag
	OCT	26	Cap
1961	MAR	15	Aqu
	AUG	12	Cap
	NOV	4	Aqu
1962	MAR	25	Pic
1963	APR	4	Ari
1964	APR	12	Tau
1965	APR	22	Gem
	SEP	21	Can
	NOV	17	Gem
1966	MAY	5	Can
	SEP	27	Leo
1967	JAN	16	Can
	MAY	23	Leo
	OCT	19	Vir
1968	FEB	27	Leo
	JUN	15	Vir
	NOV	15	Lib
1969	MAR	30	Vir
	JUL	15	Lib
	DEC	16	Scp
1970	APR	30	Lib
	AUG	15	Scp
1971	JAN	14	Sag
	JUN	5	Scp
	SEP	11	Sag
1972	FEB	6	Cap
	JUL	24	Sag
	SEP	25	Cap
1973	FEB	23	Aqu
1974	MAR	8	Pic
1975	MAR	18	Ari
1976	MAR	26	Tau
	AUG	23	Gem
	OCT	16	Tau
1977	APR	3	Gem
	AUG	20	Can
	DEC	30	Gem
1978	APR	12	Can
	SEP	5	Leo
1979	FEB	28	Can
	APR	20	Leo
	SEP	29	Vir
1980	OCT	27	Lib
1981	NOV	27	Scp
1982	DEC	26	Sag
1984	JAN	19	Cap
1985	FEB	6	Aqu
1986	FEB	20	Pic
1987	MAR	2	Ari
1988	MAR	8	Tau
	JUL	22	Gem
	NOV	30	Tau
1989	MAR	11	Gem
	JUL	30	Can
1990	AUG	18	Leo
1991	SEP	12	Vir
1992	OCT	10	Lib
1993	NOV	10	Scp
1994	DEC	9	Sag
1996	JAN	3	Cap
1997	JAN	21	Aqu
1998	FEB	4	Pic

1999	FEB	13	Ari	2003	AUG	27	Vir
	JUN	28	Tau	2004	SEP	24	Lib
	OCT	23	Ari	2005	OCT	26	Scp
2000	FEB	14	Tau	2006	NOV	24	Sag
	JUN	30	Gem	2007	DEC	17	Cap
2001	JUL	14	Can	2008			Cap
2002	AUG	1	Leo				

SATURN SIGNS 1903–2008

1903	JAN	19	Aqu		OCT	18	Pic
1905	APR	13	Pic	1938	JAN	14	Ari
	AUG	17	Aqu	1939	JUL	6	Tau
1906	JAN	8	Pic		SEP	22	Ari
1908	MAR	19	Ari	1940	MAR	20	Tau
1910	MAY	17	Tau	1942	MAY	8	Gem
	DEC	14	Ari	1944	JUN	20	Can
1911	JAN	20	Tau	1946	AUG	2	Leo
1912	JUL	7	Gem	1948	SEP	19	Vir
	NOV	30	Tau	1949	APR	3	Leo
1913	MAR	26	Gem		MAY	29	Vir
1914	AUG	24	Can	1950	NOV	20	Lib
	DEC	7	Gem	1951	MAR	7	Vir
1915	MAY	11	Can		AUG	13	Lib
1916	OCT	17	Leo	1953	OCT	22	Scp
	DEC	7	Can	1956	JAN	12	Sag
1917	JUN	24	Leo		MAY	14	Scp
1919	AUG	12	Vir		OCT	10	Sag
1921	OCT	7	Lib	1959	JAN	5	Cap
1923	DEC	20	Scp	1962	JAN	3	Aqu
1924	APR	6	Lib	1964	MAR	24	Pic
	SEP	13	Scp		SEP	16	Aqu
1926	DEC	2	Sag		DEC	16	Pic
1929	MAR	15	Cap	1967	MAR	3	Ari
	MAY	5	Sag	1969	APR	29	Tau
	NOV	30	Cap	1971	JUN	18	Gem
1932	FEB	24	Aqu	1972	JAN	10	Tau
	AUG	13	Cap		FEB	21	Gem
	NOV	20	Aqu	1973	AUG	1	Can
1935	FEB	14	Pic	1974	JAN	7	Gem
1937	APR	25	Ari		APR	18	Can

1975	SEP	17	Leo	1993	MAY	21	Pic
1976	JAN	14	Can		JUN	30	Aqu
	JUN	5	Leo	1994	JAN	28	Pic
1977	NOV	17	Vir	1996	APR	7	Ari
1978	JAN	5	Leo	1998	JUN	9	Tau
	JUL	26	Vir		OCT	25	Ari
1980	SEP	21	Lib	1999	MAR	1	Tau
1982	NOV	29	Scp	2000	AUG	10	Gem
1983	MAY	6	Lib		OCT	16	Tau
	AUG	24	Scp	2001	APR	21	Gem
1985	NOV	17	Sag	2003	JUN	3	Can
1988	FEB	13	Cap	2005	JUL	16	Leo
	JUN	10	Sag	2007	SEP	2	Vir
	NOV	12	Cap	2008			Vir
1991	FEB	6	Aqu				

CHAPTER 7

The Leader of the Parade: Your Rising Sign

Your rising sign is the degree of the zodiac ascending over the eastern horizon at the time you were born. (That's why it's often called the ascendant.) It is important to know the rising sign, because it determines *where* things happen in the horoscope chart. It marks the first point in the horoscope, the beginning of the first house, one of twelve divisions of the horoscope, each of which represents a different area of life. After the rising sign, the other houses parade around the chart in sequence, with the following sign on the house cusp.

You can learn much about a person by the signs and interactions of the sun, moon, and planets in the horoscope, but you need to know the rising sign to determine where in that person's life an activity will take place. For example, you might know that a person has Mars in Aries, which will describe that person's dynamic, fiery energy. But if you also know that the person has a Capricorn rising sign, this Mars will fall in the fourth house of home and family, so you know where that energy will operate. Without a valid rising sign, the collection of planets have no homes. One would have no idea which area of life would be influenced by a particular planet.

Due to the earth's rotation, the rising sign changes every two hours, which means that even though other babies born later or earlier on the same day in the same hospital as you were will have most planets in the same signs as you, they may not have the same rising sign and their planets may fall in different houses in the chart. For instance, if Mars is in Gemini and your rising sign is Taurus, Mars will most likely be active in the second or financial house of your chart. Someone born later in the day, when the rising sign is Virgo, would have Mars positioned at the top of the chart, energizing the tenth house of career.

Most astrologers insist on knowing the exact time of a client's birth before analyzing a chart. The more accurate your birth time, the more accurately an astrologer can position the planets in your chart by determining the correct rising sign.

How Your Rising Sign Can Influence Your Sun Sign

Your rising sign has an important relationship with your sun sign. Some will complement the sun sign; others hide it under a totally different mask, as if playing an entirely different role, making it difficult to guess the person's sun sign from outer appearances. This may be the reason why you might not look or act like your sun sign's archetype. For example, a Leo with a conservative Capricorn ascendant would come across as much more serious than a Leo with a fiery Aries or Sagittarius ascendant.

Though the rising sign usually creates the first impression you make, there are exceptions. When the sun sign is reinforced by other planets in the same sign, this might overpower the impression of the rising sign. For instance, a Leo sun plus a Leo Venus and Leo Jupiter would counteract the more conservative image that would otherwise be conveyed by the person's Capricorn ascendant.

Those born early in the morning when the sun was on the horizon will be most likely to project the image of their sun sign. These people are often called a "double Aries" or a "double Virgo" because the same sun sign and ascendant reinforce each other.

Find Your Rising Sign

Look up your rising sign from the chart at the end of this chapter. Since rising signs change every two hours, it is important to know your birth time as close to the minute as possible. Even a few minutes' difference could change the rising sign and therefore the setup of your chart. If you are unsure about the exact time, but know within a few hours, check the following descriptions to see which is most like the personality you project.

Aries Rising: Alpha Energy

You are the most aggressive version of your sun sign, with boundless energy that can be used productively if it's channeled in the right direction. Watch a tendency to overreact emotionally and blow your top. You come across as openly competitive, a positive asset in business or sports. Be on guard against impatience, which could lead to head injuries. Your walk and bearing could have the telltale head-forward Aries posture. You may wear more bright colors, especially red, than others of your sign. You may also have a tendency to drive your car faster.

Can you see the alpha Aries tendency in Barbra Streisand (a sun-sign Taurus) and Bette Midler (a sun-sign Sagittarius)?

Taurus Rising: Down to Earth

You're slow-moving, with a beautiful (or distinctive) speaking or singing voice that can be especially soothing or melodious. You probably surround yourself with comfort, good food, luxurious environments, and other sensual pleasures. You prefer welcoming others into your home to gadding about. You may have a talent for business, especially in trading, appraising, and real estate. A Taurus ascendant gives a well-padded physique that gains weight easily, like Liza Minnelli. This ascendant can also endow females with a curvaceous beauty.

Gemini Rising: A Way with Words

You're naturally sociable, with lighter, more ethereal mannerisms than others of your sign, especially if you're female.

You love to communicate with people, and express your ideas and feelings easily, like British prime minister Tony Blair. You may have a talent for writing or public speaking. You thrive on variety, a constantly changing scene, and a lively social life. However, you may relate to others at a deeper level than might be suspected. And you will be far more sympathetic and caring than you project. You will probably travel widely, changing partners and jobs several times (or juggle two at once). Physically, your nerves are quite sensitive. Occasionally, you would benefit from a calm, tranquil atmosphere away from your usual social scene.

Cancer Rising: Nurturing Instincts

You are naturally acquisitive, possessive, private, a moneymaker, like Bill Gates or Michael Bloomberg. You easily pick up on others' needs and feelings—a great gift in business, the arts, and personal relationships. But you must guard against overreacting or taking things too personally, especially during full moon periods. Find creative outlets for your natural nurturing gifts, such as helping the less fortunate, particularly children. Your insights would be helpful in psychology. Your desire to feed and care for others would be useful in the restaurant, hotel, or child-care industries. You may be especially fond of wearing romantic old clothes, collecting antiques, and, of course, dining on exquisite food. Since your body may retain fluids, pay attention to your diet. To relax, escape to places near water.

Leo Rising: Diva Dazzle

You may come across as more poised than you really feel. However, you play it to the hilt, projecting a proud royal presence. A Leo ascendant gives you a natural flair for drama, like Marilyn Monroe, and you might be accused of stealing the spotlight. You'll also project a much more outgoing, optimistic, sunny personality than others of your sign. You take care to please your public by always projecting your best star quality, probably tossing a luxuriant mane of hair, sporting a striking hairstyle, or dressing to impress. Females often dazzle with spectacular jewelry. Since you may have a strong parental nature, you could well be the regal family matriarch or patriarch, like George W. Bush.

Virgo Rising: High Standards

Virgo rising masks your inner nature with a practical, analytical outer image. You seem neat, orderly, more particular than others of your sign. Others in your life may feel they must live up to your high standards. Though at times you may be openly critical, this masks a well-meaning desire to have only the best for loved ones. Your sharp eye for details could be used in the financial world, or your literary skills could draw you to teaching or publishing. The healing arts, health care, and service-oriented professions attract many with a Virgo ascendant. You're likely to take good care of yourself, with great attention to health, diet, and exercise, like Madonna. You might even show some hypochondriac tendencies, like Woody Allen. Physically, you may have a very sensitive digestive system.

Libra Rising: The Charmer

Libra rising gives you a charming, social public persona, like Bill Clinton. You tend to avoid confrontations in relationships, preferring to smooth the way or negotiate diplomatically rather than give in to an emotional reaction. Because you are interested in all aspects of a situation, you may be slow to reach decisions. Physically, you'll have good proportions and symmetry. You will move with natural grace and balance. You're likely to have pleasing, if not beautiful, facial features, with a winning smile, like Cary Grant. You'll show natural good taste and harmony in your clothes and home decor. Legal, diplomatic, or public relations professions could draw your interest.

Scorpio Rising: An Air of Mystery

You project an intriguing air of mystery with this ascendant, as the Scorpio secretiveness and sense of underlying power combines with your sun sign. As with Jackie O, there's more to you than meets the eye. You seem like someone who is always in control and who can move comfortably in the world of power. Your physical look comes across as intense. Many of you have remarkable eyes, with a direct, penetrating gaze. But you'll never reveal your private agenda, and you tend to keep your true feelings under wraps (watch a tendency toward paranoia). You may have an interesting romantic history with secret love affairs, like Grace Kelly. Many of you heighten your air of mystery by wearing black. You're happiest near water and should provide yourself with a seaside retreat.

Sagittarius Rising: The Explorer

You travel with this ascendant. You may also be a more outdoor, sportive type, with an athletic, casual, outgoing air. Your moods are camouflaged with cheerful optimism or a philosophical attitude. Though you don't hesitate to speak your mind, like Ted Turner, who was called the Mouth of the South, you can also laugh at your troubles or crack a joke more easily than others of your sign. A Sagittarius ascendant can also draw you to the field of higher education or to spiritual life. You'll seem to have less attachment to things and people, and may explore the globe. Your strong, fast legs are a physical bonus.

Capricorn Rising: Serious Business

This rising sign makes you come across as serious, goal-oriented, disciplined, and careful with cash. You are not one of the zodiac's big spenders, though you might splurge occasionally on items with good investment value. You're the traditional, conservative type in dress and environment, and you might come across as quite normal and business-like, like Rupert Murdoch. You'll function well in a structured or corporate environment where you can climb to the top. (You are always aware of who's the boss.) In your personal life, you could be a loner or a single parent who is "father and mother" to your children.

Aquarius Rising: One of a Kind

You come across as less concerned about what others think and could even be a bit eccentric. You're more at ease with groups of people than others in your sign, and you may be attracted to public life, like Jay Leno. Your appearance may be unique, either unconventional or unimportant to you. Those of you whose sun is in a water sign (Cancer, Scorpio, Pisces) may exercise your nurturing qualities with a large group, an extended family, or a day-care or community center.

Pisces Rising: Romantic Roles

Your creative, nurturing talents are heightened and so is your ability to project emotional drama. And, like Antonio Banderas, your dreamy eyes and poetic air bring out the protective instinct in others. You could be attracted to the arts, especially theater, dance, film, and photography, or to psychology, spiritual practice, and charity work. You are happiest when you are using your creative ability to help others. Since you are vulnerable to mood swings, it is especially important for you to find interesting, creative work where you can express your talents and heighten your self-esteem. Accentuate the positive. Be wary of escapist tendencies, particularly involving alcohol or drugs to which you are supersensitive, like Whitney Houston.

RISING SIGNS—A.M. BIRTHS

	1 AM	2 AM	3 AM	4 AM	5 AM	6 AM	7 AM	8 AM	9 AM	10 AM	11 AM	12 NOON
Jan 1	Lib	Sc	Sc	Sc	Sag	Sag	Cap	Cap	Aq	Aq	Pis	Ar
Jan 9	Lib	Sc	Sc	Sag	Sag	Sag	Cap	Cap	Aq	Pis	Ar	Tau
Jan 17	Sc	Sc	Sc	Sag	Sag	Cap	Cap	Aq	Aq	Pis	Ar	Tau
Jan 25	Sc	Sc	Sag	Sag	Sag	Cap	Cap	Aq	Pis	Ar	Tau	Tau
Feb 2	Sc	Sc	Sag	Sag	Cap	Cap	Aq	Pis	Pis	Ar	Tau	Gem
Feb 10	Sc	Sag	Sag	Sag	Cap	Cap	Aq	Pis	Ar	Tau	Tau	Gem
Feb 18	Sc	Sag	Sag	Cap	Cap	Aq	Pis	Pis	Ar	Tau	Gem	Gem
Feb 26	Sag	Sag	Sag	Cap	Aq	Aq	Pis	Ar	Tau	Tau	Gem	Gem
Mar 6	Sag	Sag	Cap	Cap	Aq	Pis	Pis	Ar	Tau	Gem	Gem	Can
Mar 14	Sag	Cap	Cap	Aq	Aq	Pis	Ar	Tau	Tau	Gem	Gem	Can
Mar 22	Sag	Cap	Cap	Aq	Pis	Ar	Ar	Tau	Gem	Gem	Can	Can
Mar 30	Cap	Cap	Aq	Pis	Pis	Ar	Tau	Tau	Gem	Can	Can	Can
Apr 7	Cap	Cap	Aq	Pis	Ar	Ar	Tau	Gem	Gem	Can	Can	Leo
Apr 14	Cap	Aq	Aq	Pis	Ar	Tau	Tau	Gem	Gem	Can	Can	Leo
Apr 22	Cap	Aq	Pis	Ar	Ar	Tau	Gem	Gem	Gem	Can	Leo	Leo
Apr 30	Aq	Aq	Pis	Ar	Tau	Tau	Gem	Can	Can	Can	Leo	Leo
May 8	Aq	Pis	Ar	Ar	Tau	Gem	Gem	Can	Can	Leo	Leo	Leo
May 16	Aq	Pis	Ar	Tau	Gem	Gem	Can	Can	Can	Leo	Leo	Vir
May 24	Pis	Ar	Ar	Tau	Gem	Gem	Can	Can	Leo	Leo	Leo	Vir
June 1	Pis	Ar	Tau	Gem	Gem	Can	Can	Can	Leo	Leo	Vir	Vir
June 9	Ar	Ar	Tau	Gem	Gem	Can	Can	Leo	Leo	Leo	Vir	Vir
June 17	Ar	Tau	Gem	Gem	Can	Can	Can	Leo	Leo	Vir	Vir	Vir
June 25	Tau	Tau	Gem	Gem	Can	Can	Leo	Leo	Leo	Vir	Vir	Lib
July 3	Tau	Gem	Gem	Can	Can	Can	Leo	Leo	Vir	Vir	Vir	Lib
July 11	Tau	Gem	Gem	Can	Can	Leo	Leo	Leo	Vir	Vir	Lib	Lib
July 18	Gem	Gem	Can	Can	Can	Leo	Leo	Vir	Vir	Vir	Lib	Lib
July 26	Gem	Gem	Can	Can	Leo	Leo	Vir	Vir	Vir	Lib	Lib	Lib
Aug 3	Gem	Can	Can	Can	Leo	Leo	Vir	Vir	Vir	Lib	Lib	Sc
Aug 11	Gem	Can	Can	Leo	Leo	Leo	Vir	Vir	Lib	Lib	Lib	Sc
Aug 18	Can	Can	Can	Leo	Leo	Vir	Vir	Vir	Lib	Lib	Sc	Sc
Aug 27	Can	Can	Leo	Leo	Leo	Vir	Vir	Lib	Lib	Lib	Sc	Sc
Sept 4	Can	Can	Leo	Leo	Leo	Vir	Vir	Vir	Lib	Lib	Sc	Sc
Sept 12	Can	Leo	Leo	Leo	Vir	Vir	Lib	Lib	Lib	Sc	Sc	Sag
Sept 20	Leo	Leo	Leo	Vir	Vir	Vir	Lib	Lib	Sc	Sc	Sc	Sag
Sept 28	Leo	Leo	Leo	Vir	Vir	Lib	Lib	Lib	Sc	Sc	Sag	Sag
Oct 6	Leo	Leo	Vir	Vir	Vir	Lib	Lib	Sc	Sc	Sc	Sag	Sag
Oct 14	Leo	Vir	Vir	Vir	Lib	Lib	Lib	Sc	Sc	Sag	Sag	Cap
Oct 22	Leo	Vir	Vir	Lib	Lib	Lib	Sc	Sc	Sc	Sag	Sag	Cap
Oct 30	Vir	Vir	Vir	Lib	Lib	Sc	Sc	Sc	Sag	Sag	Cap	Cap
Nov 7	Vir	Vir	Lib	Lib	Lib	Sc	Sc	Sc	Sag	Sag	Cap	Cap
Nov 15	Vir	Vir	Lib	Lib	Sc	Sc	Sc	Sag	Sag	Cap	Cap	Aq
Nov 23	Vir	Lib	Lib	Lib	Sc	Sc	Sag	Sag	Sag	Cap	Cap	Aq
Dec 1	Vir	Lib	Lib	Sc	Sc	Sc	Sag	Sag	Cap	Cap	Aq	Aq
Dec 9	Lib	Lib	Lib	Sc	Sc	Sag	Sag	Sag	Cap	Cap	Aq	Pis
Dec 18	Lib	Lib	Sc	Sc	Sc	Sag	Sag	Cap	Cap	Aq	Aq	Pis
Dec 28	Lib	Lib	Sc	Sc	Sag	Sag	Sag	Cap	Aq	Aq	Pis	Ar

RISING SIGNS—P.M. BIRTHS

	1 PM	2 PM	3 PM	4 PM	5 PM	6 PM	7 PM	8 PM	9 PM	10 PM	11 PM	12 MID-NIGHT
Jan 1	Tau	Gem	Gem	Can	Can	Can	Leo	Leo	Vir	Vir	Vir	Lib
Jan 9	Tau	Gem	Gem	Can	Can	Leo	Leo	Leo	Vir	Vir	Vir	Lib
Jan 17	Gem	Gem	Can	Can	Can	Leo	Leo	Vir	Vir	Vir	Lib	Lib
Jan 25	Gem	Gem	Can	Can	Leo	Leo	Leo	Vir	Vir	Lib	Lib	Lib
Feb 2	Gem	Can	Can	Can	Leo	Leo	Vir	Vir	Vir	Lib	Lib	Sc
Feb 10	Gem	Can	Can	Leo	Leo	Leo	Vir	Vir	Lib	Lib	Lib	Sc
Feb 18	Can	Can	Can	Leo	Leo	Vir	Vir	Vir	Lib	Lib	Sc	Sc
Feb 26	Can	Can	Leo	Leo	Leo	Vir	Vir	Lib	Lib	Lib	Sc	Sc
Mar 6	Can	Leo	Leo	Leo	Vir	Vir	Vir	Lib	Lib	Sc	Sc	Sc
Mar 14	Can	Leo	Leo	Vir	Vir	Vir	Lib	Lib	Lib	Sc	Sc	Sag
Mar 22	Leo	Leo	Leo	Vir	Vir	Lib	Lib	Lib	Sc	Sc	Sc	Sag
Mar 30	Leo	Leo	Vir	Vir	Vir	Lib	Lib	Sc	Sc	Sc	Sag	Sag
Apr 7	Leo	Leo	Vir	Vir	Lib	Lib	Lib	Sc	Sc	Sc	Sag	Sag
Apr 14	Leo	Vir	Vir	Vir	Lib	Lib	Sc	Sc	Sc	Sag	Sag	Cap
Apr 22	Leo	Vir	Vir	Lib	Lib	Lib	Sc	Sc	Sag	Sag	Sag	Cap
Apr 30	Vir	Vir	Vir	Lib	Lib	Sc	Sc	Sc	Sag	Sag	Cap	Cap
May 8	Vir	Vir	Lib	Lib	Lib	Sc	Sc	Sag	Sag	Sag	Cap	Cap
May 16	Vir	Vir	Lib	Lib	Sc	Sc	Sc	Sag	Sag	Cap	Cap	Aq
May 24	Vir	Lib	Lib	Lib	Sc	Sc	Sag	Sag	Cap	Cap	Cap	Aq
June 1	Vir	Lib	Lib	Sc	Sc	Sc	Sag	Sag	Cap	Cap	Aq	Aq
June 9	Lib	Lib	Lib	Sc	Sc	Sag	Sag	Sag	Cap	Cap	Aq	Pis
June 17	Lib	Lib	Sc	Sc	Sc	Sag	Sag	Cap	Cap	Aq	Aq	Pis
June 25	Lib	Lib	Sc	Sc	Sag	Sag	Sag	Cap	Cap	Aq	Pis	Ar
July 3	Lib	Sc	Sc	Sc	Sag	Sag	Cap	Cap	Aq	Aq	Pis	Ar
July 11	Lib	Sc	Sc	Sag	Sag	Sag	Cap	Cap	Aq	Pis	Ar	Tau
July 18	Sc	Sc	Sc	Sag	Sag	Cap	Cap	Aq	Aq	Pis	Ar	Tau
July 26	Sc	Sc	Sag	Sag	Sag	Cap	Cap	Aq	Pis	Ar	Tau	Tau
Aug 3	Sc	Sc	Sag	Sag	Cap	Cap	Aq	Aq	Pis	Ar	Tau	Gem
Aug 11	Sc	Sag	Sag	Sag	Cap	Cap	Aq	Pis	Ar	Tau	Tau	Gem
Aug 18	Sc	Sag	Sag	Cap	Cap	Aq	Pis	Pis	Ar	Tau	Gem	Gem
Aug 27	Sag	Sag	Sag	Cap	Cap	Aq	Pis	Ar	Tau	Tau	Gem	Can
Sept 4	Sag	Sag	Cap	Cap	Aq	Pis	Pis	Ar	Tau	Gem	Gem	Can
Sept 12	Sag	Sag	Cap	Aq	Aq	Pis	Ar	Tau	Tau	Gem	Gem	Can
Sept 20	Sag	Cap	Cap	Aq	Pis	Pis	Ar	Tau	Gem	Gem	Can	Can
Sept 28	Cap	Cap	Aq	Aq	Pis	Ar	Tau	Tau	Gem	Gem	Can	Can
Oct 6	Cap	Cap	Aq	Pis	Ar	Ar	Tau	Gem	Gem	Can	Can	Leo
Oct 14	Cap	Aq	Aq	Pis	Ar	Tau	Tau	Gem	Gem	Can	Can	Leo
Oct 22	Cap	Aq	Pis	Ar	Ar	Tau	Gem	Gem	Can	Can	Leo	Leo
Oct 30	Aq	Aq	Pis	Ar	Tau	Tau	Gem	Can	Can	Can	Leo	Leo
Nov 7	Aq	Aq	Pis	Ar	Tau	Tau	Gem	Can	Can	Can	Leo	Leo
Nov 15	Aq	Pis	Ar	Tau	Gem	Gem	Can	Can	Can	Leo	Leo	Vir
Nov 23	Pis	Ar	Ar	Tau	Gem	Gem	Can	Can	Leo	Leo	Leo	Vir
Dec 1	Pis	Ar	Tau	Gem	Gem	Can	Can	Can	Leo	Leo	Vir	Vir
Dec 9	Ar	Tau	Tau	Gem	Gem	Can	Can	Leo	Leo	Leo	Vir	Vir
Dec 18	Ar	Tau	Gem	Gem	Can	Can	Can	Leo	Leo	Vir	Vir	Vir
Dec 28	Tau	Tau	Gem	Gem	Can	Can	Leo	Leo	Vir	Vir	Vir	Lib

♎ CHAPTER 8

Astrology's Magic Symbols: The Glyphs

One of the first things an astrology student learns is how to read the symbols on a horoscope chart. These symbols or *glyphs* represent a kind of code, a pictorial language understood by astrologers around the globe and used by all astrology software programs. You'll miss out if you don't learn the glyphs. Once you learn them, you can begin to find your way around the chart, beginning your journey to deeper understanding. You can also make use of free charts available on any number of Internet sites and perhaps purchase one of the many astrology software programs.

The glyphs are fascinating little pictures in themselves, with built-in clues to help you not only decipher which sign or planet each represents, but what the symbol means in a deeper, more esoteric sense. Actually the physical act of writing the symbol is a mystical experience in itself, a way to invoke the deeper meaning of the sign or planet through age-old visual elements that have been with us since time began.

Since there are only twelve signs and ten planets (not counting a few asteroids and other space objects some astrologers use), it's a lot easier than learning to read a foreign language. Here's a code cracker for the glyphs, beginning with the glyphs for the planets. To those who already know their glyphs, don't just skim over the chapter. These familiar graphics have hidden meanings you will discover!

The Glyphs for the Planets

The glyphs for the planets are easy to learn. They're simple combinations of the most basic visual elements: the circle, the semicircle or arc, and the cross. However, each component of a glyph has a special meaning in relation to the other parts of the symbol.

The circle, which has no beginning or end, is one of the oldest symbols of spirit or spiritual forces. Early diagrams of the heavens—spiritual territory—are shown in circular form. The never-ending line of the circle is the perfect symbol for eternity. The semicircle or arc is an incomplete circle, symbolizing the receptive, finite soul, which contains spiritual potential in the curving line.

The vertical line of the cross symbolizes movement from heaven to earth. The horizontal line describes temporal movement, here and now, in time and space. Combined in a cross, the vertical and horizontal planes symbolize manifestation in the material world.

The Sun Glyph ⊙

The sun is always shown by this powerful solar symbol, a circle with a point in the center. The center point is you, your spiritual center, and the symbol represents your infinite personality incarnating (the point) into the finite cycles of birth and death.

The sun has been represented by a circle or disk since ancient Egyptian times when the solar disk represented the sun god, Ra. Some archaeologists believe the great stone circles found in England were centers of sun worship. This particular version of the symbol was brought into common use in the sixteenth century after German occultist and scholar Cornelius Agrippa (1486–1535) wrote a book called *Die Occulta Philosophia,* which became accepted as the authority in the field. Agrippa collected many medieval astrological and magical symbols in this book, which have been used by astrologers since then.

The Moon Glyph ☽

The moon glyph is the most recognizable symbol on a chart, a left-facing arc stylized into the crescent moon. As part of a circle, the arc symbolizes the potential fulfillment of the entire circle, the life force that is still incomplete. Therefore, it is the ideal representation of the reactive, receptive, emotional nature of the moon.

The Mercury Glyph ☿

Mercury contains all three elemental symbols: the crescent, the circle, and the cross in vertical order. This is the "Venus with a hat" glyph (compare with the symbol of Venus). With another stretch of the imagination, can't you see the winged cap of Mercury the messenger? Think of the upturned crescent as antennae that tune in and transmit messages from the sun, reminding you that Mercury is the way you communicate, the way your mind works. The upturned arc is receiving energy into the spirit or solar circle, which will later be translated into action on the material plane, symbolized by the cross. All the elements are equally sized because Mercury is neutral; it doesn't play favorites! This planet symbolizes objective, detached, unemotional thinking.

The Venus Glyph ♀

Here the relationship is between two components: the circle of spirit and the cross of matter. Spirit is elevated over matter, pulling it upward. Venus asks, "What is beautiful? What do you like best? What do you love to have done to you?" Consequently, Venus determines both your ideal of beauty and what feels good sensually. It governs your own allure and power to attract, as well as what attracts and pleases you.

The Mars Glyph ♂

In this glyph, the cross of matter is stylized into an arrowhead pointed up and outward, propelled by the circle of spirit. With a little imagination, you can visualize it as the shield and spear of Mars, the ancient god of war. You can deduce that Mars embodies your spiritual energy projected into the outer world. It's your assertiveness, your initiative, your aggressive drive, what you like to do to others, your temper. If you know someone's Mars, you know whether they'll blow up when angry or do a slow burn. Your task is to use your outgoing Mars energy wisely and well.

The Jupiter Glyph ♃

Jupiter is the basic cross of matter, with a large stylized crescent perched on the left side of the horizontal, temporal plane. You might think of the crescent as an open hand, because one meaning of Jupiter is "luck," what's handed to you. You don't have to work for what you get from Jupiter; it comes to you, if you're open to it.

The Jupiter glyph might also remind you of a jumbo jet plane, with a huge tail fin, about to take off. This is the planet of travel, mental and spiritual, of expanding your horizons via new ideas, new spiritual dimensions, and new places. Jupiter embodies the optimism and enthusiasm of the traveler about to embark on an exciting adventure.

The Saturn Glyph ♄

Flip Jupiter over, and you've got Saturn. This might not be immediately apparent because Saturn is usually stylized into an "h" form like the one shown here. The principle it expresses is the opposite of Jupiter's expansive tendencies. Saturn pulls you back to earth: the receptive arc is pushed down underneath the cross of matter. Before there are any rewards or expansion, the duties and obligations of the material world must be considered. Saturn says, "Stop, wait, finish your chores before you take off!"

Saturn's glyph also resembles the sickle of old "Father Time." Saturn was first known as Chronos, the Greek god of time, for time brings all matter to an end. When it was the most distant planet (before the discovery of Uranus), Saturn was believed to be the place where time stopped.

After the soul departed from earth, it journeyed back to the outer reaches of the universe and finally stopped at Saturn, or at "the end of time."

The Uranus Glyph ♅

The glyph for Uranus is often stylized to form a capital *H* after Sir William Herschel, who discovered the planet. But the more esoteric version curves the two pillars of the H into crescent antennae, or "ears," like satellite disks receiving signals from space. These are perched on the horizontal material line of the cross of matter and pushed from below by the circle of the spirit. To many sci-fi fans, Uranus looks like an orbiting satellite.

Uranus channels the highest energy of all, the white electrical light of the universal spiritual force that holds the cosmos together. This pure electrical energy is gathered from all over the universe. Because Uranus energy doesn't follow any ordinary celestial drumbeat, it can't be controlled or predicted (which is also true of those who are strongly influenced by this eccentric planet). In the symbol, this energy is manifested through the balance of polarities (the two opposite arms of the glyph) like the two polarized wires of a lightbulb.

The Neptune Glyph ♆

Neptune's glyph is usually stylized to look like a trident, the weapon of the Roman god Neptune. However, on a more esoteric level, it shows the large upturned crescent of the soul pierced through by the cross of matter. Neptune nails down, or materializes, soul energy, bringing impulses from the soul level into manifestation. That is why Neptune is associated with imagination or "imagining in," making an image of the soul. Neptune works through feelings, sensitivity, and the mystical capacity to bring the divine into the earthly realm.

The Pluto Glyph ♇

Pluto is written two ways. One is a composite of the letters *PL,* the first two letters of the word Pluto and coincidentally the initials of Percival Lowell, one of the planet's discoverers. The other, more esoteric symbol is a small circle above a large open crescent that surmounts the cross of matter. This depicts Pluto's power to regenerate. Imagine a new little spirit emerging from the sheltering cup of the soul. Pluto rules the forces of life and death. After this planet has passed a sensitive point in your chart, you are transformed, reborn in some way.

Sci-fi fans might visualize this glyph as a small satellite (the circle) being launched. It was shortly after Pluto's discovery that we learned how to harness the nuclear forces that made space exploration possible. Pluto rules the transformative power of atomic energy, which totally changed our lives and from which there is no turning back.

The Glyphs for the Signs

On an astrology chart, the glyph for the sign will appear after that of the planet. For example, when you see the moon glyph followed first by a number and then by another glyph representing the sign, this means that the moon was passing over a certain degree of that astrological sign at the time of the chart. On the dividing lines between the houses on your chart, you'll find the symbol for the sign that rules the house.

Because sun sign symbols do not contain the same basic geometric components of the planetary glyphs, we must look elsewhere for clues to their meanings. Many have been passed down from ancient Egyptian and Chaldean civilizations with few modifications. Others have been adapted over the centuries.

In deciphering many of the glyphs, you'll often find that the symbols reveal a dual nature of the sign, which is not always apparent in the usual sun sign descriptions. For instance, the Gemini glyph is similar to the Roman numeral for two, and reveals this sign's longing to discover a twin soul. The Cancer glyph may be interpreted as resembling either the nurturing breasts or the self-protective claws of a crab, both symbols associated with the contrasting qualities of this sign. Libra's glyph embodies the duality of the spirit balanced with material reality. The Sagittarius glyph shows that the aspirant must also carry along the earthly animal nature in his quest. The Capricorn sea goat is another symbol with dual emphasis. The goat climbs high, yet is always pulled back by the deep waters of the unconscious. Aquarius embodies the double waves of mental detachment, balanced by the desire for connection with others, in a friendly way. Finally, the two fishes of Pisces, which are forever tied together, show the duality of the soul and the spirit that must be reconciled.

The Aries Glyph ♈

Since the symbol for Aries is the Ram, this glyph is obviously associated with a ram's horns, which characterize one aspect of the Aries personality—an aggressive, me-first, leaping-headfirst attitude. But the symbol can be interpreted in other ways as well. Some astrologers liken it to a fountain of energy, which Aries people also embody. The first sign of the zodiac bursts on the scene eagerly, ready to go. Another analogy is to the eyebrows and nose of the human head, which Aries rules, and the thinking power that is initiated by the brain.

One theory of this symbol links it to the Egyptian god Amun, represented by a ram in ancient times. As Amun-Ra, this god was believed to embody the creator of the universe, the leader of all the other gods. This relates easily to the position of Aries as the leader (or first sign) of the zodiac, which begins at the spring equinox, a time of the year when nature is renewed.

The Taurus Glyph ♉

This is another easy glyph to draw and identify. It takes little imagination to decipher the bull's head with long curving horns. Like its symbol the Bull, the archetypal Taurus is slow to anger but ferocious when provoked, as well as stubborn, steady, and sensual. Another association is the larynx (and thyroid) of the throat area (ruled by Taurus) and the eustachian tubes running up to the ears, which coincides with the relationship of Taurus to the voice, song, and music. Many famous singers, musicians, and composers have prominent Taurus influences.

Many ancient religions involved a bull as the central figure in fertility rites or initiations, usually symbolizing the victory of man over his animal nature. Another possible origin is in the sacred bull of Egypt, who embodied the incarnate form of Osiris, god of death and resurrection. In early Christian imagery, the Taurus Bull represented St. Luke.

The Gemini Glyph ♊

The standard glyph immediately calls to mind the Roman numeral for two (II) and the Twins symbol, as it is called, for Gemini. In almost all drawings and images used for this sign, the relationship between two persons is emphasized. Usually one twin will be touching the other, which signifies communication, human contact, the desire to share.

The top line of the Gemini glyph indicates mental communication, while the bottom line indicates shared physical space.

The most famous Gemini legend is that of the twin sons, Castor and Pollux, one of whom had a mortal father while the other was the son of Zeus, king of the gods. When it came time for the mortal twin to die, his grief-stricken brother pleaded with Zeus, who agreed to let them spend half the year on earth in mortal form and half in immortal life, with the gods on Mount Olympus. This reflects a basic duality of humankind, which possesses an immortal soul yet is also subject to the limits of mortality.

The Cancer Glyph ♋

Two convenient images relate to the Cancer glyph. It is easiest to decode the curving claws of the Cancer symbol, the Crab. Like the crab's, Cancer's element is water. This sensitive sign also has a hard protective shell to protect its tender interior. The crab must be wily to escape predators, scampering sideways and hiding under rocks. The crab also responds to the cycles of the moon, as do all shellfish. The other image is that of two female breasts, which Cancer rules, showing that this is a sign that nurtures and protects others as well as itself.

In ancient Egypt, Cancer was also represented by the scarab beetle, a symbol of regeneration and eternal life.

The Leo Glyph ♌

Notice that the Leo glyph seems to be an extension of Cancer's glyph, with a significant difference. In the Cancer glyph, the lines curve inward protectively. The Leo glyph expresses energy outwardly. And there is no duality in the symbol, the Lion, or in Leo, the sign.

Lions have belonged to the sign of Leo since earliest times. It is not difficult to imagine the king of beasts with his sweeping mane and curling tail from this glyph. The upward sweep of the glyph easily describes the positive energy of Leo: the flourishing tail, the flamboyant qualities. Anther analogy, perhaps a stretch of the imagination, is that of a heart leaping up with joy and enthusiasm, also very typical of Leo, which also rules the heart. In early Christian imagery, the Leo Lion represented St. Mark.

The Virgo Glyph ♍

You can read much into this mysterious glyph. For instance, it could represent the initials of "Mary Virgin," or a young woman holding a staff of wheat, or stylized female genitalia, all common interpretations. The M shape might also remind you that Virgo is ruled by Mercury. The cross beneath the symbol reveals the grounded, practical nature of this earth sign.

The earliest zodiacs link Virgo with the Egyptian goddess Isis, who gave birth to the god Horus after her husband

Osiris had been killed, in the archetype of a miraculous conception. There are many ancient statues of Isis nursing her baby son, which are reminiscent of medieval Virgin and Child motifs. This sign has also been associated with the image of the Holy Grail, when the Virgo symbol was substituted with a chalice.

The Libra Glyph ♎

It is not difficult to read the standard image for Libra, the Scales, into this glyph. There is another meaning, however, that is equally relevant: the setting sun as it descends over the horizon. Libra's natural position on the zodiac wheel is the descendant, or sunset position (as the Aries natural position is the ascendant, or rising sign). Both images relate to Libra's personality. Libra is always weighing pros and cons for a balanced decision. In the sunset image, the sun (male) hovers over the horizontal earth (female) before setting. Libra is the space between these lines, harmonizing yin and yang, spiritual and material, male and female, ideal and real worlds. The glyph has also been linked to the kidneys, which are associated with Libra.

The Scorpio Glyph ♏

With its barbed tail, this glyph is easy to identify as the Scorpion for the sign of Scorpio. It also represents the male sexual parts, over which the sign rules. From the arrowhead, you can draw the conclusion that Mars was once its ruler. Some earlier Egyptian glyphs for Scorpio represent it as an erect serpent, so the Serpent is an alternate symbol.

Another symbol for Scorpio, which is not identifiable in this glyph, is the Eagle. Scorpios can go to extremes, either in soaring like the eagle or self-destructing like the scorpion. In early Christian imagery, which often used zodiacal symbols, the Scorpio Eagle was chosen to symbolize the intense apostle St. John the Evangelist.

The Sagittarius Glyph ♐

This is one of the easiest to spot and draw: an upward pointing arrow lifting up a cross. The arrow is pointing skyward, while the cross represents the four elements of the material world, which the arrow must convey. Elevating materiality into spirituality is an important Sagittarius quality, which explains why this sign is associated with higher learning, religion, philosophy, travel—the aspiring professions. Sagittarius can also send barbed arrows of frankness in the pursuit of truth, so the Archer symbol for Sagittarius is apt. (Sagittarius is also the sign of the supersalesman.)

Sagittarius is symbolically represented by the centaur, a mythological creature who is half man, half horse, aiming his arrow toward the skies. Though Sagittarius is motivated by spiritual aspiration, it also must balance the powerful appetites of the animal nature. The centaur Chiron, a figure in Greek mythology, became a wise teacher who, after many adventures and world travels, was killed by a poisoned arrow.

The Capricorn Glyph ♑

One of the most difficult symbols to draw, this glyph may take some practice. It is a representation of the sea goat: a mythical animal that is a goat with a curving fish's tail. The goat part of Capricorn wants to leave the waters of the emotions and climb to the elevated areas of life. But the fish tail is the unconscious, the deep chaotic psychic level that draws the goat back. Capricorn is often trying to escape the deep, feeling part of life by submerging himself in work, steadily ascending to the top. To some people, the glyph represents a seated figure with a bent knee, a reminder that Capricorn governs the knee area of the body.

An interesting aspect of this glyph is the contrast of the sharp pointed horns—which represent the penetrating, shrewd, conscious side of Capricorn—with the swishing tail—which represents its serpentine, unconscious, emotional force. One Capricorn legend, which dates from Roman times, tells of the earthy fertility god, Pan, who tried to save himself from uncontrollable sexual desires by jumping into the Nile. His upper body then turned into a goat, while the lower part became a fish. Later, Jupiter gave him a safe haven as a constellation in the skies.

The Aquarius Glyph ≈

This ancient water symbol can be traced back to an Egyptian hieroglyph representing streams of life force. Symbolized by the Water Bearer, Aquarius is distributor of the waters of life—the magic liquid of regeneration. The two waves can also be linked to the positive and negative charges of the electrical energy that Aquarius rules, a sort of universal wavelength. Aquarius is tuned in intuitively to higher forces via this electrical force. The duality of the glyph could also refer to the dual nature of Aquarius, a sign that runs hot and cold and that is friendly but also detached in the mental world of air signs.

In Greek legends, Aquarius is represented by Ganymede, who was carried to heaven by an eagle in order to become the cupbearer of Zeus and to supervise the annual flooding of the Nile. The sign later became associated with aviation and notions of flight.

The Pisces Glyph)(

Here is an abstraction of the familiar image of Pisces, two Fishes swimming in opposite directions yet bound together by a cord. The Fishes represent the spirit—which yearns for the freedom of heaven—and the soul—which remains attached to the desires of the temporal world. During life on earth, the spirit and the soul are bound together. When they complement each other, instead of pulling in opposite directions, they facilitate the Pisces creativity. The ancient version of this glyph, taken from the Egyptians, had no connecting line, which was added in the fourteenth century.

In another interpretation, it is said that the left fish indicates the direction of involution or the beginning of a cycle, while the right fish signifies the direction of evolution, the way to completion of a cycle. It's an appropriate grand finale for Pisces, the last sign of the zodiac.

♎ CHAPTER 9

High-Tech Astrology: The Best Software for Your Budget and Ability

After you've acquired some basic knowledge—the signs, houses, planets, and glyphs—you have the tools to take astrology to the next level by reading charts and relating the planets to the lives of friends, relatives, and daily events.

If you have a computer, the easiest way to do this is to use astrology software that can put a chart on the screen in seconds and even help you interpret it.

When it comes to astrology software, there are endless options. How do you make the right choice? First, define your goals. Do you want to do charts of friends and family, study celebrity charts, or check the aspects every day on your Palm Pilot? Do you want to invest in a more comprehensive program that adapts to your changing needs as you learn astrology?

The good news is that there's a program for every level of interest in all price points—starting with free. For the dabbler, there are the affordable Winstar Express and Time Passages. For the serious student, there are Astrolog (free), Solar Fire, Kepler, Winstar Plus—software that does every technique on planets and gives you beautiful chart printouts. You can do a chart of someone you've just met on your PDA with Astracadabra. If you're a Mac user, you'll be satisfied with the wonderful IO and Time Passages software.

However, since all the programs use the astrology symbols, or glyphs, for planets and signs, rather than written words, you should learn the glyphs before you purchase your software. Our chapter on the glyphs in this book will help you do just that. Here are some software options for you to explore.

Easy for Beginners

Time Passages

Designed for either a Macintosh or Windows computer, Time Passages is straightforward and easy to use. It allows you to generate charts and interpretation reports for yourself or friends and loved ones at the touch of a button. If you haven't yet learned the astrology symbols, this might be the program for you; just roll your mouse over any symbol of the planets, signs, or house cusps, and you'll be shown a description in plain English below the chart. Then click on the planet, sign, or house cusp and up pops a detailed interpretation. It couldn't be easier. A new basic edition, under fifty dollars at this writing, is bargain priced and ideal for beginners.

Time Passages
(866) 772-7876 (866-77-ASTRO)
Web site: www.astrograph.com

Growth Opportunities

Astrolabe

Astrolabe is one of the top astrology software resources. Check out the latest version of their powerful Solar Fire software for Windows. A breeze to use, it will grow with your increasing knowledge of astrology to the most sophisticated levels. This company also markets a variety of programs for all levels of expertise and a wide selection of computer-generated astrology readings. This is a good resource for innovative software as well as applications for older computers.

The Astrolabe Web site is a great place to start your astrology tour of the Internet. Visitors to the site are greeted with a chart of the time you log on. And you can get your chart calculated, also free, with an interpretation e-mailed to you.

Astrolabe
Box 1750-R
Brewster, MA 02631
Phone: (800) 843-6682
Web site: www.alabe.com

Matrix Software

You'll find a wide variety of software at student and advanced levels in all price ranges, demo disks, and lots of interesting readings. Check out Winstar Express, a powerful but reasonably priced program suitable for all skill levels. The Matrix Web site offers lots of fun activities for Web surfers, such as free readings from the *I Ching,* the runes, and the tarot. There are many free desktop backgrounds with astrology themes. Go here to connect with news groups and online discussions. Their online almanac helps you schedule the best day to sign on the dotted line, ask for a raise, or plant your tomatoes.

Matrix Software
126 South Michigan Avenue
Big Rapids, MI 49307
Phone: (800) 416-3924
Web site: www.astrologysoftware.com

Astro Communications Services (ACS)

Books, software for Mac and IBM compatibles, individual charts, and telephone readings are offered by this California company. Their freebies include astrology greeting cards and new moon reports. Find technical astrology materials here, such as *The American Ephemeris* and PC atlases. ACS will calculate and send charts to you, a valuable service if you do not have a computer.

ACS Publications
P.O. Box 1646
El Cajon, CA 92022-1646
Phone: (800) 514-5070
Fax: (619) 631-0180
Web site: www.astrocom.com

Air Software

Here you'll find powerful, creative astrology software, and current stock market analysis. Financial astrology programs for stock market traders are a specialty. There are some interesting freebies at this site; check out the maps of eclipse paths for any year and a free astrology clock program.

Air Software
115 Caya Avenue
West Hartford, CT 06110
Phone: (800) 659-1247
Web site: www.alphee.com

Kepler: State of the Art

Here's a program that has everything. Gorgeous graphic images, audio-visual effects, and myriad sophisticated chart options are built into this fascinating software. It's even got an astrological encyclopedia, plus diagrams and images to help you understand advanced concepts. This program is expensive, but if you're serious about learning astrology, it's an investment that will grow with you! Check out its features at www.astrologysoftwareshop.com.

Time Cycles Research: For Mac Users

Here's where Mac users can find astrology software that's as sophisticated as it gets. If you have a Mac, you'll love their beautiful graphic IO Series programs.

Time Cycles Research
P.O. Box 797
Waterford, CT 06385
Web site: www.timecycles.com
(800) 827-2240

Shareware and Freeware: The Price Is Right!

Halloran Software: A Super Shareware Program

Check out Halloran Software's Web site (www.halloran. com), which offers several levels of Windows astrology software. Beginners should consider their Astrology for Windows shareware program, which is available in unregistered demo form as a free download and in registered form for a very reasonable price.

Halloran Software
P.O. Box 75713
Los Angeles, CA 90075
(800) 732-4628

Astrolog

If you're computer-savvy, you can't go wrong with Walter Pullen's amazingly complete Astrolog program, which is offered absolutely free at the site. The Web address is www.astrolog.org/astrolog.htm.

Astrolog is an ultrasophisticated program with all the features of much more expensive programs. It comes in versions for all formats—DOS, Windows, Mac, UNIX—and has some cool features, such as a revolving globe and a constellation map. If you are looking for astrology software with bells and whistles that doesn't cost big bucks, this program has it all!

Programs for the Pocket PDA and Palm Pilot

Would you like to have astrology at your fingertips everywhere you go? No need to drag along your laptop. You can check the chart of the moment or of someone you've just met on your pocket PDA or Palm Pilot. As with most other programs, you'll need to know the astrological symbols in order to read the charts.

For the pocket PC that has the Microsoft Pocket PC 2002 or the Microsoft Windows Mobile 2003 operating system, there is the versatile Astracadabra, which can interchange charts with the popular Solar Fire software. It can be ordered at www.leelehman.com or www.astrologysoftwareshop.com.

For the Palm OS5 and compatible handheld devices, there is Astropocket from www.yves.robert.org/features.html. This is a shareware program, which allows you to use all the features free. However, you cannot store more than one chart at a time until you pay a mere twenty-eight-dollar registration fee for the complete version.

♎ CHAPTER 10

Travel the World of Astrology

There's a world of astrology waiting to welcome you, and thanks to the Internet, it's now possible to connect instantly with astrology fans and events around the globe. There are so many ways out there to expand your knowledge and share with others. Consider studying with a famous astrologer or attending a local astrology club or regional workshop. You could even combine your vacation with an astrological workshop in an exotic locale such as Bali or Mexico.

You need only type the word *astrology* into any Internet search engine and watch hundreds of listings of astrology-related sites pop up. There are local meetings and international conferences where you can connect with other astrologers, and books and tapes to help you study at home.

To help you sort out the variety of options available, here are our top picks of the Internet and the astrological community at large.

Nationwide Astrology Organizations and Conferences

Meet the World's Best Astrologers at UAC!

From May 14 to 21, 2008, the best astrologers from around the world will gather in Denver, Colorado, site of the United

Astrology Conference. UAC is jointly sponsored by three nonprofit educational organizations: AFAN (Association for Astrological Networking), ISAR (International Society for Astrological Research), and NCGR (National Council for Geocosmic Research). This conference attracts astrology fans from North and South America, Europe, Russia, India, Japan, South Africa, Australia, and New Zealand.

Here's your chance to meet and socialize with the world's top astrologers, who'll be participating in a global forum on modern astrology. There will be an all-star lineup of lectures on a variety of financial, metaphysical, psychological, and scientific topics for astrology professionals, students, and beginners. Whatever your level of expertise, there's a track for you at UAC.

Preview the conference at the convention site Web site, www.uacastrology.com.

National Council for Geocosmic Research (NCGR)

Whether you'd like to know more about such specialties as financial astrology or techniques for timing events, or if you'd prefer the psychological or mythological approach, you'll meet the top astrologers at conferences sponsored by the National Council for Geocosmic Research. NCGR is dedicated to providing quality education, bringing astrologers and astrology fans together at conferences, and promoting fellowship. Their course structure provides a systematized study of the many facets of astrology. The organization sponsors educational workshops, taped lectures, conferences, and a directory of professional astrologers. For an annual membership fee, you get their excellent publications and newsletters, plus the opportunity to network with other astrology buffs at local chapter events. (At this writing there are chapters in twenty-six states and four countries.)

To join NCGR for the latest information on upcoming events and chapters in your city, consult their Web site: www.geocosmic.org.

American Federation of Astrologers (AFA)

Established in 1938, this is one of the oldest astrological organizations in the United States. AFA offers conferences, conventions, and a thorough correspondence course. If you are looking for a reading, their interesting Web site will refer you to an accredited AFA astrologer.

AFA
6535 S. Rural Road
Tempe, AZ 85283
Phone: (888) 301-7630 or (480) 838-1751
Fax: (480) 838-8293
Web site: www.astrologers.com

Association for Astrological Networking (AFAN)

Did you know that astrologers are still being harassed for practicing astrology? AFAN provides support and legal information and works toward improving the public image of astrology. AFAN's network of local astrologers links with the international astrological community. Here are the people who will go to bat for astrology when it is attacked in the media. Everyone who cares about astrology should join!

AFAN
8306 Wilshire Boulevard
PMB 537
Beverly Hills, CA 90211
Phone: (800) 578-2326
E-mail: info@afan.org
Web site: www.afan.org

International Society for Astrology Research (ISAR)

An international organization of professional astrologers dedicated to encouraging the highest standards of quality in the field of astrology with an emphasis on research. Among ISAR's benefits are a quarterly journal, a weekly e-mail newsletter, frequent conferences, and a free membership directory.

ISAR
P.O. Box 38613
Los Angeles, CA 90038
Fax: (805) 933-0301
Web site: www.isarastrology.com

Astrology Magazines

In addition to articles by top astrologers, most of these have listings of astrology conferences, events, and local happenings.

Horoscope Guide
Kappa Publishing Group
6198 Butler Pike
Suite 200
Blue Bell, PA 19422-2600
Web site: www.kappapublishing.com/astrology

Dell Horoscope
Their Web site (www.dellhoroscope.com) features a listing of local astrological meetings.

Customer Service
6 Prowitt Street
Norwalk, CT 06855
(800) 220-7443

The Mountain Astrologer

A favorite magazine of astrology fans! *The Mountain Astrologer* also has an interesting Web site featuring the latest news from an astrological point of view, plus feature articles from the magazine.

The Mountain Astrologer
P.O. Box 970
Cedar Ridge, CA 95924
Phone: (800) 247-4828
Web site: www.mountainastrologer.com

Astrology College

Kepler College of Astrological Arts and Sciences

A degree-granting college, which is also a center of astrology, has long been the dream of the astrological community and is a giant step forward in providing credibility to the profession. Therefore, the opening of Kepler College in 2000 was a historical event for astrology. It is the only college in the western hemisphere authorized to issue B.A. and M.A. degrees in Astrological Studies. Here is where to study with the best scholars, teachers, and communicators in the field. A long-distance study program is available for those interested.

For more information, contact:

Kepler College of Astrological Arts and Sciences
4630 200th Street SW
Suite A-1
Lynnwood, WA 98036
Phone: (425) 673-4292
Fax: (425) 673-4983
Web site: www.kepler.edu

Our Favorite Web Sites

Of the thousands of astrological Web sites that come and go on the Internet, these have stood the test of time and are likely to still be operating when this book is published.

Astrodienst (www.astro.com)

Don't miss this fabulous international site that has long
been one of the best astrology resources on the Internet.
It's also a great place to view and download your own
astrology chart. The world atlas on this site will give you
the accurate longitude and latitude of your birthplace for
setting up your horoscope. Then you can print out your
free chart in a range of easy-to-read formats. Other attrac-
tions: a list of famous people born on your birth date, a
feature that helps you choose the best vacation spot, plus
articles by world-famous astrologers.

AstroDatabank (www.astrodatabank.com)

When the news is breaking, you can bet this site will be
the first to get accurate birthdays of the headliners. The
late astrologer Lois Rodden was a stickler for factual information and her meticulous research is being continued,
much to the benefit of the astrological community. The
Web site specializes in charts of current newsmakers, political figures, and international celebrities. You can also participate in discussions and analysis of the charts and see
what some of the world's best astrologers have to say about
them. Their AstroDatabank program, which you can purchase at the site, provides thousands of verified birthdays
sorted into categories. It's an excellent research tool.

StarIQ (www.stariq.com)

Find out how top astrologers view the latest headlines at
the must-see StarIQ site. Many of the best minds in astrology comment on the latest news, stock market ups and
downs, political contenders. You can sign up to receive e-
mail forecasts at the most important times keyed to your
individual chart. (This is one of the best of the many online forecasts.)

Astro-Noetics (www.astro-noetics.com)

For those who are ready to explore astrology's interface with politics, popular culture, and current events, here is a sophisticated site with in-depth articles and personality profiles. Lots of depth and content here for the astrology-savvy surfer.

Astrology Books (www.astroamerica.com)

The Astrology Center of America sells a wide selection of books on all aspects of astrology, from the basics to the most advanced, at this online bookstore. Also available are many hard-to-find and recycled books.

Astrology Scholars' Sites

See what one of astrology's great teachers, Robert Hand, has to offer on his site: www.robhand.com. A leading expert on the history of astrology, he's on the cutting edge of the latest research.

The Project Hindsight group of astrologers is devoted to restoring the astrology of the Hellenistic period, the primary source for all later Western astrology. There are fascinating articles for astrology fans on this site, www.project-hindsight.com.

Financial Astrology Sites

Financial astrology is a hot specialty, with many tipsters, players, and theorists. There are online columns, newsletters, specialized financial astrology software, and mutual funds run by astrology seers. One of the more respected financial astrologers is Ray Merriman, whose stock market comments on www.mmacycles.com are a must read for those following the bulls and bears. Other top financial astrologers offer tips and forecasts at the www.afund.com and www.alphee.com sites.

CHAPTER 11

Is It Time for a Personal Reading?

Looking for answers to a burning personal question? A reading with a professional astrologer might help. A reading can be an empowering experience if you want to reach your full potential. You could use it for sizing up a lover or business situation to find out what the future has in store. If you're in a quandary about a problem, some astrological perspective could be an eye-opener. It might help you make over your life by choosing a more satisfying career or moving to a more favorable location. You could use it to find the optimum time for an important event such as a wedding or get the competitive edge in a meeting.

Another good reason for a reading is to refine your knowledge of astrology by consulting with someone who has years of experience analyzing charts. You might choose someone with a special technique that intrigues you. Armed with the knowledge of your chart that you have acquired so far, you can then learn to interpret subtle nuances or gain insight on your talents and abilities.

How do you choose when there are so many different kinds of readings available, especially since the Internet has brought astrology into the mainstream? Besides individual one-on-one readings with a professional astrologer, there are personal readings by mail, telephone, Internet, and tape. Well-advertised computer-generated reports and celebrity-sponsored readings are sure to attract your attention on commercial Web sites and in magazines. Then there are astrologers who specialize in certain areas such as finance or medical astrology. And unfortunately, there are many questionable practitioners who range from streetwise gypsy fortune-tellers to unscrupulous scam artists.

The following basic guidelines can help you sort out your options to find the reading that's right for you.

One-on-One Consultations with a Professional Astrologer

Nothing compares to a one-on-one consultation with a professional astrologer who has analyzed thousands of charts and can pinpoint the potential in yours. During your reading, you can get your specific questions answered. For instance, how to get along better with your mate or coworker. There are many astrologers who now combine their skills with training in psychology and are well-suited to help you examine your alternatives.

To give you an accurate reading, an astrologer needs certain information from you: the date, time, and place where you were born. (A horoscope can be cast about anyone or anything that has a specific time and place.) Most astrologers will then enter this information into a computer, which will calculate a chart in seconds. From the resulting chart, the astrologer will do an interpretation.

If you don't know your exact birth time, you can usually locate it at the Bureau of Vital Statistics at the city hall or county seat of the state where you were born. If you still have no success in getting your time of birth, some astrologers can estimate an approximate birth time by using past events in your life to determine the chart. This technique is called *rectification*.

How to Find an Astrologer

Choose your astrologer with the same care as you would any trusted adviser such as a doctor, lawyer, or banker. Unfortunately, anyone can claim to be an astrologer—to date, there is no licensing of astrologers or universally established professional criteria. However, there are nation-wide organizations of serious, committed astrologers that can help you in your search.

Good places to start your investigation are organizations such as the American Federation of Astrologers (AFA) or the National Council for Geocosmic Research (NCGR), which offer a program of study and certification. If you live near a major city, there is sure to be an active NCGR chapter or astrology club in your area; many are listed in astrology magazines available at your local newsstand. In response to many requests for referrals, both the AFA and the NCGR have directories of professional astrologers listed on their Web sites; these directories include a glossary of terms and an explanation of specialties within the astrological field. Contact the NCGR and AFA headquarters for information (see chapter 10 in this book).

Warning Signals

As a potentially lucrative freelance business, astrology has always attracted self-styled experts who may not have the knowledge or the counseling experience to give a helpful reading. These astrologers can range from the well-meaning amateur to the charlatan or street-corner gypsy who has for many years given astrology a bad name. Be very wary of astrologers who claim to have occult powers or who make pretentious claims of celebrated clients or miraculous achievements. You can often tell from the initial phone conversation if the astrologer is legitimate. He or she should ask for your birthday time and place, then conduct the conversation in a professional manner. Any astrologer who gives a reading based only on your sun sign is highly suspect.

When you arrive at the reading, the astrologer should be prepared. The consultation should be conducted in a private, quiet place. The astrologer should be interested in your problems of the moment. A good reading involves feedback on your part. So if the reading is not relating to your concerns, you should let the astrologer know. You should feel free to ask questions and get clarifications of technical terms. The more you actively participate, rather than expecting the astrologer to carry the reading or come forth with oracular predictions, the more meaningful your experience will be. An astrologer should help you validate your current experience and be frank about possible negative happenings, but also suggest a positive course of action.

In their approach to a reading, some astrologers may be more literal, others more intuitive. Those who have had counseling training may take a more psychological approach. Though some astrologers may seem to have an almost psychic ability, extrasensory perception or any other parapsychological talent is not essential. A very accurate picture can be drawn from the data in your horoscope chart.

An astrologer may do several charts for each client, including one for the time of birth and a *progressed chart,* showing the evolution from birth to the present time. According to your individual needs, there are many other possibilities, such as a chart for a different location if you are contemplating a change of place. Relationships between any two people, things, or events can be interpreted with a chart that compares one partner's horoscope with the other's. A composite chart, which uses the midpoint between planets in two individual charts to describe the relationship, is another commonly used device.

An astrologer will be particularly interested in transits, those times when cycling planets activate the planets or sensitive points in your birth chart. These indicate important events in your life.

Many astrologers offer tape-recorded readings, another option to consider, especially if the astrologer you choose lives at a distance. In this case, you'll be mailed a taped reading based on your birth chart. This type of reading is more personal than a computer printout and can give you valuable insights, though it is not equivalent to a live dialogue with the astrologer when you can discuss your specific interests and issues of the moment.

The Telephone Reading

Telephone readings come in two varieties: a dial-in taped reading, usually recorded in advance by an astrologer, or a live consultation with an "astrologer" on the other end of the line. The taped readings are general daily or weekly forecasts, applied to all members of your sign and charged by the minute. The quality depends on the astrologer. One caution: Be aware that these readings can run up quite a telephone bill, especially if you get into the habit of calling every day. Be sure that you are aware of the per-minute cost of each call beforehand.

Live telephone readings also vary with the expertise of the astrologer. Ideally, the astrologer at the other end of the line enters your birth date into a computer, which then quickly calculates your chart. This chart will be referred to during the consultation. The advantage of a live telephone reading is that your individual chart is used and you can ask about a specific problem. However, before you invest in any reading, be sure that your astrologer is qualified and that you fully understand in advance how much you will be charged. There should be no unpleasant financial surprises later.

Computer-Generated Reports

Companies that offer computer programs (such as ACS, Matrix, Astrolabe) also offer a variety of computer-generated horoscope readings. These can be quite comprehensive, offering a beautiful printout of the chart plus many pages of detailed information about each planet and aspect of the chart. You can then study it at your convenience. Of course, the interpretations will be general, since there is no personal input from you, and may not cover your immediate concerns. Since computer-generated horoscopes are much lower in cost than live consultations, you might consider one as either a supplement or a preparation for an eventual live reading. You'll then be more familiar with your chart and able to plan specific questions in advance. They also make terrific gifts for astrology fans. There are several companies, listed in chapter 9, that offer computerized readings prepared by reputable astrologers.

Whichever option you decide to pursue, may your reading be an empowering one!

♎ CHAPTER 12

Your Baby-scope: Children Born in 2008

Parents of several children may see a marked difference between children born in 2008 and their older siblings, as the cosmic atmosphere is changing, which should imprint the personalities of this year's children.

Astrologers look to the slow-moving outer planets—Uranus, Neptune, and Pluto—to describe a generation. This year, Uranus and Neptune are still passing through Pisces and Aquarius, both visionary and spiritual signs. However, there is also much more earth-sign emphasis than in previous years due to the earthly pull of Pluto in Capricorn, plus the closer planets, Jupiter and Saturn, also in earth signs, which will counterbalance this spirituality with extreme practicality and pragmatism. This generation will be focused on getting the job done, on fixing up the planet, and on making things work.

Astrology can be an especially helpful tool that can be used to design an environment that will enhance and encourage each child's positive qualities. Some parents start before conception, planning the birth of their child as far as possible to harmonize with the signs of other family members. However, each baby has its own schedule, so if yours arrives a week early or late, or elects a different sign than you'd planned, recognize that the new sign may be more in line with the mission your child is here to accomplish. In other words, if you were hoping for a Libra child and he arrives during Virgo, that Virgo energy may be just what is needed to stimulate or complement your family. Remember that there are many astrological elements besides the sun sign that indicate strong family ties. Usually each child will share a particular planetary placement, an emphasis on a particular sign or house, or a certain chart configuration with his parents and other family members. Often there is a significant planetary angle that will define the parent-child relationship, such as family sun signs that form a T-square or a triangle.

One important thing you can do is to be sure the exact moment of birth is recorded. This will be essential in calculating an accurate astrological chart. The following descriptions can be applied to the sun or moon sign (if known) of a child—the sun sign will describe basic personality and the moon sign indicates the child's emotional needs.

The Aries Child

Baby Aries is quite a handful! This energetic child will walk—and run—as soon as possible and perform daring feats of exploration. Caregivers should be vigilant. Little Aries seems to know no fear (and is especially vulnerable to head injuries). Many Aries children, in their rush to get on with life, seem hyperactive and are easily frustrated when they can't get their own way. Violent temper tantrums and dramatic physical displays are par for the course with these children, necessitating a time-out chair.

The very young Aries should be monitored carefully, since he is prone to take risks and may injure himself. An Aries loves to take things apart and may break toys easily, but with encouragement, the child will develop formidable coordination. Aries's bossy tendencies should be molded into leadership qualities, rather than bullying. Otherwise, the me-first Aries will have many clashes with other strong-willed youngsters. Encourage these children to take out aggressions and frustrations in active, competitive sports, where they usually excel. When a young Aries learns to focus his energies long enough to master a subject and learns consideration for others, the indomitable Aries spirit will rise to the head of the class.

Aries born in 2008 will be a more subdued version of

this sign, but still loaded with energy. The Capricorn effect should make little Aries easier to discipline and more focused on achievement. A natural leader!

The Taurus Child

This is a cuddly, affectionate child who eagerly explores the world of the senses, especially the senses of taste and touch. The Taurus child can be a big eater and will put on weight easily if not encouraged to exercise. Since this child likes comfort and gravitates to beauty, try coaxing little Taurus to exercise to music or take him outdoors for hikes or long walks. Though Taurus may be a slow learner, this sign has an excellent retentive memory and generally masters a subject thoroughly. Taurus is interested in results and will see each project patiently through to completion, continuing long after others have given up. This year's earth-sign planet will give him a wonderful sense of support and accomplishment.

Choose Taurus toys carefully to help develop innate talents. Construction toys, such as blocks or erector sets, appeal to their love of building. Paints or crayons develop their sense of color. Many Taurus have musical talents and love to sing, which is apparent at a young age.

This year's Taurus will want a pet or two and a few plants of his own. Give little Taurus a minigarden and watch the natural green thumb develop. This child has a strong sense of acquisition and an early grasp of material value. After filling a piggy bank, Taurus graduates to a savings account, before other children have started to learn the value of money.

This year's Taurus gets a bonanza of good luck and support from Jupiter, Pluto, and Saturn—all in compatible earth signs. These should give little Taurus an especially easygoing disposition and provide many opportunities to live up to his sign's potential.

The Gemini Child

Little Gemini will talk as soon as possible, filing the air with questions and chatter. This is a friendly child who enjoys social contact, seems to require company, and adapts quickly to different surroundings. Geminis have quick minds that easily grasp the use of words, books, and telephones and will probably learn to talk and read at an earlier age than most. Though they are fast learners, Gemini may have a short attention span, darting from subject to subject. Projects and games that help focus the mind could be used to help them concentrate. Musical instruments, typewriters, and computers help older Gemini children combine mental with manual dexterity. Geminis should be encouraged to finish what they start before they go on to another project. Otherwise, they can become jack-of-all-trade types who have trouble completing anything they do. Their dispositions are usually cheerful and witty, making these children popular with their peers and delightful company at home.

This year's Gemini baby should go to the head of the class. Uranus in Pisces could inspire Gemini to make an unusual career choice, perhaps in a financial field. When he grows up, this year's Gemini may change jobs several times before he finds a position that satisfies his need for stimulation and variety.

The Cancer Child

This emotional, sensitive child is especially influenced by patterns set early in life. Young Cancers cling to their first memories as well as their childhood possessions. They thrive in calm emotional waters, with a loving, protective mother, and usually remain close to her (even if their relationship with her was difficult) throughout their lives. Divorce, death—anything that disturbs the safe family unit—

are devastating to Cancers, who may need extra support and reassurance during a family crisis.

They sometimes need a firm hand to push the positive, creative side of their personality and discourage them from getting swept away by emotional moods or resorting to emotional manipulation to get their way. Praised and encouraged to find creative expression, Cancer will be able to express his positive side consistently on a firm, secure foundation.

This year's Cancer baby should be a social, cooperative child, oriented toward others, thanks to Jupiter and Pluto blessing relationships.

The Leo Child

Leo children love the limelight and will plot to get the lion's share of attention. These children assert themselves with flair and drama and can behave like tiny tyrants to get their way. But in general, they have sunny, positive dispositions and are rarely subject to blue moods. At school, they're the ones who are voted most popular, head cheerleader, or homecoming queen. Leo is sure to be noticed for personality, if not for stunning looks or academic work; the homely Leo will be a class clown and the unhappy Leo may be the class bully.

Above all, a Leo child cannot tolerate being ignored for long. Drama or performing-arts classes, sports, and school politics are healthy ways for Leo to be a star. But Leos must learn to take lesser roles occasionally, or they will have some painful put-downs in store. Usually, the popularity of Leos is well earned; they are hard workers who try to measure up to their own high standards—and usually succeed.

This year's Leo should be a less flamboyant, more down-to-earth version of his sign, as the earthy planets exert their influence. This should add more financial and practical talents to the expressive Leo personality.

The Virgo Child

The young Virgo can be a quiet, rather serious child, with a quick, intelligent mind. Early on, little Virgo shows far more attention to detail and concern with small things than other children do. Little Virgo has a built-in sense of order and a fascination with how things work. It is important for these children to have a place of their own, which they can order as they wish and where they can read or busy themselves with crafts and hobbies.

This child's personality can be very sensitive. Little Virgo may get hyper and overreact to seemingly small irritations, which can take the form of stomach upsets or delicate digestive systems. But this child will flourish where there is mental stimulation and a sense of order. Virgos thrive in school, especially in writing or language skills, and seem truly happy when buried in books. Chances are, young Virgo will learn to read ahead of classmates. Hobbies that involve detail work or that develop fine craftsmanship are especially suited to young Virgos.

Baby Virgo of 2008 is likely to be an especially high achiever with Saturn also in Virgo, adding focus and discipline, while Jupiter transiting the house of self-expression endows extra creativity.

The Libra Child

The Libra child learns early about the power of charm and appearance. This is often a very physically appealing child with an enchanting dimpled smile, who is naturally sociable and enjoys the company of both children and adults. It is a rare Libra child who is a discipline problem, but when their behavior is unacceptable, they respond better to calm discussion than displays of emotion, especially if the discussion revolves around fairness. Because young Libras without a strong direction tend to drift with the mood of the group, these children should be encouraged to develop their unique talents and powers of discrimination so they can later stand on their own.

In school, this child is usually popular and will often have to choose between social invitations and studies. In the teen years, social pressures mount as the young Libra begins to look for a partner. This is the sign of best friends, so Libra's choice of companions can have a strong effect on his future direction. Beautiful Libra girls may be tempted to go steady or have an unwise early marriage. Chances are, both sexes will fall in and out of love several times in their search for the ideal partner.

Little Libra of 2008 is an especially social, talkative child who gets along well with siblings because Jupiter in Capricorn enhances family life. This child is endowed with much imagination and creativity, as well as communication skills.

The Scorpio Child

The Scorpio child may seem quiet and shy, but will surprise others with intense feelings and formidable willpower. Scorpio children are single-minded when they want something and intensely passionate about whatever they do. One of a caregiver's tasks is to teach this child to balance activities and emotions, yet at the same time to make the most of his or her great concentration and intense commitment.

Since young Scorpios do not show their depth of feelings easily, parents will have to learn to read almost imperceptible signs that troubles are brewing beneath the surface. Both Scorpio boys and girls enjoy games of power and control on or off the playground. Scorpio girls may take an early interest in the opposite sex, masquerading as tomboys, while Scorpio boys may be intensely competitive and loners. When their powerful energies are directed into work, sports, or challenging studies, Scorpio is a superachiever, focused on a goal. With trusted friends, young Scorpio is devoted and caring—the proverbial friend through thick and thin, loyal for life.

Scorpio 2008 has a strong financial emphasis, which could make these children big money earners in adulthood. Uranus in Pisces in their house of creativity should put them on the cutting edge of whichever field they choose.

The Sagittarius Child

This restless, athletic child will be out of the playpen and off on adventures as soon as possible. Little Sagittarius is remarkably well-coordinated, attempting daredevil feats on any wheeled vehicle from scooters to skateboards. These natural athletes need little encouragement to channel their energies into sports. Their cheerful, friendly dispositions earn them popularity in school, and once they have found a subject where their talent and imagination can soar, they will do well academically. They love animals, especially horses, and will be sure to have a pet or two, if not a home zoo. When they are old enough to take care of themselves, they'll clamor to be off on adventures of their own, away from home, if possible.

This child loves to travel, will not get homesick at summer camp, and may sign up to be a foreign-exchange student or spend summers abroad. Outdoor adventure appeals to little Sagittarius, especially if it involves an active sport, such as skiing, cycling, or mountain climbing. Give them enough space and encouragement, and their fiery spirit will propel them to achieve high goals.

Baby Sagittarius of 2008 has a natural generosity of spirit and an optimistic, expansive nature. He will also demand a great deal of freedom. He may need reality checks from time to time, since he may be a risk taker, especially in the financial area. He should learn early in life how to handle money.

The Capricorn Child

These purposeful, goal-oriented children will work to capacity if they feel this will bring results. They're not ones who enjoy work for its own sake—there must be an end in sight. Authority figures can do much to motivate these children, but once set on an upward path, young Capricorns will mobilize energy and talent and work harder, and with more perseverance, than any other sign. Capricorn has built-in self-discipline that can achieve remarkable results, even if lacking the flashy personality, quick brain power, or penetrating insight of others. Once involved, young Capricorn will stick to a task until it is mastered. These children also know how to use others to their advantage and may well become team captains or class presidents.

A wise parent will set realistic goals for the Capricorn child, paving the way for the early thrill of achievement. Youngsters should be encouraged to express their caring, feeling side to others, as well as their natural aptitude for leadership. Capricorn children may be especially fond of grandparents and older relatives and will enjoy spending time with them and learning from them. It is not uncommon for young Capricorns to have an older mentor or teacher who guides them. With their great respect for authority, Capricorn children will take this influence very much to heart.

The Capricorn born in 2008 will have an upbeat, cheerful personality, thanks to the presence of lucky Jupiter in Capricorn. This child should have a generous, expansive nature and be more outgoing than the usual member of this sign.

The Aquarius Child

The Aquarius child has an innovative, well-focused mind that often streaks so far ahead of those of peers that this child seems like an oddball. Routine studies never hold the restless youngster for long; he will look for another, more experimental place to try out his ideas and develop his inventions. Life is a laboratory to the inquiring Aquarius mind. School politics, sports, science, and the arts offer scope for such talents. But if there is no room for expression within approved social limits, Aquarius is sure to rebel. Questioning institutions and religions comes naturally, so these children may find an outlet elsewhere, becoming rebels with a cause. It is better not to force this child to conform, but rather to channel forward-thinking young minds into constructive group activities.

This year's Aquarius will have far-out glamour as well as charisma, thanks to his ruler, Uranus, in a friendly bond with Neptune. This could be a rock star, a statesman, or a scientist.

The Pisces Child

Give young Pisces praise, applause, and a gentle, but firm, push in the right direction. Lovable Pisces children may be abundantly talented, but may be hesitant to express themselves, because they are quite sensitive and easily hurt. It is a parent's challenge to help them gain self-esteem and self-confidence. However, this same sensitivity makes them trusted friends who'll have many confidants as they develop socially. It also endows many Pisces with spectacular creative talent.

Pisces adores drama and theatrics of all sorts; therefore, encourage them to channel their creativity into art forms rather than indulging in emotional dramas. Understand that they may need more solitude than other children, as they develop their creative ideas. But though daydreaming can be creative, it is important that these natural dreamers not dwell too long in the world of fantasy. Teach them practical coping skills for the real world. Since Pisces are physically sensitive, parents should help them build strong bodies with proper diet and regular exercise. Young Pisces may gravitate to more individual sports, such as swimming, sailing, and skiing, rather than to team sports. Or they may prefer more artistic physical activities like dance or ice skating.

Born givers, these children are often drawn to the underdog (they fall quickly for sob stories) and attract those who might take advantage of their empathic nature. Teach them to choose friends wisely and to set boundaries in relationships, to protect their emotional vulnerability—invaluable lessons in later life.

With the planet Uranus now in Pisces, the 2008 baby

belongs to a generation of Pisces movers and shakers. This child may have a rebellious streak that rattles the status quo. But this generation also has a visionary nature, which will be much concerned with the welfare of the world at large.

CHAPTER 13

Your Leap Year Guide to Love

The year 2008 is a leap year, when ladies traditionally make the first romantic moves. However, it's no longer unusual for women to pursue the object of their desire aggressively, no matter what the year. So if you want to charm a Capricorn, hook a Pisces, or corral a Taurus, here are sun-sign seduction tips guaranteed to keep your lover begging for more.

How to Love Every Sign

Aries: Daredevil Lover

This highly physical sign is walking dynamite with a brief attention span. Don't be too easy to get, ladies. A little challenge, a lively debate, and a merry chase only heat up your admirers. They want to see what you're made of. Once you've lured them into your lair, be a challenge, a bit of a daredevil, and pull out your X-rated tricks. Don't give your all—let them know there's more where that came from. Make it exciting, show you're up for adventure. Wear bright red somewhere interesting. Since Aries rules the head and face, be sure to focus on these areas in your lovemaking. Use your lips, tongue, breath, and even your eyelashes to the max. Practice scalp massages and deep-kissing techniques. Aries won't wait, so when you make your move, be sure you're ready to follow through. No head games or teasing!

To keep you happy, you've got to voice your own needs, because this lover will be focused on his. Teach him how to please, or this could be a one-sided adventure.

Taurus: Sweet Treats

Taurus wins as the most sensual sign, with the most sexual stamina. This man is earthy and lusty in bed; he can go on all night. This is not a sign to tease. Like the Bull, he'll see red, not bed. So make him comfortable, then bombard all his senses. Good food gets Taurus in the mood. So do the right music and fragrance, revealing clothes, and luxurious bed linens. Give him a massage with delicious-smelling and -tasting oils; focus on the neck area.

Don't forget to turn off the phone! Taurus hates interruptions. Since they can be very vocal lovers, choose a setting where you won't be disturbed. And don't ever rush; enjoy a long, slow, delicious encounter.

Gemini: Playtime

Playful Gemini loves games, so make your seduction fun. Be their lost twin soul, their confidant. Good communication is essential, so share deep secrets, live out fantasies. This sign adores variety. Nothing bores Gemini more than making love the same way all the time, or bringing on the heavy emotions. So trot out all the roles you've been longing to play. Here's the perfect partner. But remember to keep it light and fun. Gemini's turn-on zone is the hands, and this sign gives the best massages. Gadgets that can be activated with a touch amuse Gemini. This sign is great at doing two things at once, like making love while watching an erotic film. Turn the cell phone off unless you want company. On the other hand, Gemini is your sign for superhot phone sex.

Gemini loves a change of scene. So experiment on the floor, in the shower, or on the kitchen table. Borrow a friend's apartment or rent a room in a hotel for variety.

Cancer: In the Mood

The key to Cancer is to get this moon child in the mood. Consult the moon—a full moon is best. Wining, dining, old-fashioned courtship, and breakfast in bed are turn-ons. Whatever makes your Cancer feel secure will promote shedding inhibitions in the sack. (Don't try any of your Aries daredevil techniques here!) Cancer prefers familiar, comfortable, homey surroundings. Cancer's turn-on zone is the breasts. Cancer women often have naturally inflated chests. Cancer men may fantasize about a well-endowed playmate. If your breasts are enhanced, show them off. Cancer will want to know all your deepest secrets, so invent a few good ones. But lots of luck delving into their innermost thoughts!

A sure thing: Take your Cancer near water. The sight and sound of the sea can be their aphrodisiac. A moonlit beach, a deserted swimming pool, a Jacuzzi, and a bubble bath are good seduction spots. Listen to the rain patter on the roof in a mountain cabin.

Leo: The Royal Treatment

Leo must be the best and hear it from you often. In return, they'll perform for you, telling you just what you want to hear (true or not). They like a lover with style and endurance, to be swept off their feet and into bed. Leos like to go first-class all the way, so build them up with lots of attention, wining and dining, special gifts.

Never mention other lovers or make them feel like second best. A sure signal for Leo to look elsewhere is a competitive spouse. Leos take great pride in their body, so you should pour on the admiration. A few well-placed mirrors could inspire them. So would a striptease of beautiful lingerie, expensive fragrance on the sheets, and, if female, an occasional luxury hotel room, with champagne and caviar delivered by room service. Leo's erogenous zone is the lower back, so a massage with expensive oils would make your lion purr with pleasure.

Virgo: Pedestal Perfect

Virgo's standards are so sky-high that you may feel intimidated at first. The key to pleasing fussy Virgo lovers is to look for the hot fantasy beneath their cool surface. Secret tip: They're really looking for someone to make over. So let Virgo play teacher and you play willing student; the doctor-patient routine works as well.

Let Virgo help you improve your life, quit smoking, learn French, or diet. Read an erotic book together, then practice the techniques. Or study the esoteric, erotic exercises from Asia.

The Virgo erogenous zone is the tummy area, which should be your base of operations. Virgo likes things pristine and clean. Fall into crisp, immaculate white sheets. Wear a sheer white nightie. Smell shower-fresh with no heavy perfume. Be sure your surroundings pass the hospital test. A shower together afterward (with great-smelling soap) could get the ball rolling again.

Libra: The Beauty Lover

Libra must be turned on aesthetically. Make sure you look as beautiful as possible and wear something stylishly seductive but never vulgar. Have a mental affair first, as you flirt and flatter this sign. Then proceed to the physical. Approach Libra like a dance partner, ready to waltz or tango.

Libra must be in the mood for love; otherwise, forget it. Any kind of ugliness is a turnoff. Provide the right atmosphere, elegant and harmonious. No loud noise, clashing colors, or uncomfortable beds. Libra is not an especially spontaneous lover, so it is best to spend time warming them up. Libra's back is his erogenous zone, your cue to provide back rubs with scented potions. Once in bed, you can be a bit aggressive sexually. Libra loves strong, decisive moves. Set the scene, know what you want, and let Libra be happy to provide it.

Scorpio: The Legendary Lover

Scorpio is legendary in bed, often called the sex sign of the zodiac. But seducing them is often a power game. Scorpio likes to be in control, even the quiet, unassuming ones. Scorpio loves a mystery, so don't tell all. Keep them guessing about you, offering tantalizing hints along the way. The hint of danger often turns Scorpio on, so you'll find members of this sign experimenting with the exotic and highly erotic forms of sex. Sadomasochism and bondage, anything that tests the limits of power could be a turn-on for Scorpio.

Invest in some sexy black leather and some powerful music (depending on your tastes). Clothes that lace, buckle, or zip tempt Scorpio to untie you. Present yourself as a mysterious package just waiting to be unwrapped.

Once in bed, there are no holds barred with Scorpio. They'll find your most pleasurable pressure points and touch you as you've never been touched before. They are quickly aroused (the genital area belongs to this sign) and willing to try anything. But they can be possessive. Don't expect your Scorpio to share you with anyone. It's all or nothing for them.

Sagittarius: The Sexual Athletes

Sagittarius men are the Don Juans of the zodiac, love-'em-and-leave-'em types who are difficult to pin down. Your seduction strategy is to join them in their many pursuits, then hook them with love on the road. Sagittarius enjoys sex in venues that suggest movement: planes, SUVs, or boats. But a favorite turn-on place is outdoors, in nature. A deserted hiking path, a field of tall grass, a remote woodland glade all give the Centaur sexy ideas. Athletic Sagittarius might go for some personal training in an empty gym. Join your Sagittarius for amorous aerobics, meditate together, or explore the tantric forms of sex. Lovemaking after hiking and skiing would be healthy fun.

Sagittarius enjoys lovers from exotic ethnic backgrounds or lovers met in spiritual pursuits or on college campuses. Sagittarius are great cheerleaders and motivators, and will enjoy feeling that they have inspired you to be all that you can be.

There may be a canine or feline companion sharing your Sagittarius lover's bed with you, so check your allergies. And bring Fido or Felix a toy to keep him occupied.

Capricorn: Animal Instincts

The great news about Capricorn lovers is that they improve with age. They are probably the sexiest seniors. So stick around, if you have a young one. They're lusty in bed (it's not the sign of the Goat for nothing), and can be quite raunchy and turned on by X-rated words and deeds. If this is not your thing, let them know. The Capricorn erogenous zone is the knees. Some discreet fondling in public places could be your opener. Capricorn tends to think of sex as part of a game plan for the future. They are well-organized, and might regard lovemaking as relaxation after a long day's work. This sign often combines business with pleasure. So look for a Capricorn where there's a convention, trade show, or work-related conference.

Getting Capricorn's mind off his agenda and onto yours could take some doing. Separate him from his buddies by whispering sexy secrets in his ear. Then convince him you're an asset to his image and a boon to his health. Though he may seem uptight at first, you'll soon discover he's a love animal who makes a wonderful and permanent pet.

Aquarius: Far-Out Lover

This sign really does not want an all-consuming passion or an all-or-nothing relationship. Aquarius need space. But once they feel free to experiment with a spontaneous and exciting partner, Aquarius can give you a far-out sexual adventure.

Passion begins in the mind, so a good mental buildup is key. Aquarius is an inventive sign who believes love is a playground without rules. Plan surprise, unpredictable encounters in unusual places. Find ways to make love transcendental, an extraordinary and unique experience. Be ready to try anything Aquarius suggests, if only once. Calves and ankles are the special Aquarius erogenous zones, so perfect your legwork.

Be careful not to be too possessive. Your Aquarius needs lots of space, tolerance for friends (including old lovers), and their many outside interests.

Pisces: Fantasy Time

Pisces is the sign of fantasy and imagination. This sign has great theatrical talent. Pisces looks for lovers who will take care of them. Pisces will return the favor! Here is someone who can psych out your deepest desires without mentioning them. Pisces falls for sob stories and is always ready to empathize. It wouldn't hurt to have a small problem for Pisces to help you overcome. It might help if you cry on his shoulder, for this sign needs to be needed. Use your imagination when setting the scene for love. A dramatic setting brings out Pisces theatrical talents. Or creatively use the element of water. Rain on the roof, waterfalls, showers, beach houses, waterbeds, and Jacuzzis could turn up the heat. Experiment with pulsating jets of water. Skinny-dip at midnight in deserted pools.

The Pisces erogenous zone is the feet. This is your cue to give a sensuous foot massage using scented lotions. Let him paint your toes. Beautiful toenails in sexy sandals are a special turn-on.

Your Hot Planets: Mars and Venus Tango Together

Here's a tip for finding your hottest love match. If your lover's Mars sign makes favorable aspects to your Venus, is in the same element (earth, air, fire, water), or is in the same sign, your lover will do what you want done! Mars influences how we act when we make love, while Venus shows what we like done to us. Sometimes fighting and making up is the sexiest fun of all. If you're the type who needs a spark to keep lust alive (you know who you are!), then look for Mars and Venus in different signs of the same quality (fixed or cardinal or mutable). For instance, a fixed sign (Taurus, Leo, Scorpio, Aquarius) paired with another fixed sign can have a sexy standoff, a hot tug of war before you finally surrender. Two cardinal signs (Aries, Cancer, Libra, Capricorn) set off passionate fireworks when they clash. Mutable signs (Gemini, Virgo, Sagittarius, Pisces) play a fascinating game of cat and mouse, never quite catching each other.

The Best Time for Love

The best time for love is when Venus is in your sign, making you the most desirable sign in the zodiac. This only lasts about three weeks (unless Venus is retrograde), so don't waste time! And find out the time this year when Venus is in your sign by consulting the Venus chart at the end of chapter 6.

Who's the Sexiest Sign of the Zodiac?

It depends on what sign you are. Astrology has traditionally given this honor to Scorpio, the sign associated with the sex organs. However, we are all a combination of different signs (and turn-ons). Gemini's communicating ability and manual dexterity could deliver the magic touch. Cancer's tenderness and understanding could bring out your passion more than regal Leo.

Who'll Be Faithful?

The earth signs of Capricorn, Taurus, and Virgo are usually the most faithful. They tend to be more home-oriented and family-oriented, and they are usually choosy about their mates. It's impractical, inconvenient, and probably expensive to play around, so they think.

Who's Most Likely to Cheat?

The mutable signs of Gemini, Pisces, and Sagittarius win the playboy or playgirl sweepstakes. These signs tend to be changeable, fickle, and easily bored. But they're so much fun!

⚖️ CHAPTER 14

Signs of Success: Wealth-Building Advice from the Stars

Are you a serial spender or a savvy saver? Here's where to find out your sign's bottom line when it comes to managing money. Though no sign wins the financial sweepstakes—all have their share of billionaires and paupers—the signs of success are those who make the most of their particular financial talents. This year's financial winners are the earth signs (Taurus, Virgo, and especially Capricorn), who should profit from the lucky rays of Jupiter in Capricorn. Yet all of us could benefit from some of Capricorn's self-discipline when it comes to spending wisely and budgeting carefully.

Aries

You've got a taste for fast money, quick turnover, and edgy investments, with no patience for gradual long-term gains. You're an impulse buyer with the nerve for risky tactics that could backfire. On the other hand, you're a pioneer who can see into the future, who dares to take a gamble on a new idea or product that could change the world . . . like Sam Walton of the Wal-mart stores who changed the way we shop. You need a backup plan in case one of your big ideas burns out. To protect your money, get a backup plan you can follow without thinking about it. Have an automatic percentage of your income put into a savings or retirement plan. Then give yourself some extra funds to play with. Your weak point is your impatience; you're not one to wait out a slow market or watch savings slowly accumulate.

Taurus

You're a saver who loves to see your cash accumulate, as well as your possessions. You have no qualms about steadily increasing your fortune. You're a savvy trader and a shrewd investor, in there for long-term gains. You have low toleration for risk, hate to lose anything. But you do enjoy luxuries, may need to reward yourself frequently. You might pass up an opportunity because it seems too risky. Take a chance once in a while. You're especially lucky in real estate.

Gemini

With Gemini, the cash can flow in and then out just as quickly. You naturally multitask and are sure to have several projects going at once, as well as several credit cards, which can easily get out of hand. Saving is not one of your strong points . . . too boring. You fall in and out of love with different ideas, have probably tried a round of savings techniques. Diversification is your best strategy. Have several different kinds of investments—at least one should be a long-term plan. Set savings goals and then regularly deposit small amounts into your accounts.

Cancer

You can be a natural moneymaker with your peerless intuition. You can spot a winner that everyone else misses. Consider Cancer success stories like those of cosmetics queen Estée Lauder and Roxanne Quimby, of Burt's Bees, who turned her friend's stash of beeswax into a thriving cosmetics business. Who knew? So trust your intuition. You are a saver who always has a backup plan just in case. Remember to treat and nurture yourself as well as others. Investments in the food industry, restaurants, hotels, shipping, and water-related industries are Cancer territory.

Leo

You love the first-class lifestyle, but may not always have the resources to support it. Finding a way to fund your extravagant tastes is the Leo challenge. Some courses in money management or an expert financial coach could set you on the right track. However, you're also a terrific salesperson, fabulous in high-profile jobs that pay a lot. You're the community tastemaker. Satisfy your appetite for "the best" by working for a quality company that sells luxury goods, splendid real estate, dream vacations, first-class travel—that way you'll have access to the lifestyle without having to pay for it.

Virgo

Your sign is a stickler for details and that includes your money management. You like to follow your spending and saving closely and enjoy planning and budgeting and price comparison. Your sign usually has no problem sticking to a savings or investment plan. You have a critical eye for quality and like to bargain—shop to get the best value. In fact, Virgo billionaire Warren Buffet is known for value investing. You buy cheap and sell at a profit. Investing in health care and organic products and food could be profitable for you.

Libra

Oh, do you ever love to shop! And you often have an irresistible urge to acquire an exquisite object, like a designer dress you can't really afford, or splurge on the perfect antique armoire once you've found it. You don't like to settle for second-rate or bargain buys. Learning to prioritize your spending is especially difficult for your sign, so try to find a good money manager to do it for you. Following a strictly balanced budget is your key to financial success. With Libra's keen eye for quality and good taste, you are a savvy picker at auctions and antiques fairs, so you might be able to turn around your purchase for a profit.

Scorpio

Scorpios prefer to stay in control of their finances at all times. You're sure to have a financial-tracking program on your computer. You're not an impulse buyer, unless you see something that immediately turns you on. Rely on your instincts! Scorpio is the sign of credit cards, taxes, and loans, so you are able to use these tools cleverly. Investing for Scorpio is rarely casual. You'll do extensive research and track your investments—reading the financial pages, annual reports, and profit-and-loss statements.

Sagittarius

Sagittarius is a natural gambler, with a high tolerance for risk. It's important for you to learn when to hold 'em, and when to fold 'em, as the song goes, by setting limits on your risk taking and covering your assets. You enjoy the thrill of playing the stock market, where you could win big and lose big. Money itself is rarely the object for Sagittarius—it's the game that counts. Since your sign rarely saves for a rainy day, your best strategy might be an automatic-savings plan that deducts a certain amount without your knowing it. Regular bill-paying plans are another strategy to keep you on track. You could benefit from an inspirational money manager who gets you fired up about an investment plan.

Capricorn

You're one of the strongest money managers in the zodiac, which should serve you well this year when Jupiter, the planet of luck and expansion, is blessing Capricorn. You're a born bargain hunter and clever negotiator, a saver rather than a spender. You are the sign of self-discipline, which works well when it comes to sticking with a budget and living frugally while waiting for resources to accumulate. You are likely to plan carefully for your elder years, profiting from long-term investments. You have a keen sense of value and will pick up a bargain, then turn it around at a nice profit.

Aquarius

The Aquarius trait of unpredictability extends to your financial life, where you surprise us all with your ability to turn something totally unique into a money spinner. Consider your wealthy sign mates Oprah Winfrey and Paris Hilton, who are able to intuit what the public will buy at a given moment. Some of your ideas might sound far-out, but turn out to be right on the money. Investing in high-tech companies that are on the cutting edge of their field is good for Aquarius. You'll probably intuit which ones will stay the course. You'll feel good about investing in companies that improve the environment, such as new types of fuel, or ones that are related to your favorite cause.

Pisces

The typical Pisces is probably the sign least interested in money management. However, there are many billionaires born under your sign, such as Michael Dell, David Geffen, and Steve Jobs. Generally they have made money from innovative ideas and left the details to others. That might work for you. Find a Scorpio, Capricorn, or Virgo to help you set a profitable course and systematically save (which is not in your nature). Sign up for automatic bill paying, so you won't have to think about it. If you keep in mind how much less stressful life will be and how much more you can do when you're not worried about paying bills, you might be motivated enough to stick to a sensible budget. Investmentwise, consider anything to do with water—offshore drilling, water conservation and purifying, shipping, and seafood. Petroleum is also ruled by your sign, as are institutions related to hospitals.

⚖️ CHAPTER 15

Keep Father Time in His Place: Antiaging Tips

In 2008, both Jupiter and Pluto enter the sign of Capricorn, the Saturn-ruled sign associated with Father Time and the elder years. This is especially meaningful for the baby boomer generation, the millions of Americans born between 1946 and 1964. For the post–World War II generation, who are looking forward to a long and vital life span, age sixty is the beginning of middle age, not old age. This active generation will be reinventing our concept of how to spend the senior years, as they play a much more vocal and demanding role in society.

It will not be unusual to live to be over one hundred, say the experts, but baby boomers will be concerned with how well they live, not just how long. Innovative medical technologies in areas such as joint replacement and management of cardiovascular disease assure this generation of more pep and productivity, while drugs like Viagra boost their sex lives. Americans will be well able to skip retirement and continue in the workforce or choose to start a second, more rewarding career.

Astrology has many ideas for keeping baby boomers healthy and happy. Each sign is associated with a part of the body that could become vulnerable in later years. Within the personality of a sign are other clues for having a productive old age.

Aries

The Aries baby boomer is one who plans on staying forever young. You'll stay up-to-date and may identify with the younger generation rather than your peers. If something is wrong physically, you'll fix it quickly with the latest medical technology. It's important, Aries, that you learn to pace yourself and be realistic about what you can do. (You are the sign that goes snowboarding at age sixty.) Be sure to take physical precautions to safeguard yourself when doing sports. Guard your head area with the right gear and rein in your impulsiveness when in crowded or traffic situations. More patience could be the greatest gift of your elder years.

Taurus

As the zodiac's gourmet, Taurus needs to watch your diet and craving for sweets as you grow older, since you're more likely to overindulge and gain weight. Exercise is not your favorite activity, so trick yourself by combining a workout with a walk in a beautiful nature preserve or bike path. Since you are a great shopper, you could combine bargain hunting with a power walk in your local mall. Gardening and playing with a lively pet are pleasant ways to get moving or get a fun workout playing with young grandchildren. Combining movement with your everyday activities is the key for sedentary Taurus.

Gemini

Yours is one of the active signs that rarely has a serious weight problem. Your lungs may be vulnerable, however, so do everything you can to stop smoking, get regular flu shots, and improve the air quality in your home. Gemini thrives on social contact and mental stimulation and should remain active in the community. Expand your social network as much as possible to include young people with innovative ideas. Take courses at your local college and challenge yourself by learning new skills. It is important for Gemini to protect your nerve pathways, so be sure your chairs are ergonomic and watch for carpal tunnel syndrome if you use a computer.

Cancer

Cancer is family-oriented in the elder years and thrives on close contact with loving relatives. It is even better if your home is near water, where you can exercise with long walks on the beach and swimming. If not, join a local water-aerobics class at your local pool. Cancer can be moody, so combat any tendency to get depressed by doing creative projects and spending time with loved ones. A positive attitude is one of your best antiaging techniques.

Leo

Leo's vulnerable area is the heart, which you should check frequently as you grow older, even if you appear to be the picture of health, like Leos Arnold Schwarzenegger and Bill Clinton, who have had cardiac surgery. Adopting a heart-healthy diet will help stave off problems. Sun-ruled Leos should take preventive measures to avoid skin cancer by using a high SPF sunscreen, especially if you live in a Southern climate. Leos thrive on the attention they get from performing, so why not share skills by lecturing or teaching a local class. Share that hard-won wisdom!

Virgo

As one of the most health-conscious signs, Virgo usually sticks to a sensible diet and gets regular checkups. Staying mentally active can ward off age-related depression, so investigate your local community college, take education-oriented trips, and expand your social circle with new friends. Virgo thrives when being of service to the community and should seek opportunities to do volunteer work. Teaching or coaching young people can be especially rewarding to your sign.

Libra

Libra's key to youth is to keep the social, family, mental, and physical areas of your life in balance. Strengthen your body with balancing exercises like tai chi and yoga or artistic and social exercises like dancing. Exercises done in a sociable group are more to Libra's liking. Your back and kidneys are vulnerable areas to keep in good condition. In later years, Libra has the time to become more involved in intellectual pursuits and arts and crafts. Libra enjoys entertaining and throwing parties for friends and family. Cultivating relationships with like-minded friends by joining a club or group with a common cause is a good idea.

Scorpio

You're the sexy senior! The sign of Scorpio is associated with the sex organs and known for having an active sex life in the senior years. Your partner may well need Viagra! Scorpio is often likened to a phoenix rising from the ashes for your ability to survive illness and regain health. However, you should pay special attention to the elimination and sexual functions of the body with regular examinations and colonoscopies. Water sports and vacations near the sea are excellent therapy for stressed-out Scorpios. Getting involved in something you care passionately about keeps Scorpio young at heart.

Sagittarius

You're no stay-at-home senior! You'll enjoy the independence you have, which gives you the chance to pursue your many interests, including travel to places you've always wanted to explore and having fun times with pals. Active Sagittarius is one of the most athletic signs and may continue to play your favorite sports in senior years, right alongside your grandchildren. Now's your time to motivate the younger generation, so find ways to pass on your hard-won wisdom via teaching or writing, perhaps continuing your career on a part-time basis. Many Sagittarius will get involved in promoting an idealistic or political cause.

Capricorn

The Capricorn senior likes to stay actively involved in community life. Yours is a disciplined, organized sign that may not retire from business or may continue your career on a part-time basis. Some may pursue an entirely different career, with great success. You could well represent the seniors in your community on boards and committees. It is important for Capricorn to continue doing productive work, even if it is on a volunteer basis. Physically Capricorn is one of the longer-lived signs. It is associated with bones and knees, so protect these areas and watch a tendency toward arthritis and osteoporosis.

Aquarius

Aquarius is on the cutting edge and usually on top of the latest trends, even later in life. You won't let advanced years hold you back! You're likely to play computer games with grandchildren and even have your own Web site. You remain young if you stay involved in a cause and pursue your multiple interests. You'll share your wisdom by teaching a class, lecturing, or writing. Physically, protect yourself against airborne allergies, and exercise to prevent circulation problems. Group activities appeal to Aquarius, especially if you are promoting a cause.

Pisces

Elder Pisces is happiest when pursuing creative activities, such as filmmaking, painting, writing, or a hobby or craft in which you can express your imagination. Places near water are particularly healthful for Pisces. Water sports, especially swimming, can maintain your health. Avoid addictive substances and stick to a balanced diet of organic foods, including plenty of fish. Lymphatic drainage massage is good therapy for Pisces, which is associated with the lymphatic system. Pay special attention to the condition of your feet, and wear the appropriate shoes for each activity.

⚖️ CHAPTER 16

The Mystic Properties of Your Birthstone

Who hasn't at one time or another received a special piece of jewelry with a birthstone? We enjoy the idea that wearing a special gem resonates with our personality and might even bring us luck. However, there is quite a bit of confusion over which stone is best for each sign, because we are often given birthstones according to the month of our birthday rather than our zodiac sign. You may be wondering if the amethyst is more suitable for a February-born Pisces than the aquamarine, or you might prefer the gems associated with your moon sign, which resonate with your emotional nature, or your Venus sign, which appeal to your sense of fashion and good taste.

There are many ways to approach the subject of birthstones. Lovers of precious gems could choose one that reflects the element of your sun sign. Earth signs (Taurus, Virgo, Capricorn) resonate to the bright green emerald. Fire signs (Aries, Leo, Sagittarius) belong to the flaming ruby. Water signs (Cancer, Scorpio, Pisces) might prefer the deep blue sapphire. And air signs (Gemini, Libra, Aquarius) may gravitate to the clear, brilliant diamond.

If you don't care for your birthstone, you could choose a talisman by color. Choose a stone that is associated with your sun, moon, or Venus sign. An Aries with moon in Cancer might prefer a pale lunar jewel like the pearl or moonstone. A Pisces with Venus in Aries might love to wear bright red stones like ruby or spinel.

In ancient India, Egypt, and Babylonia, rare and beautiful gemstones were thought to have magical properties. People are said to have consulted astrologers for advice on wearing the appropriate gem for each occasion. Ancient Egyptians carried scarabs and tiny figures of their gods for protection and luck. These were carved in semiprecious stones like lapis lazuli, carnelian, and turquoise. In India, one of the most powerful talismans was an amulet designed with precious stones representing the known planets at the time. Another astrological connection was the wearing of gems associated with a planet on that planet's special day. Mars-ruled rubies would be worn on the Mars day, Tuesday, for instance. It is still possible to find special astrological talismans created by astrologer-jewelers, who will make up a special pendant or necklace displaying your horoscope's special stones in a beautiful design.

In the Judeo-Christian tradition, the astrological association with gemstones dates from the sacred twelve-gem breastplate of Aaron, recorded in Exodus. Each gem symbolized one of the twelve tribes of Israel. Later these gems became connected with the twelve signs of the zodiac. However, it was not until the eighteenth century that people began to wear their special birthstones. For more information on the history and mystery of gemstones, including their astrological use, read *The Curious Lore of Precious Stones* by George Frederick Kunz.

Here are some suggestions for choosing stones associated with a given zodiac sign. Bear in mind that there are no hard-and-fast rules; you might find yourself attracted to a certain gem without fully understanding why. That might well be the gem you are supposed to wear, regardless of your sign.

Aries

Though most sources give the birthstone for April as the diamond, Aries may feel more affinity for Mars-ruled stones with red hues, such as ruby, spinels, fire opals, garnets, coral, and carnelian.

Taurus

Emeralds are most associated with Taurus. However, Taurus might gravitate toward some of the earthy agates and green stones such as tourmaline, jade, serpentine (which is believed to draw good fortune), and green quartz.

Gemini

Pearls and agates are associated with Gemini, but you might prefer fascinating gems like alexandrite or tanzanite, which change color according to the angle of light. Or watermelon tourmaline, which has dual colorations. Interesting rutilated quartzes with fine hairlike inclusions are associated with communication and might be perfect for your sign.

Cancer

July has often been linked with the ruby; however, that fiery stone might be better suited to Leos born in late July. Cancer seems to resonate more with the elegant blue sapphire, moonstone, chalcedony, and the deep blue flashes of laboradorite and rainbow moonstone.

Leo

The yellow-green peridot and all golden stones belong to sun-ruled Leos. You may also love the ruby, yellow diamonds, amber, and citrine. Go for the golden tones!

Virgo

Sapphires, which come in many colors, carnelian, onyx, and pink jasper are associated with Virgo. You may also respond to the earthy agates and the green tones of emerald and jade.

Libra

Opal, which was once considered exclusive to Libra, comes in many variations. In fact, the opal was deemed unlucky for any other sign. This beautiful stone comes in many color variations, from the deeper Australian opals to the pale Russian opals. You might try the blue-and-pink Peruvian opal or the mysterious, earthy boulder opal. Libra is also associated with the color pink, as in rose quartz, pink sapphires, pink diamonds, and kunzite. Apple green chrysoprase is another beautiful choice.

Scorpio

This mysterious sign was given the topaz, which comes in blue or golden variations. You might also respond to the deep tones of smoky quartz, tiger's eye, black onyx, rainbow obsidian, black diamonds, or black South Sea pearls.

Sagittarius

Visionary Sagittarius responds to turquoise, the mystical stone of Native Americans and Tibetans. No medicine man's outfit was complete without a turquoise. It was treasured by the Persians, who believed that turquoise could protect from evil and bring good fortune. Also consider lapis lazuli, blue topaz, and ruby.

Capricorn

The burgundy red garnet is the usual stone for Capricorn, but garnets are now available in many other colors, such as the green tsavorite garnet. Also consider the beautifully marked green malachite. Onyx in all its color variations is compatible with Capricorn.

Aquarius

Aquarius is associated with the purple amethyst, a type of quartz that was once thought to prevent drunkenness. This sign might respond to some of the newer stones on the market, such as laboradorite, a gray stone that flashes electric blue, or to some of the other purple stones, such as sugilite, tanzanite, or purple jade. The colorful quartzes, which are able to conduct electricity, could be your gem. Diamonds of all kinds also resonate with Aquarius, according to the glamorous Aquarius Gabor sisters and Carol Channing, who sang "Diamonds Are a Girl's Best Friend."

Pisces

The blue-green aquamarine and the earthy bloodstone are usually associated with Pisces. During the sixteenth century, bloodstone was believed to cure hemorrhages caused by the plague. Jasper is also a Pisces stone, now available in many beautiful colors such as "picture jasper" and "poppy jasper," which look like miniature paintings. Pisces also responds to jewels from the sea: pearls and coral and ocean blue sapphires. Elizabeth Taylor, a great Pisces jewel collector, owns the famous Peregrina pearl as well as many deep blue sapphires.

♎ CHAPTER 17

Give the Perfect Gift to Every Sign

So often we're in a quandary about what to give a loved one, someone who has everything, that hard-to-please friend, or a fascinating new person in your life, or about the right present for a wedding, birthday, or hostess gift. Why not let astrology help you make the perfect choice by appealing to each sun sign's personality. When you're giving a gift, you're also making a memory, so it should be a special occasion. The gift that's most appreciated is one that touches the heart, reminds you both of a shared experience, or shows that the giver has really cared enough to consider the recipient's personality.

In general, the water signs (Cancer, Pisces, Scorpio) enjoy romantic, sentimental, and imaginative gifts given in a very personal way. Write your loved one a poem or a song to express your feelings. Assemble an album of photos or mementos of all the good times you've shared. Appeal to their sense of fantasy. Scorpio Richard Burton had the right idea when he gave Pisces Elizabeth Taylor a diamond bracelet hidden in lavender roses (her favorite color).

Fire signs (Aries, Leo, Sagittarius) appreciate a gift presented with lots of flair. Pull out the drama, like the actor who dazzled his Aries sweetheart by presenting her with trash cans overflowing with daisies.

Air signs (Gemini, Libra, Aquarius) love to be surprised with unusual gifts. The Duke of Windsor gave his elegant Gemini duchess, Wallis Windsor, fabulous jewels engraved with love notes and secret messages in their own special code.

Earth signs (Taurus, Virgo, Capricorn) value solid, tangible gifts or ones that appeal to all the senses. Delicious gourmet treats, scented body lotions, the newest CDs, the gift of a massage, or stocks and bonds are sure winners! Capricorn Elvis Presley once received a gold-plated piano from his wife.

Here are some specific ideas for each sign:

Aries

These are the trendsetters of the zodiac, who appreciate the latest thing! For Aries, it's the excitement that counts, so present your gift in a way that will knock their socks off. Aries is associated with the head, so a jaunty hat, hair ornaments, chandelier earrings, sunglasses, and hair-taming devices are good possibilities. Aries love games of any kind that offer a real challenge, like war video games, military themes, or rousing music with a beat. Anything red is a good bet: red flowers, red gems, and red accessories. How about giving Aries a way to let off steam with a gym membership or aerobic-dancing classes? Monogram a robe with a nickname in red.

Taurus

These are touchy-feely people who love things that appeal to all their senses. Find something that sounds, tastes, smells, feels, or looks good. And don't stint on quality or comfort. Taurus know the value of everything and will be aware of the price tag. Taurus foodies will appreciate chef-worthy kitchen gadgets, the latest cookbook, and gourmet treats. Taurus is a great collector. Find out what their passion is and present them with a rare item or a beautiful storage container such as an antique jewelry box. Green-thumb Taurus would love some special plants or flowers, garden tools, beautiful plant containers. Appeal to their sense of touch with fine fabrics—high-thread-count sheets, cashmere, satin, and mohair. One of the animal-loving

179

signs, Taurus might appreciate a retractable leash or soft bed for the dog or cat. Get them a fine wallet or checkbook cover. They'll use it often.

Gemini

Mercury-ruled Gemini appreciates gifts that appeal to their mind. The latest book or novel, a talked-about film, a CD from a hot new singer, or a high-tech gadget might appeal. A beautiful diary or a tape recorder would record their adventures. Since Geminis often do two things at once, a telephone gadget that leaves their hands free would be appreciated. In fact, a new telephone device or superphone would appeal to these great communicators. Gloves, rings, and bracelets accent their expressive hands. Clothes from an interesting new designer appeal to their sense of style. You might try giving Gemini a variety of little gifts in a beautiful box or a Christmas stocking. A tranquil massage at a local spa would calm Gemini's sensitive nerves. Find an interesting way to wrap your gift. Nothing boring, please!

Cancer

Cancer is associated with home and family, so anything to do with food, entertaining at home, and family life is a good bet. Beautiful dishes or serving platters, silver items, fine crystal and linen, gourmet cookware, cooking classes or the latest DVD from a cooking teacher might be appreciated. Cancer designers Vera Wang and Giorgio Armani have perfected the Cancer style and have many home products available, as well as their elegant designer clothing. Naturally, anything to do with the sea is a possibility: pearls, coral, or shell jewelry. Boat and water-sports equipment might work. Consider cruise wear for traveling Cancers. Sentimental Cancer loves antiques and silver frames for family photos. Cancer people are often good photographers, so consider frames, albums, and projectors to showcase their work. Present your gift in a personal way with a special note.

Leo

Think big with Leo and appeal to this sign's sense of drama. Go for the gold (Leo's color) with gold jewelry, designer clothing, or big attention-getting accessories. Follow their signature style, which could be superelegant, like Jacqueline Onassis, or superstar, like Madonna or Jennifer Lopez. This sign is always ready for the red carpet and stays beautifully groomed, so stay within these guidelines when choosing your gift. Feline motifs and animal prints are usually a hit. The latest grooming aids, high-ticket cosmetics, and mirrors reflect their best image. Beautiful hairbrushes tame their manes. Think champagne, high-thread-count linens, and luxurious loungewear or lingerie. Make Leo feel special with a custom portrait or photo shoot with your local star photographer. Be sure to go for spectacular wrapping, with beautiful paper and ribbons. Present your gift with a flourish!

Virgo

Virgo usually has a special subject of interest and would appreciate relevant books, films, lectures, or classes. Choose health-oriented things: gifts to do with fitness and self-improvement. Virgo enjoys brainteasers, crossword puzzles, computer programs, organizers, and digital planners. Fluffy robes, bath products, and special soaps appeal to Virgo's sense of cleanliness. Virgo loves examples of good, practical design: efficient telephones, beautiful briefcases, computer cases, desk accessories. Choose natural fibers and quiet colors when choosing clothes for Virgo. Virgo has high standards, so go for quality when choosing a gift.

Libra

Whatever you give this romantic sign, go for beauty and romance. Libra loves accessories, decorative objects, whatever makes him or his surroundings more aesthetically pleasing. Beautiful flowers in pastel colors are always welcome. Libras are great hosts and hostesses, who might appreciate a gift related to fine dining: serving pieces, linens, glassware, flower vases. Evening or party clothes please since Libra has a gadabout social life. Interesting books, objets d'art, memberships to museums, and tickets to cultural events are good ideas. Fashion or home-decorating magazine subscriptions usually please Libra women. Steer away from anything loud, garish, or extreme. Think pink, one of their special colors, when giving Libra jewelry, clothing, or accessories. It's a very romantic sign, so be sure to remember birthdays, holidays, and anniversaries with a token of affection.

Scorpio

Scorpios love mystery, so bear that in mind when you buy these folks a present. You could take this literally and buy them a good thriller DVD, novel, or video game. Scorpios are power players, so a book about one of their sign might please. Bill Gates, Jack Welch, Condoleezza Rice, and Hillary Clinton are hot Scorpio subjects. Scorpios love black leather, suede, fur, anything to do with the sea, power tools, tiny spy tape recorders, and items with secret compartments or intricate locks. When buying a handbag for Scorpio, go for simple shapes with lots of interior pockets. Sensuous Scorpios appreciate hot lingerie, sexy linens, body lotions, and perfumed candles. Black is the favored color for Scorpio clothing—go for sexy textures like cashmere and satin in simple shapes by designers like Calvin Klein. This sign is fascinated with the occult, so give them an astrology or tarot-card reading, beautiful crystals, or an astrology program for the computer.

Sagittarius

For these outdoor people, consider adventure trips, designer sportswear, gear for their favorite sports. A funny gift or something for their pets pleases Sagittarius. For clothing and accessories, the fashionista of this sign tends to like bright colors and dramatic innovative styles. Otherwise, casual sportswear is a good idea. These travelers usually have a favorite getaway place; give them a travel guide, DVD, novel, or history book that would make their trip more interesting. Luggage is also a good bet. Sleek carry-ons, travel wallets, ticket holders, business-card cases, and wheeled computer bags might please these wanderers. Anything that makes travel more comfortable and pleasant is good for Sagittarius, including a good book to read en route. This sign is the great gambler of the zodiac, so gifts related to their favorite gambling venue would be appreciated.

Capricorn

For this quality-conscious sign, go for a status label from the best store in town. Get Capricorns something good for their image and career. They could be fond of things Spanish, like flamenco or tango music, or of country-and-western music and motifs. In the bookstore, go for biographies of the rich and famous, or advice books to help Capricorn get to the top. Capricorns take their gifts seriously, so steer away from anything too frivolous. Garnet, onyx, or malachite jewelry, Carolina Herrera fragrance and clothing, and beautiful briefcases and wallets are good ideas. Glamorous status tote bags carry business gear in style. Capricorns like golf, tennis, and sports that involve climbing, cycling, or hiking, so presents could be geared to their outdoor interests. Elegant evening accessories would be fine for this sign, which often entertains for business.

Aquarius

Give Aquarius a surprise gift. This sign is never impressed with things that are too predictable. So use your imagination to present the gift in an unusual way or at an unexpected time. With Aquarius, originality counts. When in doubt, give them something to think about, a new electronic gadget, perhaps a small robot, or an advanced computer game. Or something New Age, like an amethyst-crystal cluster. Aquarius like innovative materials with a space-age look. They are the ones with the wraparound glasses, the titanium computer cases. This air sign loves to fly—an airplane ticket always pleases. Books should be on innovative subjects, politics, or adventures of the mind. Aquarius goes for unusual color combinations—especially electric blue or hot pink—and abstract patterns. They like the newest, coolest looks on the cutting edge of fashion and are not afraid to experiment. Think of Paris Hilton's constantly changing looks. Look for an Aquarius gift in an out-of-the-way boutique or local hipster hangout. They'd be touched if you find out Aquarius's special worthy cause and make a donation. Spirit them off to hear their favorite guru.

Pisces

Pisces respond to gifts that have a touch of fantasy, magic, and romance. Look for mystical gifts with a touch of the occult. Romantic music (a customized CD of favorite love songs) and love stories appeal to Pisces sentimentalists. Pisces is associated with perfume and fragrant oils, so help this sign indulge with their favorite scent in many forms. Anything to do with the ocean, fish, and water sports appeals to Pisces. How about a whirlpool, a water-therapy spa treatment, or a sea salt rub. Appeal to this sign with treats for the feet: foot massages, pedicures, ballet tickets, and dance lessons. Cashmere socks and metallic evening sandals are other Pisces pleasers. A romantic dinner overlooking the water is Pisces paradise. A case of fine wine or another favorite liquid is always appreciated. Write a love poem and enclose it with your gift.

CHAPTER 18

The Meaning of Numbers

What exactly is a number 9 day, and how did it get to be that number? If you've been reading the dailies, you've no doubt seen such numerological references. Usually you'll find these numbers on the days when the moon is transiting from one sign to another.

If you're familiar with numerology, you probably know your life-path number, which is derived from your birth date. That number represents who you were at birth and the traits that you'll carry throughout your life. There are numerous books and Web sites that will provide you with details on what the numbers mean regarding your life path.

The numbers used in the dailies are found by adding the numbers related to the astrological sign (1 for Aries, 2 for Taurus, etc.), the year, the months, and the day. For example, June 14, 2008 for a Libra would be 7 for Libra, plus 1 (adding together the numbers in 2008), plus 6 for June, plus 7 (1+6) for the day. That would be 7+1+6+5 (sign+year+month+day)=19=1 (1+9=10 [1+0=1]).

So on that number 1 day, you might be advised that you're getting a fresh start, a new beginning. You can take the lead on something new. Stress originality and creativity. Explore and discover. You're inventive and make connections that others overlook.

Briefly, here are the meanings of the numbers, which are included in more detail in the dailies themselves.

1: taking the lead, getting a fresh start, a new beginning
2: cooperation, partnership, a new relationship, sensitivity
3: harmony, beauty, pleasures of life, warm, receptive

4: getting organized, hard work, being methodical, rebuilding, fulfilling your obligations

5: freedom of thought and action, change, variety, thinking outside the box

6: a service day, being diplomatic, generous, tolerant, sympathetic

7: mystery, secrets, investigations, research, detecting deception, exploration of the unknown, of the spiritual realms

8: your power day, financial success, unexpected money, a windfall

9: finishing a project, looking beyond the immediate, setting your goals, reflection, expansion

—Rob MacGregor

Rob MacGregor is the author of seventeen novels and ten nonfiction books, including *Psychic Power*, *Star Power for Teens*, and *Romancing the Raven*. For more information, go to www.robmacgregor.net.

CHAPTER 19

All About Libra: Your Personality, Family, Career, Relationships, and Lifestyle

Have you tapped in to your Libra power? Knowing and using your positive Libra sun-sign traits (and downplaying the negative ones) could be your key to achieving more happiness and success in all areas of your life. That's because every part of your life has a strong Libra influence: That includes what and whom you like, your family relationships, your strengths on the job, even the decor of your home. The more you understand the Libra in you, the better you can use your personal solar power to help you make good decisions. You can use it every day from something as basic as choosing what to wear to more important issues such as getting along with your boss or spicing up your love life.

So get ready for your close-up! In the following chapters, you'll be empowered with tools to control your destiny and make your dreams come true by moving in harmony with your natural inclinations.

Before we begin, here's how we determine what a Libra personality is. Astrologers describe a Libra using a type of recipe. The basic personality of a Libra is determined by blending several ingredients. First there's your Libra element: air. An air sign, you are mentally oriented. You're a doer, like the other active, cardinal signs (Aries and Capricorn). Libra has a positive masculine yang polarity, which adds yet another dimension. Then there's the influence of your planetary ruler, Venus, the planet of attraction, love, beauty, relationships. Add your sign's place in the zodiac: seventh, in the house of partnership, the place of relating. Finally, stir in your symbol: the Scales of Justice, balance.

This recipe influences everything we say about Libra. For example, you could deduce that a mentally oriented, Venus-ruled sign would thrive in an atmosphere of beauty and harmony, tend to avoid confrontations. You would be likely to enjoy relationships, seek marriage and partnerships, rather than going it alone. Your favorite colors might be flattering pastels. You may have a charming, diplomatic manner with others. But remember that your total astrological personality contains a blend of many other planets, colored by the signs they occupy, plus factors such as the sign coming over the horizon at the exact moment of your birth. The more Libra planets in your horoscope, the more likely you'll follow your sun sign's prototype. On the other hand, if planets are grouped together in a different sign, they will color your horoscope accordingly, sometimes making a low-key, mellow sun sign come on much stronger. So if the Libra traits mentioned here don't describe you, there could be other factors flavoring your cosmic stew. (Look up your other planets in the tables in this book to find out what they might be!)

The Libra Man: Well-Balanced

The typical Libra man appears charming, cool, and well mannered at all times. But your delicately balanced nervous system is highly sensitive to disharmony of any sort. Whether the cause is blatantly rude behavior or simply a picture tilted out of alignment or a color mismatched, you will pick it up instantly. And when you are seriously offended, you will vanish into thin air, often before airing your grievances.

The Libra man appreciates (some might say, worships) style. Beauty of ideas and beauty of form are priorities, and you'd scrimp on mundane necessities to buy a beautiful object. You always look put together, even in the most casual clothes. It took a Libra designer like Ralph Lauren to make coveted items of Indian blankets, blue jeans, and polo shirts. But Libra is not easy to please. You are never truly satisfied until you've achieved perfect balance.

Striving for harmony at all costs, Libra often retreats into an ivory tower to avoid the messy world of emotions. Your real potential lies in blending the two, bringing the ideals of your ivory tower down to the human earthly level.

You need companionship to exchange ideas and to help you define what you really think. Libras have been known to infuriate others by not offering an opinion until they have weighed the pros and cons and considered every possible angle. Too many alternatives could leave you suspended in a quandary. But, like Vaclav Havel or Jesse Jackson, you'll find a strong authoritative voice quickly when there is obvious injustice.

The Libra man functions better when performing the role of mediator or moderator than in a situation where you must make quick decisions. You are scrupulously fair when it comes to presenting each side of a question, but you can debate endlessly before taking action. Usually you excel on a team where others make the final decisions based on your evaluation.

In a Relationship

Partnerships are necessary for you; they make you feel complete. You'll truly enjoy sharing all the happenings in your life and participating in lots of outside activities with your partner on your arm.

Unlike many other men, the Libra man is a perennial romantic who truly enjoys the company of women, especially if they are lovely to look at and stylishly dressed. You'll be quick to notice details of dress and grooming. If your mate changes her hairstyle or the length of her skirts, you'll have a strong opinion pro or con. You love to see your mate looking beautiful, and may even pick out or design her clothes. You have probably searched long and hard to find the perfect partner, one who shares your aesthetic values, appeals to your tastes, and balances out your other qualities. Though it is difficult for you to express dissatisfaction openly (or tell your mate how you dislike the color of the new sofa), you'll do your best to encourage calm discussion of problems. However, you'll avoid emotional scenes and any confrontation that throws you off balance.

The Libra Woman: A Fair Lady

The balance of masculine and feminine energies is nowhere more evident than in the Libra woman. Strikingly feminine, elegant, and stylish in appearance, you are oft idealized as a love goddess or a fashion plate. But anyone who thinks of the Libra woman as a frivolous beauty should carefully study Eleanor Roosevelt, England's former Prime Minister Margaret Thatcher, or France's Segolene Royal. Libra women, under their elegant facade, are active and strong-willed, with considerable drive. The Libra woman is busy, energetic, and involved in life around her. She often prefers the company of men, which allows her to balance her feminity with the other, masculine, side of her nature.

One of the most charming and social beings, Libras such as Brigitte Bardot, Catherine Deneuve, Rita Hayworth, and Gwyneth Paltrow have often been the love goddess of their time. But your feminine appearance usually hides a cool intellect, which is at ease working with abstract concepts. The logical side to your personality often surprises those who perceive you as a woman preoccupied with superficialities, who happily spends the day at the mall or the beauty salon.

Because you are constantly searching for balance in your life, you usually get involved in a variety of activities, rarely focusing on one aspect of anything to the exclusion of other interests. You can be most successful in a career that blends your artistic and social skills and that involves either a partner or teamwork. You are a talented peacemaker or strategist, guiding others to the right course. Your good looks, style, and diplomacy are great social assets, making you popular with a wide scope of friends.

In a Relationship

Born under the sign that rules relationships of all sorts, the Libra woman is naturally geared for marriage. You thrive on a committed partnership because you need someone who complements your energies and shares your experiences. To the right mate, you offer support and well-considered advice, as well as a beautiful home where you can entertain friends and business associates.

Since your major challenge is indecisiveness, you must find a partner who is not only compatible but who also helps balance the male and female elements within yourself. To do this, Libra women cultivate male attention (sometimes at the expense of female friends). Most Libra women will have a group of male courtiers who offer flattering, romantic attention and with whom she can flirt. But your real goal in a male-female relationship is an equal partnership where each supplies what the other lacks.

Once married, the other side of your personality that demands an active public life comes to the fore. Again, you'll find yourself balancing the scales between two polarities—in this case, your home and the outside world. Though your home will be in exquisite taste, you're not the stay-at-home type and will get involved in social life as soon as possible. If the marriage is lacking, Libra will compensate with a full schedule of outside activities, artistic pursuits, political or charitable activities, or an engrossing career.

Libra in the Family

The Libra Parent

Ideally, your family group will contain attractive, intelligent, well-mannered children raised in a calm, rational, harmonious environment. The reality, however, may set your scales swinging, especially if your children are strong-willed, competitive, and aggressive. Discipline by discussion is more your style than confrontation or a show of power. You'll coolly withdraw from emotional scenes or become irritable if your scales are tipped.

Keep the peace by focusing on shared creative or social activities, and be the impartial judge when conflicts arise. You are more equipped than most parents to teach children how the art of compromise and adjustment can bring even the most diverse personalities together. You'll be especially supportive of the child who shows artistic or intellectual ability, providing them with an excellent education suited to their special needs.

The Libra Stepparent

Creating a new family equilibrium is Libra's talent as a stepparent. You are a sharing person who enjoys an extended family. You'll create a calm, accepting, and hospitable atmosphere ready to receive the children as soon as they feel ready. You'll never push them, or be overly demonstrative or insincere. Because you give much consideration to what is right in the situation, you will treat stepchildren fairly and encourage their biological parent to spend time with them, even planning special activities for everyone to enjoy. But if the children are very demanding, you may not take on caregiving responsibilities that are not rightfully yours. Your charm, fairness, and diplomacy will help everyone make this new family situation work.

The Libra Grandparent

Libras are charming, elegant grandparents who remain stylish and beautifully groomed. Libra grandmas are up-to-date on all the latest fashion trends and understand just how to wear them, regardless of age. You'll enjoy sharing your beautiful home and many interests with well-behaved grandchildren. When asked, you'll offer excellent advice and guidance to parents—unless you're asked for spur-of-the-moment babysitting (you may be going out on date yourself!). You'll still have an active social life and will be very occupied with your own interests. Libras treat grandchildren as young companions rather than charges. You'll never take over for Mother, but you will insist that the children be under control. You do not like your hard-earned peace and quiet to be upset by noisy disturbances. But you'll love sharing projects with young friends, perhaps introducing them to new interests or teaching them skills and crafts. You'll teach children that sharing good times knows no age limits!

CHAPTER 20

The Libra Lifestyle: How to Make Your Libra Sign Shine

Astrology's personal insights follow through to the way you dress and live. Here's how to polish your Libra image with tips tailored specifically for your sign. Improve your atmosphere by using your best colors and surrounding yourself with Libra-loving sounds. Find out how to create a living environment that reflects your personality, where you'll feel totally at home. And how to make the most of your sign's special fashion flair. Even your vacations might be more fun and relaxing if you tailor them to your sun sign's natural inclinations.

The Libra Fashion Image

Libra is most creative in packaging yourself beautifully. Your look is always complete from head to toe; you'd never wear the wrong shoes or carry an odd-looking handbag. Your style is extremely feminine, flirty, and sometimes girlish; it's sexy without ever being vulgar.

You're a nonstop shopper who is sure to know the fashion contents of the best stores in town. But before you make a major purchase, you'll be sure it suits your style and complements the contents of your closet. You usually have an extensive wardrobe with plenty of options for every occasion, but such is your fashion flair that you could combine a few basic everyday items with knockout scarves and jewelry to create a stunning outfit. Your natural sense of balance and suitability rarely fails you in any fashion emergency.

Your sun sign usually endows its members with curly hair and well-balanced features. To complement your look, style your hair in a soft and romantic way and use subtle makeup, just enough to give definition to your features.

Your Libra Fashion Colors

Pastels, especially delicate pale shell colors, are usually most becoming to Libra. Pale cosmetic shades are flattering to everyone, promote tranquility and a calm, harmonious feeling. Pink and sky blue are special Libra favorites.

Your Libra Fashion Role Models

Catherine Zeta-Jones, Naomi Watts, Monica Bellucci, and Gwyneth Paltrow have the classic beauty your sign is famous for. Gwen Stefani and Nicky Hilton have a slightly more dramatic Libra look with flair in every detail. They're style-setting Libras in tune with the latest trends who also design striking accessories.

Libran designers Isaac Mizrahi, Ralph Lauren, and Donna Karan understand your style completely. Like typical Libras, they are known for their total look, including perfume, lingerie, and designs for the home. That way, there's no chance that a single element can be off-balance. They also understand that style knows no budget limitations and create collections for discount outlets and lower-priced chains as well as luxury couture-level boutiques.

Libra at Home

Libra is the sign of good taste. You have a natural eye for proportion, color harmony, and furniture arrangement. Generally, you prefer a classic look, with carefully coordinated furniture, color, and fabrics. Effects that are jarring, too avant-garde, too dramatic are not for you. You probably have a collection of objets d'art, which you display skillfully in lovely still-life settings. Lighting in your rooms is unobtrusive and flattering to your guests.

Libra loves to decorate and usually has definite ideas. Any discordant note can upset your equilibrium, so assert your preferences when decorating or renovation is done by others.

Create a dreamy serene paradise using delicate shades of pink and airy blues. A little (or a lot of) pink makes everyone look good and uplifts the general mood of a room, promoting a graceful, social atmosphere. Pale colors also serve as a complementary background for your artworks and antiques. Ultrafeminine bedrooms with ruffles, fabric flourishes, extravagant bed linens, and perhaps a canopy bed are a Libra specialty.

There are Libra designers whose visions might suit you. Ralph Lauren's brand of classical home furnishings has conservative flair, enabling you to re-create the look of the country club lifestyle. Donna Karan's home furnishings express a more modern vision, with the coordinated, beautifully balanced Libra flair.

Since you are one of the zodiac's great hosts, you'll want elegant table settings and well-chosen background music. You will serve food that is as beautiful to look at as it is delicious.

Your Libra Background Music

Romantic music makes your heart sing. Libra artists Luciano Pavarotti, Yo-Yo Ma, Julio Iglesias, and Johnny

Mathis strike the right notes. Verdi, Liszt, and John Lennon wrote your kind of music. In the right mood, you can rock with Bruce Springsteen, Jerry Lee Lewis, Patti LaBelle, and Sting.

Libra Travel Guide

Vacations should appeal to Libra aesthetic and social tastes. Libras usually prefer to stay close to civilization rather than explore the wilderness. Beautiful surroundings, good company, excellent food, and wonderful shopping make Libra happy.

Libra loves to do things with a partner, so take a favorite companion along on your trips. You'll enjoy a vacation in elegant surroundings (no camping out, please), where you can dress up and socialize with other well-mannered people. With pleasant company, you could unwind on a trip through the castles of the Loire Valley; spend a weekend at an aristocratic English country house; waltz in Vienna; float through the vale of Kashmir; breathe the clear, clean air of the Swiss Alps or Tibet. Lacking a partner, tour with a special-interest group, perhaps one devoted to exploring the antique markets, museums, and design centers of Europe.

You'll enjoy getting the royal treatment in a gorgeous grand hotel or cruise ship, and especially dressing up for dinner.

Romantic weekends with the one you love are perfect Libra escapes. Keep a list of beautiful bed-and-breakfasts in the country or resorts that cater to lovers. Rent an exotic car for the trip (or a bicycle built for two when you get there). If you're single, plan trips with kindred souls around interests you all share, such as visiting antiques fairs, art shows, music festivals, or historic homes.

Since you're one of the great shoppers of the zodiac, be sure to go somewhere with a selection of stores. Of course, you will take along an empty bag to stash your treasures.

♎ CHAPTER 21

Libra Health and Well-Being

Astrology can clue you in to the tendencies that contribute to good or ill health (especially when it comes to controlling your appetite). So follow these tips on how best to lose those extra pounds, and make this your healthiest year ever.

Resist Sweet Temptations

Dr. Robert Atkins, one of the most famous diet doctors, was a Libra. A well-spoken gentleman with a liking for sweets, he fit your sign's profile. At first, the low-carbohydrate diet he advocated was vilified by nutritional "experts." However, in recent years, the effectiveness of the Atkins Diet has been proven, though it has been modified to suit our current lifestyles. It could be the perfect diet for Libras who often put on too much weight from indulging their famous sweet tooth. Because your sign rules the kidneys, it's no surprise that this diet advocates drinking plenty of water to cleanse the system as you reduce.

Since you are one of the most social signs, you may entertain or be entertained often. If possible, plan your food choices before you go out so you'll know exactly what to order and will be more likely to resist sweet temptations. Dieting with your mate or group of friends could provide the support you need and keep you on track when you go out to dinner.

Stay in Balance

Restoring and maintaining equilibrium is the Libra key to health. Balance in all things should be your mantra. If you have been working too hard or taking life too seriously, a dose of art, music, or perhaps some social activity will balance your scales. Make time to entertain friends, be romantic with the one you love, and enjoy the cultural life of your city.

Since Libra is associated with the kidneys and lower back, watch these areas for misalignment or health problems. Consider yoga, spinal adjustments, or a detoxification program if your body is out of balance.

Make Exercise a Social Occasion

Working out in a no-frills gym might be unappealing to an aesthetic Libra, so choose one that is well-designed. Attractive instructors or sociable exercise buddies could make a big difference in your motivation. Treat yourself to some good-looking exercise clothing as well.

Since yours is the sign of relationships, you may prefer exercising with a partner or with loved ones in a more imaginative and aesthetic way. Take morning walks in a beautiful local park or weekend hikes in the mountains with your family. Take a romantic bicycle tour, ending with a picnic in the autumn countryside.

Libra is also the sign of grace, so any kind of dancing may appeal to you. Dancing combines art, music, romance, relaxation, graceful movement, social contact, and exercise. Ballroom dancing would be the perfect way to exercise while flirting with your partner and showing off your dazzling evening wardrobe.

Put more beauty in all areas of your life, and you'll be healthier and happier.

⚖️ CHAPTER 22

Your Libra Career Guide: What It Takes to Succeed in 2008

Find the Right Career for You

Libra has a special combination of talents and abilities that can make you a natural winner. Develop and nurture these sun-sign strengths, and you'll be likely to find a career you truly enjoy, one where you'll be most successful. The great philosopher and teacher Joseph Campbell gave you the best advice: Follow your bliss!

Your Ideal Work Environment

Your job should be one that engages your mind, gives you social contacts, and has pleasant surroundings. You'll also be happiest when your work satisfies your ideals in some way. That is why Libras so often choose careers in design, law, diplomacy, labor relations, art, fashion, strategic planning, or education. These are fields where you can work out abstract concepts of beauty and justice.

Your innate feeling for balance might lead you to a health-oriented field where you are especially good at diagnosis, massage, chiropractic work, or nutrition. You work very well with partners or on a team, thriving on the social contact and exchange of ideas. Though you are able to mediate between different groups, getting people to work together toward a common goal, you will be happiest if your immediate surroundings are harmonious. Avoid clashing egos and offices that assault your aesthetic tastes. Difficult working conditions such as these can take a toll on your mental and physical health in the long run.

The Libra Leader

You are a charming, social boss and you rarely raise your voice or handle anyone harshly. Even when annoyed, you prefer to take a diplomatic approach, solving problems with calm discussion. You bring together a winning team and keep everyone working in harmony. You are extremely fair with subordinates, delegating work so that no one has an excessive workload. You may have problems with direct confrontations. You are much better at smoothing over a difficult situation than coming to grips with it head-on or making a quick turnaround. You may leave the face-off scenes to a partner, while you assume the role of mediator. Your office is always neat and harmonious, since you are very conscious of appearances. You are careful to represent your company in the most elegant ways. You enjoy business entertaining and probably have a generous expense account.

One of the keys to Libra success is to find your own brand of personal style and market it well. Libra designer Ralph Lauren marketed his own classic personal style into a billion-dollar company and one of the most recognizable and consistently popular brands in the world. He sold his style not only in clothing, but followed it through to home furnishings. An astute businessman, he has managed to adapt to consumers' changing needs and the fickle fashion world, yet retain the elegant, classic image of his brand. That's quite a Libra balancing act!

The Libra Team Player

Libra thrives when working with others, though you avoid getting too personally involved. You prefer to be the peacemaker, the one in the middle who brings opposing factions together. You have a charming telephone manner and work well in a spot where you meet the public directly or indirectly. Your workspace is always harmonious and well organized, and you've probably given it some aesthetic touches because your work may suffer in an ugly or disorderly environment. You are a hard worker, but not a workaholic, sensing that you must balance your work life with play and exercise. Your good looks, personal style, and natural diplomacy make you a good advertisement for your company in a public position.

The Libra Way to Get Ahead

As a Libra, you bring some important assets to the table, such as your sense of style, your social skills, and your analytical ability. It's up to you to decide how to best utilize your talents and abilities to bring you the very highest return on the investment of your time and energy. Choose a job in an aesthetically pleasing environment where you deal with the public or with idealistic issues. Play up these Libra characteristics:

- Intelligence
- Sense of fairness
- Grace under pressure
- Balanced judgment
- Artistic talent
- Social skills
- Elegant taste

♎ CHAPTER 23

Libra on the Red Carpet

Are you a fan of tabloids and gossip columns? Your fascination with the rich and famous could have a fringe benefit. It's also a terrific way to learn more about astrology. A celebrity's attraction for the public tells much about the planetary influences of a given time and the special star quality of his or her sun sign. You may even have a celebrity astro twin who shares both your birthday and the same year.

You're sure to have many of the same traits as your famous sun-sign siblings. Ralph Lauren and Ray Kroc can motivate you to develop your business savvy. Barbara Walters shows gracious Libra poise and diplomacy. The classic timeless fashion look of Catherine Deneuve or Gwyneth Paltrow might become you. For sex appeal, think of legendary Brigitte Bardot or Rita Hayworth or the modern look of Gwen Stefani and Catherine Zeta-Jones.

The lives of the famous can be fascinating textbooks with full-color illustrations of the different planetary combinations. If someone intrigues you, explore his personality further by looking up his other planets using the tables in this book. Then apply the effects of Venus, Mars, Saturn, and Jupiter to his sun-sign traits. It's a fun way to get up close and personal with your famous friend, maybe learn some secrets not revealed to the public.

Then why not move on from the red carpet to world leaders and current newsmakers? You can find accurate data online at Internet sites such as www.Stariq.com or www.astrodatabank.com, which have the charts of world events and headline makers. Then compare notes with other fans, including many professional astrologers who frequent the forums on these sites.

Libra Celebrities

Ray Charles (9/23/32)
Bruce Springsteen (9/23/49)
F. Scott Fitzgerald (9/24/1896)
Anthony Newley (9/24/31)
Jim Henson (9/24/36)
Linda McCartney (9/24/41)
Barbara Walters (9/25/31)
Juliet Prowse (9/25/37)
Michael Douglas (9/25/44)
Mark Hamill (9/25/51)
Christopher Reeve (9/25/52)
Heather Locklear (9/25/61)
Catherine Zeta-Jones (9/25/69)
Julio Iglesias (9/26/43)
Olivia Newton-John (9/26/48)
James Caviezel (9/26/68)
Serena Williams (9/26/81)
Louis Auchincloss (9/27/17)
Misha Dichter (9/27/45)
Cheryl Tiegs (9/27/47)
Avril Lavigne (9/27/84)
Peter Finch (9/28/16)
Marcello Mastroianni (9/28/24)
Brigitte Bardot (9/28/34)
Mira Sorvino (9/28/67)
Naomi Watts (9/28/68)
Carre Otis (9/28/68)
Gwyneth Paltrow (9/28/72)
Hilary Duff (9/28/87)
Gene Autry (9/29/10)
Trevor Howard (9/29/16)
Anita Ekberg (9/29/31)
Jerry Lee Lewis (9/29/37)
Bryant Gumbel (9/29/48)

Deborah Kerr (9/30/21)
Robert Duvall (9/30/29)
Angie Dickinson (9/30/31)
Truman Capote (9/30/34)
Johnny Mathis (9/30/37)
Victoria Tennant (9/30/50)
Fran Drescher (9/30/57)
Monica Bellucci (9/30/68)
Jimmy Carter (10/1/27)
Walter Matthau (10/1/30)
George Peppard (10/1/30)
Richard Harris (10/1/32)
Julie Andrews (10/1/37)
Mary McFadden (10/1/38)
Randy Quaid (10/1/50)
Groucho Marx (10/2/1890)
Rex Reed (10/2/40)
Don Maclean (10/2/45)
Donna Karan (10/2/48)
Sting (10/2/51)
Lorraine Bracco (10/2/54)
Kelly Ripa (10/2/69)
Tiffany (10/2/71)
Jack La Lanne (10/31/14)
Gore Vidal (10/3/25)
Chubby Checker (10/3/41)
Dave Winfield (10/3/51)
Al Sharpton (10/3/54)
Gwen Stefani (10/3/69)
Neve Campbell (10/3/73)
Ashlee Simpson (10/3/84)
Charlton Heston (10/4/23)
Anne Rice (10/4/41)
Patti LaBelle (10/4/44)
Susan Sarandon (10/4/45)
Armand Assante (10/4/49)
Alicia Silverstone (10/4/76)
Ray Kroc (10/5/1892)
Vaclav Havel (10/5/36)
Karen Allen (10/5/51)
Kate Winslet (10/5/75)
Carole Lombard (10/6/1908)

Stephanie Zimbalist (10/6/56)
Elizabeth Shue (10/6/63)
June Allison (10/7/23)
Yo-Yo Ma (10/7/55)
Simon Cowell (10/7/59)
Paul Hogan (10/8/36)
David Carradine (10/8/40)
Jesse Jackson (10/8/41)
Sigourney Weaver (10/8/49)
Matt Damon (10/8/70)
John Lennon (10/9/40)
Sean Lennon (10/9/75)
Helen Hayes (10/10/1900)
Tanya Tucker (10/10/58)
Bai Ling (10/10/70)
Eleanor Roosevelt (10/11/1884)
Mackenzie Phillips (10/11/59)
Joan Cusack (10/11/62)
Michelle Trachtenberg (10/11/85)
Dick Gregory (10/12/32)
Luciano Pavarotti (10/12/35)
Susan Anton (10/12/51)
Hugh Jackman (10/12/68)
Lillian Gish (10/13/1896)
Yves Montand (10/13/21)
Paul Simon (10/13/41)
Marie Osmond (10/13/59)
Kelly Preston (10/13/62)
Ralph Lauren (10/14/39)
Isaac Mizrahi (10/14/61)
Penny Marshall (10/15/42)
Roger Moore (10/15/42)
Sarah Ferguson (10/15/59)
Angela Lansbury (10/16/25)
Suzanne Somers (10/16/46)
Tim Robbins (10/16/58)
Rita Hayworth (10/17/18)
Montgomery Clift (10/17/20)
Dr. Robert Atkins (10/17/30)
Eminem (10/18/74)
Melina Mercouri (10/18/25)
George C. Scott (10/18/27)

Peter Boyle (10/18/35)
Pam Dawber (10/18/51)
Martina Navratilova (10/18/56)
John Lithgow (10/19/45)
Evander Holyfield (10/19/62)
Bela Lugosi (10/20/1882)
Ellery Queen (10/20/1905)
Mickey Mantle (10/20/31)
Snoop Dogg (10/20/72)
Dizzy Gillespie (10/21/17)
Michael Landon (10/21/37)
Patti Davis (1/21/52)
Carrie Fisher (10/21/56)
Joan Fontaine (10/22/17)
Catherine Deneuve (10/22/43)
Jeff Goldblum (10/22/53)
Brian Boitano (10/22/63)

♎ CHAPTER 24

Star Wars or Passionate Supernovas? How Libra Partners with Every Other Sign

After learning all about your own sun sign, it's time to consider how you interact with others. Knowing how your sun sign works with other signs can give you valuable insight into the future of all your relationships. Once you understand how another sun sign is likely to view yours, you'll be in a much better position to judge whether this combination will burn and crash or have lasting happiness potential.

The celebrity couples are used as examples to help you visualize each sun-sign combination. Note that some legendary couples have stood the test of time, others blazed bright and then burned out, and a few existed only in the fantasy world of film or television (but still captured our imagination). Is there a magic formula for compatibility? Traditional astrological wisdom holds that signs of the same element, in your case other air signs (Gemini and Aquarius), are naturally compatible. So are signs of complementary elements, such as air signs with fire signs. In these relationships communication supposedly flows easily and you'll feel most comfortable with each other. However, there are no hard-and-fast rules with sun-sign combinations. Many lasting marriages happen between incompatible sun signs, while some ideally matched couples fizzle after a few years.

When sparks fly, and an irresistible magnetic pull draws you together, when disagreements and challenges fuel intrigue, mystery, passion, and sexy sparring matches, don't rule the relationship out. That person may provide the diversity, excitement, and challenge you need for an unforgettable romance, a stimulating friendship, or a successful business partnership!

Libra/Aries

THE ATTRACTION:

This attraction of opposite signs is about sharing (Libra) versus going it alone (Aries), the judge (Libra) versus the crusader (Aries). Libra admires the decision maker in Aries and adores having a true romantic lead. In this combination, Aries supplies the push and energy; Libra, the charm and diplomacy. Libra learns to take a stand; Aries learns to see the opposite point of view.

THE ISSUES:

Libra indecisiveness can make Aries see red. Aries views vacillation as a serious weakness—he who hesitates is lost or last! Aries lack of consideration and pushy manner is a Libra no-no. Aries enjoys a rousing confrontation, while Libra avoids disharmony. Discuss differences frequently and calmly in an elegant setting.

SIGN MATES:

Libra Kelly Ripa and Aries Mark Consuelos

Libra/Taurus

THE ATTRACTION:

Both Venus-ruled signs are turned on by beauty and luxury, and enjoy indulging each other. Libra brings intellectual sparkle and social savvy to Taurus. Taurus gives Libra financial stability and adoration. And Libra profits from the strong Taurus sense of direction and decisiveness.

THE ISSUES:

Taurus is possessive and enjoys staying at home. Libra loves social life and flirting. Taurus must watch out for jealousy because Libra flirtations are rarely serious. Libra can be extravagant, while Taurus sticks to a budget, another cause for resentment.

SIGN MATES;

Libra Juan Peron and Taurus Evita Peron

Libra/Gemini

THE ATTRACTION:

Air signs Gemini and Libra have both mental and physical rapport. This is an outgoing combination, full of good talk. You'll never be bored. Your Libra good looks and charm, as well as your fine mind, could keep restless Gemini close to home.

THE ISSUES:

Both of you have a low tolerance for the boredom of practical chores. The question of who will provide, do the chores, and clean up can be the subject of many a debate. There could be more talk than action here, leaving you turning elsewhere for substance.

SIGN MATES:

Tiger tamers Libra Roy Horn and Gemini Siegfried

Libra/Cancer

THE ATTRACTION:

You'll bring out each other's creativity, as Cancer sensitivity merges with your Libra balanced aesthetic sense. Your Libra innate sense of harmony could create a serenely elegant atmosphere where Cancer flourishes. You'll create an especially beautiful and welcoming home together.

THE ISSUES:

Libra detachment could be mistaken for rejection by Cancer, while Cancer hypersensitivity could throw your Libra scales off balance. Libra avoids emotional confrontations, so Cancer may look elsewhere for sympathy and nurturing.

SIGN MATES:

Libra Heather Locklear and Cancer Richie Sambora

Libra/Leo

THE ATTRACTION:

Libra is the perfect audience for Leo theatrics. As a Libra, you know how to package Leo for stardom. You both love the best things in life; you both are intelligent, stylish, and social. Since you have similar priorities, and stroke each other the right way, you could have a long-lasting relationship.

THE ISSUES:

Getting the financial area of your life under control could be a problem for these two big spenders. Since you both love to make an elegant impression, you may find yourselves perennially living beyond your means. You are both flirts, which is easier for Libra to tolerate than Leo, who could unleash lethal jealousy.

SIGN MATES:

Libra Eric Benet and Leo Halle Berry

Libra/Virgo

THE ATTRACTION:

You are intelligent companions with refined tastes, both perfectionists in different ways. Your Libra charm and elegant style work well with Virgo clear-headed decision making. You both listen to reason and treat each other fairly.

THE ISSUES:

Libra responds to admiration, but will turn off to criticism or too much negativity. Virgo must use diplomacy to keep your Libra scales in balance. Virgo values function as well as form, and sticks to a carefully thought-out budget. Extravagant Libra spends for beauty alone.

SIGN MATES:

Libra Will Smith and Virgo Jada Pinkett Smith

Libra/Libra

THE ATTRACTION:

Two Libras are a double dose of charm and style. You'll understand each other's need for beautiful, harmonious surroundings. And you'll be each other's perfect social escort. It's the light, lively, elegant romance seen in Hollywood films of the 1940s.

THE ISSUES:

This couple is long on glamour, short on practicality. Someone has to make the decisions, balance the budget, and handle the chores. Who will it be? Discuss matters gracefully and objectively; then delegate fairly.

SIGN MATES:

Libras Catherine Zeta-Jones and Michael Douglas
Libras Susan Sarandon and Tim Robbins

Libra/Scorpio

THE ATTRACTION:

The interplay of Scorpio intensity and Libra objectivity makes an exciting cat-and-mouse game. Your Libra intellect and flair will balance the powerful Scorpio charisma. Scorpio will add warmth and substance to your cool Libra demeanor.

THE ISSUES:

Libra must learn to handle Scorpio sensitive feelings with velvet gloves. When not taken seriously, Scorpio retaliates with a force that could send your Libra scales swinging off balance. On the other hand, Scorpio must give Libra room to exercise his or her mental and social skills.

SIGN MATES:

Libra Gwen Stefani and Scorpio Gavin Rossdale

Libra/Sagittarius

THE ATTRACTION:

Libra charm smooths the rough spots, while Sagittarius provides lofty goals and a spirit of adventure. This can be a blazing romance, full of action and fun on the town together. Neither of you likes to stay at home.

THE ISSUES:

Libra vacillation and Sagittarius wanderlust could keep you from making a firm commitment. You both need to find a solid launchpad (either mutual interests or career goals) to give this relationship structure. Libra needs a partner, but Sagittarius, who travels fastest alone, resents being pinned down in any way.

SIGN MATES:

Libra Teresa Heinz Kerry and Sagittarius John Kerry

Libra/Capricorn

THE ATTRACTION:

Capricorn is quick to spot Libra potential as a social asset, as well as a romantic partner. Libra loves the Capricorn dignified demeanor and elegant taste. You can climb the heights together, helping each other get the lifestyle you both want.

THE ISSUES:

Capricorn is a loner and a home lover, while Libra is a party person who likes to do things in tandem. Your expensive Libra tastes could create tension with frugal Capricorn. Libra must learn to watch the budget.

SIGN MATES:

Libra Marcello Mastroianni and Capricorn Faye Dunaway

Libra/Aquarius

THE ATTRACTION:

Shared interests and common causes are the keys to keeping this relationship on track. You'll have excellent communication, which blends friendship with romantic chemistry. You both understand how to be there for each other without making demands and how to mix public with private life.

THE ISSUES:

Libra needs flattery and romance, which Aquarius is too busy to provide. Aquarius must remember to send Libra valentines as well as never forget your birthday, ever. Aquarius needs freedom (too much togetherness is confining). Libra, remember to let this sign fly solo occasionally.

SIGN MATES:

Libra John Lennon and Aquarius Yoko Ono
Libra Kelly Preston and Aquarius John Travolta

Libra/Pisces

THE ATTRACTION:

You're one of the most creative couples. Libra keeps the delicate Pisces ego on an even keel, while Pisces provides the romance and attention Libra craves. You are ideal collaborators. Pisces appreciates your Libra aesthetic judgment. Libra refines Pisces ideas without dampening their creative spirit or deflating their ego.

THE ISSUES:

Pisces swims in emotional waters where Libra gets seasick. Fluctuating moods rock the boat here, unless you find a way to give each other stability and support. Turn to calm reason, avoiding emotional scenes, to solve problems.

SIGN MATES:

Libra Sarah "Fergie" Ferguson and Pisces Prince Andrew
Libra Gwyneth Paltrow and Pisces Chris Martin of Coldplay

CHAPTER 25

The Big Picture for Libra in 2008

Welcome to 2008, Libra! Let's start with the magnificent news first—and that's Jupiter in Capricorn, your fourth house—your house of home and family. Jupiter, as the planet of expansion, promises at least one of several possibilities. You move to a larger home or expand your existing home; your family grows—a baby or someone moves in with you; a generally luckier feeling about your home life; or the purchase of property, perhaps for investment purposes. Your connection to the collective unconscious deepens and grows in some way, perhaps through a creative project or through a broadening of your spiritual beliefs.

On January 25, Pluto joins Jupiter in your fourth house. Pluto is about profound and permanent transformation, so you can expect monumental changes in your home and family life. Pluto retrogrades back into Sagittarius and your fourth house through the year, then finally enters Capricorn for good on November 26. This means you'll feel Pluto's impact in your third house of communication off and on this year. But you already know what that means, since you have been living it since 1995.

Saturn enters Virgo in the fall of 2007 and is now in your twelfth house, which governs all that is hidden in our lives. In a sense, for the next year, you'll be clearing out long-standing issues so that you begin with a clean slate when Saturn enters your sign in the fall of 2009. Saturn governs the rules of physical existence—that's probably why it's known as the planet of karma. So your exploration of your own unconscious should be put into some sort of context.

Meditation, for instance. Or therapy. Or even just a trusted partner, friend, or family member in whom you can confide.

Uranus, the planet of sudden, unpredictable events, continues its transit of Pisces and your sixth house. The angle it forms to your sun indicates that you must make adjustments in your attitude throughout the year when it comes to your work and health. Maybe a boss or coworker is driving you crazy. Rather than placing the blame on the other person, ask yourself what lesson you're supposed to learn from this individual. Chances are that once you learn the lesson, whatever it is, the problem will disappear. You, after all, are the consummate charmer of the zodiac and should be able to charm your way through any challenge.

Neptune is still transiting Aquarius and your fifth house, which its been doing since 1998. Since it's the planet of higher inspiration and illusion, you may not be seeing your romantic partners as they really are. You may put these people on pedestals or your idealism gets in the way of an honest relationship. Another possibility is that your idealism is what binds you to your romantic partners.

Neptune in the fifth house is excellent for artistic and creative projects: dance, art, music, fiction writing, photography, acting, movies. If you have interests in any of these areas, dive in, Libra. Indulge yourself.

Best Time for Romance

Mark the dates between August 30 and September 22, when Venus is in your sign. Your romantic quota soars. You're artistic, and others see you in a flattering light. You feel confident, and your sex appeal rises. Great backup dates for romance fall between February 17 and March 11, when Venus is transiting your fifth house of love and forming a beautiful angle to your sun.

Other excellent dates for romance (and just about anything else) fall between May 11 and 13, and September 3 and 5, when the sun and Jupiter see eye to eye and there's a nice flow of energy between them.

Best Time for Career Decisions

Make career decisions between June 18 and July 11, when Venus is transiting your tenth house of careers. This should be quite a smooth time professionally. In fact, things may be going along so smoothly that you'll be tempted to kick back and relax. Don't. Seize the opportunity. There will be a lot of traveling and socializing during this period. Communication will be vital.

Mercury Retrogrades

Every year, there are three periods when Mercury—the planet of communication and travel—turns retrograde. During these periods, it's wisest not to negotiate or sign contracts, travel, submit manuscripts, or make major decisions. Granted, we can't live our lives entirely by Mercury retrogrades! However, if you have to travel during the periods listed below, then expect changes in your itinerary. If you have to sign a contract, expect to revisit it.

It's also a good idea to back up computer files before Mercury turns retrograde. Quite often, computers and other communication devices act up. Be sure your virus software is up-to-date. Pay special attention to the house in which Mercury retrograde falls. It will tell you the area of your life most likely to be impacted. The periods to watch for in 2008 are:

January 28–February 18: retrograde in Aquarius, your fifth house of romance and creativity. Best course? Review and revise all creative projects and don't start a new relationship unless it's with someone from the past who reappears in your life.

May 26–June 19: retrograde in Gemini, your ninth house, your worldview. It definitely won't be a propitious time for overseas travel or for signing up for college or graduate school courses. Someone may challenge your beliefs. Defend yourself, but without being confrontational.

September 24–October 15: retrograde in Libra. Whenever Mercury turns retrograde in your own sign, your life feels like you're on a bumper car.

Eclipses

Every year, there are four eclipses, two solar and two lunar. Solar eclipses trigger external events that allow us to see something that eluded us before. They can bring about beginnings and endings. When an eclipse hits one of your natal planets, it's especially important. Take note of the sign and house placement. Lunar eclipses bring up emotional issues related to the sign and house into which they fall.

Here are the dates to watch for:

February 6: solar eclipse at 17 degrees Aquarius, your fifth house of health and work. You'll be able to see something about your romantic partnerships and creative projects that you haven't perceived before. A new relationship may appear, or new creative opportunities.

February 20: lunar eclipse at 10 degrees Virgo, your twelfth house. Expect external events to reveal something about your motives or those of the people around you. You may spend time visiting someone in a hospital or nursing home. You may spend time in solitude.

August 1: solar eclipse, 9 degrees Leo, in your eleventh house. Something about a friend or a group to which you belong becomes glaringly obvious.

August 16: lunar eclipse at 24 degrees Aquarius, your fifth house of romance and creativity. This house seems to take a lot of hits this year, but roll with the punches, Libra, and you'll come out just fine.

Luckiest Days in 2008

Every year, Jupiter forms a beneficial angle with the sun, usually a conjunction, when both planets are in the same sign. In 2008, the angle is a lovely trine and it occurs during two time periods: May 11–13 and September 3–5. If you're going to buy a Lotto ticket, do it during these periods!

Now let's take a look at what 2008 has in store for you day by day.

CHAPTER 26

Eighteen Months of Day-by-Day Predictions—July 2007 to December 2008

Moon sign times are calculated for Eastern Standard Time and Eastern Daylight Time. Please adjust for your local time zone.

JULY 2007

Sunday, July 1 (Moon in Capricorn)   Your home life may need attention, especially if you haven't been spending much time at home. Be conservative in your decisions. Don't take any unnecessary risks. Stay grounded and maintain your emotional equilibrium.

Monday, July 2 (Moon in Capricorn to Aquarius 1:25 a.m.)   There's mystery in the air. Go with the flow. Try to avoid any confusion and conflicts. Maintain emotional balance. Gather information, but don't make any absolute decisions until tomorrow.

Tuesday, July 3 (Moon in Aquarius)   The moon is in your fifth house of creativity and children. Pursue creative endeavors. You have an ability to tap deep into the collective unconscious. There's emotional depth in a relationship, and you're possessive toward loved ones, especially children.

223

Wednesday, July 4 (Moon in Aquarius to Pisces 6:53 a.m.)   It's all about finishing the old and contemplating the new. Hold off on starting a new project. Ask someone to read the Declaration of Independence. How do the words and sentiments apply? Happy Fourth of July!

Thursday, July 5 (Moon in Pisces)   The moon is in your sixth house. Your personal health occupies your attention. Attend to details. Watch your diet; remember to exercise. Take a yoga class, even if it's your first one. Help others however you can.

Friday, July 6 (Moon in Pisces to Aries 10:57 a.m.)   Don't make waves. Be cooperative. Other people may nag, but don't show resentment. Don't rush or take on any major jobs. Use your intuition.

Saturday, July 7 (Moon in Aries)   The moon is in your seventh house. The energy that began yesterday continues with added emphasis on partnerships, both business and personal. Be careful that others don't manipulate your feelings. Any conflicts you have will be emotional.

Sunday, July 8 (Moon in Aries to Taurus 1:54 p.m.)   Be methodical and thorough. Clean out the old so there's room for the new. Revise and rewrite. Emphasize quality. You can overcome obstacles or bureaucratic red tape. You're at the right place at the right time.

Monday, July 9 (Moon in Taurus)   Mercury goes direct. Your communications with others, both individuals and groups, will go smoothly. You get your point across. Misunderstandings are resolved. Forgive and forget. You and your partner get along.

Tuesday, July 10 (Moon in Taurus to Gemini 4:10 p.m.)   It's a day for service. Be understanding and tolerant. Focus on making people happy, especially those close to you. Make a purchase for the home.

Wednesday, July 11 (Moon in Gemini)   The moon is in your ninth house. You may feel a need to get away from the regular routine. Plan for a long trip, or sign up for a workshop or seminar that interests you. Look to the big picture. How can you grow and expand?

Thursday, July 12 (Moon in Gemini to Cancer 6:40 p.m.)   You hit the jackpot. Expect a financial coup. You have an opportunity to gain recognition, fame, and power. Be courageous.

Friday, July 13 (Moon in Cancer)   The moon is in your tenth house. Career and professional goals are at center stage. You may seek a raise in status or pay. You could reach for fame. Your success will depend on how emotionally connected you are to your career or profession.

Saturday, July 14 (Moon in Cancer to Leo 10:44 p.m.)   Venus enters your twelfth house. A secret romance could blossom. You may want to keep your feelings to yourself. You benefit from any activities that take place behind the scenes. Seek out a therapist to deal with issues related to the past.

Sunday, July 15 (Moon in Leo)   The moon is in your eleventh house. You're ready to take center stage. You're passionate about whatever interests you. Romance is not secret. You're impulsive, honest, and creative.

Monday, July 16 (Moon in Leo)   Get together with friends who share a similar interest with you. You find strength through the group. Make sure your goals are an expression of who you are.

Tuesday, July 17 (Moon in Leo to Virgo 5:40 a.m.)   Put your organizational skills to use. Persevere to get things done. Be methodical and thorough. Don't get sloppy. You're building a creative base. You may feel inhibited about showing affection.

Wednesday, July 18 (Moon in Virgo) The moon is in your twelfth house. You could deal with institutions, such as hospitals, government offices, or prisons. Pay attention to details. Do as much work behind the scenes as possible.

Thursday, July 19 (Moon in Virgo to Libra 3:54 p.m.) It's all about service to others. Visit or call a sick family member or friend. Do a good deed for someone, but avoid scattering your energies. Be diplomatic, but dance to your own tune.

Friday, July 20 (Moon in Libra) The moon is in your first house. You're particularly sensitive to others' feelings, and you can be somewhat moody. Your thoughts and emotions are aligned. Pay attention to your health needs.

Saturday, July 21 (Moon in Libra) You get recharged and revitalized. Your appeal to the public is strong. Relations with the opposite sex go well. A flirtation could turn serious.

Sunday, July 22 (Moon in Libra to Scorpio 4:19 a.m.) Spiritual values surface. Nurture your intuition. Clear up odds and ends. Clear your desk for new beginnings. Accept whatever comes your way. Reflect and conclude projects.

Monday, July 23 (Moon in Scorpio) The moon is in your second house. Finances are key. You get a new start. Watch your spending. You may equate money with emotional security. Be careful about mixing love and financial security.

Tuesday, July 24 (Moon in Scorpio to Sagittarius 4:31 p.m.) Spotlight cooperation. Marriage takes on importance. Pay attention to the direction you are moving and the reasons you're going that way.

Wednesday, July 25 (Moon in Sagittarius) The moon is in your third house of communications. Relatives and neighbors play an important role. You communicate with them either verbally or in writing, and you express your opinions on a matter close to your heart. You share your thoughts and opinions with a female relative.

Thursday, July 26 (Moon in Sagittarius)   Look for ways to expand your horizons. Your thoughts turn to big ideas. You could prepare for a long journey or deal with a publishing project or legal matter. Prosperity and abundance are key.

Friday, July 27 (Moon in Sagittarius to Capricorn 2:23 a.m.)   Venus goes retrograde in your twelfth house. If you start a secret affair, it won't be secret after Venus goes direct. Watch your diet to avoid indigestion. You may be attracted to rich foods.

Saturday, July 28 (Moon in Capricorn)   The moon is in your fourth house of the home. Take time to retreat to a private place. Spend some time meditating. You feel relaxed in the home setting and nurturing toward those close to you.

Sunday, July 29 (Moon in Capricorn to Aquarius 9:14 a.m.)   Go with the flow. See things as they are, not as you wish them to be. Keep any secrets entrusted to you. Research and investigate. Dig deep for information; avoid self-deception. Knowledge is essential to your success. Maintain your emotional balance.

Monday, July 30 (Moon in Aquarius)   The moon is in your fifth house of creativity. Be yourself. Explore your creative talents. You have the ability to tap deep into the collective unconscious. You're involved with children; animals may play a role.

Tuesday, July 31 (Moon in Aquarius to Pisces 1:41 p.m.)   Discard preconceived notions. Visualize for the future. Set your goals. Then get to work. Be confident, not obsequious. Your sex appeal is heightened.

Wednesday, August 1 (Moon in Pisces)   The moon is in your sixth house of health and daily work. You could feel emotionally repressed or physically drained. Get a good night's sleep. Be helpful, but don't allow yourself to become a martyr for someone else's cause.

Thursday, August 2 (Moon in Pisces to Aries 4:43 p.m.)   Be courageous. Be aware that fear of failure, or fear that you won't measure up, will attract tangible experiences that reinforce the feeling. Appear successful, even if you don't feel that way.

Friday, August 3 (Moon in Aries) ·   The moon is in the seventh house of partnerships. Any conflicts with loved ones or business partners will be emotional. Remain detached and objective. It won't be easy. Be careful that others don't manipulate your feelings.

Saturday, August 4 (Moon in Aries to Taurus 7:16 p.m.)   Mercury moves into your eleventh house. Your communications with friends go well. You make new contacts and rethink your goals. Any activities with a group of friends who have similar interests work to your favor.

Sunday, August 5 (Moon in Taurus)   The moon is in the eighth house. Romance is in the air. A flirtation turns serious. You let go of any old stagnant energy or ideas in order to renew yourself.

Monday, August 6 (Moon in Taurus to Gemini 10:02 p.m.)   Jupiter goes direct in your third house. You could look for a better neighborhood to live in or a larger house. You could take a short trip that might involve contact with a brother or sister. Pursue a writing project.

Tuesday, August 7 (Moon in Gemini)   Mars moves into your ninth house, which bodes well for foreign travel or higher education. Don't speed, or you could end up in court. You could start an affair with a foreign-born person or have an affair while overseas.

Wednesday, August 8 (Moon in Gemini) The moon, along with Mars, is in your ninth house. Yesterday's energy related to foreign travel or the pursuit of higher education continues and strengthens. Or an affair that's with a foreign-born person or that takes place in a foreign land grows stronger.

Thursday, August 9 (Moon in Gemini to Cancer 1:37 a.m.) Do a good deed for someone. Attend to matters at home. Make some alterations in your living environment. It's a good day for a domestic purchase. Be diplomatic when dealing with others.

Friday, August 10 (Moon in Cancer) The moon is in your tenth house of profession and career. You get a raise, a bonus, or a promotion. You're responsive to the needs of a group. It's a good day for sales or dealing with the public.

Saturday, August 11 (Moon in Cancer to Leo 6:42 a.m.) You can attract success in business. Just open your mind to a new approach. Make it a goal-oriented day. Expect a financial coup. You may feel like you've won the lottery before the day is over!

Sunday, August 12 (Moon in Leo) The moon is in your eleventh house of wishes and dreams. Friends play an important role. Make sure your goals are an expression of who you are. Any group activity will work to your benefit.

Monday, August 13 (Moon in Leo to Virgo 2:04 p.m.) You're at the top of your cycle. You get a fresh start. Emphasize your individuality. Don't follow others. Stress originality; express your opinions dynamically.

Tuesday, August 14 (Moon in Virgo) The moon is in your twelfth house. Lie low. Keep your feelings to yourself; work behind the scenes. You could have dealings with institutions, such as hospitals, courts, or prisons. Use your intuition in such dealings; keep your opinions to yourself.

Wednesday, August 15 (Moon in Virgo)   Your popularity is on the rise. Your charm and wit are appreciated. Your attitude determines everything. Make time to listen to others.

Thursday, August 16 (Moon in Virgo to Libra 12:05 a.m.)   The moon is in your first house of the self. You're sensitive to other people's feelings. You may be withdrawn one moment and happy the next. Your feelings and thoughts are aligned.

Friday, August 17 (Moon in Libra)   The moon is in your sign. Be independent and creative. Make room for a new love, if that's what you want. Trust your hunches. Get out and meet new people; have new experiences.

Saturday, August 18 (Moon in Libra to Scorpio 12:14 a.m.)   Diplomacy wins the way. Do a good deed for someone. Make an adjustment in your home life. Emotional outbursts that make unfair demands on your time are likely. Be generous and tolerant, but avoid scattering your energies.

Sunday, August 19 (Moon in Scorpio)   Mercury moves into your twelfth house. Communications with people associated with institutions, such as a hospital or government office, go well. You confide in a close friend.

Monday, August 20 (Moon in Scorpio)   You're being watched by people in power. Expect a financial coup. Business discussions go well. Expand. Gain recognition, fame, and power.

Tuesday, August 21 (Moon in Scorpio to Sagittarius 12:45 a.m.)   The moon is in your third house. Your communications with others are subjective. Your thinking may be unduly influenced by the past, especially when relating to relatives. Your contact with neighbors becomes important.

Wednesday, August 22 (Moon in Sagittarius) You see the big picture. Plan a long trip, perhaps to another country. Or sign up for a workshop or seminar on a subject that interests you. Keep your good humor. Any publishing project you're working on takes off.

Thursday, August 23 (Moon in Sagittarius to Capricorn 11:20 a.m.) The spotlight is on cooperative efforts, partnerships. Be kind and understanding. Don't make waves or show any resentment. Don't rush about or take on any major projects.

Friday, August 24 (Moon in Capricorn) The moon is in your fourth house of the home. Stick close to home; spend time with your family. You feel comfortable and grounded in your home. Be nurturing toward family members.

Saturday, August 25 (Moon in Capricorn to Aquarius 6:35 p.m.) You may feel like working hard and getting things accomplished. You can overcome any obstacles. Emphasize quality. You're in the right place at the right time.

Sunday, August 26 (Moon in Aquarius) The moon is in your fifth house of creativity. In love, you'll find great depth in a relationship. You're possessive toward loved ones, especially children. Pursue creative endeavors. You can reach deep into the collective unconscious for ideas.

Monday, August 27 (Moon in Aquarius to Pisces 10:35 p.m.) Do a good deed for someone. Focus on making people happy. Be generous and tolerant. It's a day for service, but dance to your own tune.

Tuesday, August 28 (Moon in Pisces) There's a lunar eclipse in your sixth house. Emotional issues related to work arise. They could involve coworkers. You might feel

231

concerned about your health or appearance and take action to change your habits.

Wednesday, August 29 (Moon in Pisces)   Unexpected money arrives. Open your mind to a new approach and watch the results. You're playing with power, so be careful not to hurt others.

Thursday, August 30 (Moon in Pisces to Aries 12:25 a.m.)   The moon is in your seventh house of partnerships. You may hear about someone getting married soon. Loved ones and partners play an important role. A legal matter could come to your attention. Any conflicts will be emotional.

Friday, August 31 (Moon in Aries)   Initiate a new project; launch new ideas. Emotions could be volatile. Try not to be impatient with others. Your power of persuasion is strong, especially if you're passionate about what you're doing.

SEPTEMBER 2007

Saturday, September 1 (Moon in Aries to Taurus 1:36 a.m.) Play it your way. Watch for unexpected money or a surprise opportunity. Your success story could gain attention from others who want to follow your example.

Sunday, September 2 (Moon in Taurus)   You could feel fixed in your opinions. If you're not careful, someone might even call you stubborn. Go to a concert, or visit a museum. Or enjoy the early fall weather, and go for a hike or a picnic.

Monday, September 3 (Moon in Taurus to Gemini 3:31 a.m.)   Be independent and creative. Take the initiative to start something new; don't be afraid of turning in a new direction. Stress originality. A flirtation could turn serious.

Tuesday, September 4 (Moon in Gemini)   The moon is in your ninth house of higher education and long-distance travel. You feel restless and long to break away from the usual routine. Sign up for a workshop or seminar, or plan a long trip to a foreign country. In romance, a foreign-born person plays a role.

Wednesday, September 5 (Moon in Gemini to Cancer 7:09 a.m.)   Mercury is in your first house. You're in the public spotlight and communicating your ideas. People are attracted to you and pay close attention to what you have to say. You get a lot of feedback from people around you.

Thursday, September 6 (Moon in Cancer)   The moon is in your tenth house of profession and career. Like yesterday, your life is in the public view. You're responsive to the needs of a group. Be careful to avoid any emotional displays in public. You feel close to fellow workers.

Friday, September 7 (Moon in Cancer to Leo 1:00 p.m.)   You're versatile and changeable. Variety is the spice of life. Freedom of thought and action is highlighted. Take a risk. You can overcome obstacles with ease.

Saturday, September 8 (Moon in Leo)   Venus goes direct. Relations take a turn for the better. Physical discomforts end. Your love life perks up.

Sunday, September 9 (Moon in Leo to Virgo 9:11 p.m.)   Spirituality is emphasized. Look for secret matters, mystery, and intrigue. Knowledge is essential to success. See things as they are, not as you wish them to be.

Monday, September 10 (Moon in Virgo)   The moon is in your twelfth house. Yesterday's energy related to secrecy continues. You feel a need to withdraw and work behind the scenes. Pursue a mystical or spiritual discipline.

Tuesday, September 11 (Moon in Virgo)   There's a lunar eclipse in your twelfth house. Some buried issue

233

comes to the surface and triggers a strong emotional response. Your reaction may surprise you.

Wednesday, September 12 (Moon in Virgo to Libra 7:32 a.m.) You get a fresh start. Stress your individuality. Take the lead. Don't follow others. Be independent and creative. Seek originality, and you'll find it.

Thursday, September 13 (Moon in Libra) With the moon in the same sign as your sun sign, your thoughts and emotions are aligned. You get your batteries recharged. You feel physically vital. Relations with the opposite sex go well.

Friday, September 14 (Moon in Libra to Scorpio 7:37 p.m.) Intuition is highlighted. Your popularity is on the rise. Relax and enjoy yourself. Listen to others, and spread your good news. Your attitude determines everything.

Saturday, September 15 (Moon in Scorpio) The moon is in your second house of finances. You identify closely with your possessions, which make you feel comfortable. It's not to the objects themselves, but the emotions that you connect with them. Catch up on paying bills and collecting what's owed to you. Put off any big purchases for a few days.

Sunday, September 16 (Moon in Scorpio) Things could get intense and passionate. You could discuss religion or a philosophy of life with someone who disagrees. Things could get heated. What's at the heart of the issue? Make your point and back off. Be tolerant and open-minded.

Monday, September 17 (Moon in Scorpio to Sagittarius 8:21 a.m.) Service is key. Do a good deed for someone, even if there's no reward. The more kindness you offer others, the more kindness you'll reap.

Tuesday, September 18 (Moon in Sagittarius) The moon is in your third house of communications and short-distance travel. Something's going on in the neighborhood—maybe a meeting over an issue affecting everyone or maybe you get invited to a social gathering involving neighbors and relatives. Your opinion is heard loud and clear.

Wednesday, September 19 (Moon in Sagittarius to Capricorn 7:52 p.m.)   You're in the driver's seat. Take advantage of it; strive to make a deal. You get what you want, and you might get an unexpected financial windfall. Go for it!

Thursday, September 20 (Moon in Capricorn)   The moon is in your fourth house. Take the day off or work at home. Or do some work on your house. Sit quietly, relax, and meditate.

Friday, September 21 (Moon in Capricorn)   You could deal with elderly people, possibly your parents. Banks and institutions could be involved. You deal with an authority figure. You may feel stressed and overworked. Your ambition and drive to succeed might take their toll if you don't recharge your batteries.

Saturday, September 22 (Moon in Capricorn to Aquarius 4:18 a.m.)   It's all about partnerships and cooperative efforts. Be kind and understanding with your partner, whether it's a business or personal relationship. Make sure you've got a good handle on where you're going with your partner.

Sunday, September 23 (Moon in Aquarius)   The moon is in your fifth house. Take time for your animals. Walk the dog. Groom your cat. Extra treats are called for. You feel close to animals and children, who also play a big role.

Monday, September 24 (Moon in Aquarius to Pisces 8:56 a.m.)   Get organized. Control your impulses to let your mind wander. Persevere. Be methodical and thorough. Get rid of the old stuff cluttering your work or living area.

Tuesday, September 25 (Moon in Pisces)   The moon is in your sixth house. The work-oriented energy from yesterday keeps flowing, but you may feel somewhat glum and overworked. Get your work done, but don't be a martyr. Don't overlook your health needs. Exercise. Relax and get recharged.

Wednesday, September 26 (Moon in Pisces to Aries 10:23 a.m.)   It's a service day. Help others wherever you can. Be generous with your time and tolerant of others who can't keep up with your pace. Instead of being demanding, try to make others happy.

Thursday, September 27 (Moon in Aries)   Mercury moves into your seventh house. You could deal with a legal matter. If a partnership is involved, don't hide your true feelings. Express your opinions; lay out the facts. Make sure everything is clearly understood in personal and business partnerships.

Friday, September 28 (Moon in Aries to Taurus 10:18 a.m.)   Mars moves into your ninth house. You feel very strong about a matter that could deal with higher education or long-distance travel. Whatever it is, you want it very badly. Try not to get angry with someone who is attempting to temper your expansive goals.

Saturday, September 29 (Moon in Taurus)   Mars moves into your eighth house. Like yesterday, your experiences could get somewhat tense and emotional. Today it could be about possessions that you share. Is it really worth all the emotional effort? Some powerful people could be looking your way. How will you react?

Sunday, September 30 (Moon in Taurus to Gemini 10:35 a.m.)   You get a fresh start. Get out and meet new people; have new experiences. You could connect with someone who will be attracted to you or helpful in a business matter.

OCTOBER 2007

Monday, October 1 (Moon in Gemini)   The moon is in
your ninth house. Start your week off by planning for a
long trip, whether it's for pleasure or knowledge. Gather
information on your destination. Talk to someone who's
been there. Get the inside information that will make the
trip special.

*Tuesday, October 2 (Moon in Gemini to Cancer 12:58
p.m.)*   You're at the top of your cycle. Be independent;
don't be afraid to turn in a new direction. You get a fresh
start. A flirtation turns serious.

Wednesday, October 3 (Moon in Cancer)   The moon is
in your tenth house. You could deal with a boss. Business
matters are highlighted. Avoid any emotional displays in
public. It's a good day for sales and marketing or contact
with the public.

*Thursday, October 4 (Moon in Cancer to Leo 6:28
p.m.)*   People pay attention to you. You have a natural
ability to express yourself. Your positive energy attracts
them. Stay optimistic. Use your charm and wit. Ease up on
your routines; take time to listen to others.

Friday, October 5 (Moon in Leo)   The moon is in your
eleventh house. Focus on your wishes and dreams. Make
sure your overall goals are an expression of who you are.
You have deep contact with friends; they can help you get
what you want.

Saturday, October 6 (Moon in Leo)   You're at center
stage. Drama is highlighted. You're passionate and possessive of loved ones. You're impulsive and honest. Your creativity is highlighted.

*Sunday, October 7 (Moon in Leo to Virgo 3:04
a.m.)*   Be of service to others. Be generous with your
time. Be patient and diplomatic, even if someone close to

you makes unfair demands. Buy something special for your home.

Monday, October 8 (Moon in Virgo)   Venus moves into your twelfth house. A secret love affair could be the focus of your day. Work behind the scenes. Matters related to the unconscious mind and dreams could play a role.

Tuesday, October 9 (Moon in Virgo to Libra 1:58 p.m.)   You have power. Make good use of it. Avoid hurting others. Expect a windfall. Things go well in any business-related meetings. Play it your way.

Wednesday, October 10 (Moon in Libra)   The moon is in your first house of the self. You're particularly sensitive to other people's feelings. Your own feelings are closely aligned with your thoughts, which allows you to move in the direction that feels right and makes sense. You may be moody at times, but that feeling won't last.

Thursday, October 11 (Moon in Libra)   Mercury goes retrograde and stays that way until November 1. Communications can be difficult during this period. There could be disruption of plans, especially with groups. If you sign any contracts, make sure you read the fine print. To avoid arguments with those close to you, make sure you explain important matters clearly.

Friday, October 12 (Moon in Libra to Scorpio 2:14 a.m.) Cooperation and partnerships are important. You could enter into a new relationship. Expect some soul searching! Show appreciation to others. Help comes through friends, loved ones, or a partner.

Saturday, October 13 (Moon in Scorpio)   The moon is in your second house of finances. Take care of payments, and collect what's owed to you. You identify emotionally with your possessions or whatever you value. Watch your spending. Put off any major purchases for a few days.

Sunday, October 14 (Moon in Scorpio to Sagittarius 2:58 p.m.)   Clear out the old and make room for the new. Clean your closet, your attic, or your garage. Be methodical and thorough. You find a missing object or papers.

Monday, October 15 (Moon in Sagittarius)   The moon is in your third house. Your communications with relatives or neighbors could become very opinionated. Make sure that you are clearly understood. A female relative could play a role. Your thinking could be unduly influenced by the past.

Tuesday, October 16 (Moon in Sagittarius)   You see the big picture in your life. Don't limit yourself. You may feel restless and look ahead to a long trip. You could deal with a legal matter. Abundance and prosperity are in sight.

Wednesday, October 17 (Moon in Sagittarius to Capricorn 3:04 a.m.)   You could begin a journey into the unknown or a new venture of some sort. Knowledge is key to your success. Go with the flow. Avoid self-deception. Keep any secrets entrusted to you.

Thursday, October 18 (Moon in Capricorn)   The moon is in your fourth house. Spend time at home with your loved ones. It's a good day for any type of work on your home-improvement or real estate dealings. Take time to retreat to a private place to meditate.

Friday, October 19 (Moon in Capricorn to Aquarius 12:52 p.m.)   Clear up odds and ends, and get ready for a new cycle. Finish what you've started, but don't begin anything new. Visualize your future. Set your goals. Then get to work.

Saturday, October 20 (Moon in Aquarius)   The moon is in your fifth house of creativity and children. You gain great pleasure from romance and your children. Seek pleasure, even if it means taking a risk.

Sunday, October 21 (Moon in Aquarius to Pisces 7:03 p.m.)   Go with the flow. Don't rock the boat. Be cooperative. Share your abilities and talents with others. You gain through a partnership. Be supportive and patient.

Monday, October 22 (Moon in Pisces)   The moon is in your sixth house of health and daily work. You tend to your daily duties and serve others through your work. Deal with adversity by staying strong and healthy, even if you feel overworked. Face your fears, and you'll overcome them.

Tuesday, October 23 (Moon in Pisces to Aries 9:25 p.m.)   The work-oriented energy from yesterday continues. Focus on getting everything organized. Take care of your obligations. Persevere to get things done. Don't get sloppy. You're building a creative base.

Wednesday, October 24 (Moon in Aries)   The moon is in your seventh house of partnerships. Loved ones and partners are important to you. Try to keep everything in balance. Any conflicts will be emotional.

Thursday, October 25 (Moon in Aries to Taurus 9:08 p.m.)   Continue the balancing act that began yesterday. It's all about service to others and remaining diplomatic, even in the face of emotional outbursts. Be understanding, generous, and tolerant. At the same time, avoid scattering your energies; balance your needs against the wishes of others.

Friday, October 26 (Moon in Taurus)   The moon is in your eighth house. Your experiences are particularly intense, especially when dealing with relationships. Sex is in the air! So are death and rebirth. A part of us dies, and we are reborn.

Saturday, October 27 (Moon in Taurus to Gemini 8:12 p.m.)   You're being watched by those in power. Be courageous. Play it your way. You have a chance to gain prestige.

Sunday, October 28 (Moon in Gemini) The moon is in your ninth house. You play with ideas and philosophies. Religion or mythology interests you. You talk about your worldviews. A foreign-born person could be involved.

Monday, October 29 (Moon in Gemini to Cancer 8:50 p.m.) You get your way. You get a fresh start. Stress originality. Trust your hunches. Get out and discover something new. Creativity is highlighted.

Tuesday, October 30 (Moon in Cancer) The moon is in your tenth house. Professional concerns are the focus. You're emotional and warm toward coworkers. Your life turns public. Business matters are highlighted. You gain prestige.

Wednesday, October 31 (Moon in Cancer) Attitude determines everything. Be happy, positive, and upbeat. Spend time with family or a small group of friends. Remember a special anniversary or birthday. Relax and enjoy yourself!

NOVEMBER 2007

Thursday, November 1 (Moon in Cancer to Leo 12:48 a.m.) Mercury goes direct. The bumpy ride regarding communications these past three weeks turns smooth. You relate better with others. Misunderstandings are resolved. Forgive and forget. You and your friends get along better.

Friday, November 2 (Moon in Leo) The moon is in your eleventh house. Go to lunch with coworkers for a social and business gathering. You benefit by acting as an arbitrator and keeping everything in balance. You gain power through your association with the group.

Saturday, November 3 (Moon in Leo to Virgo 8:45 a.m.)
Relax and recharge your battery. Ease up on your routines. Have fun in preparation for next week's discipline and focus. Make time to listen to others. Spread your good news.

Sunday, November 4—Daylight Saving Time Ends (Moon in Virgo) The moon is in your twelfth house. Work behind the scenes. Stay out of the public view for the present. Keep your feelings to yourself, or confide in a close friend or a therapist. Matters dealing with the past arise.

Monday, November 5 (Moon in Virgo to Libra 6:47 p.m.) It's all about freedom of thought and action. Take risks. Change your perspective. Approach the day with an unconventional mind-set. You may look for a change of scenery.

Tuesday, November 6 (Moon in Libra) The moon is in your sign. Get revitalized for the month ahead. You're physically vital and appealing to the public. Relations with the opposite sex go well.

Wednesday, November 7 (Moon in Libra) The moon is in your first house of the self. It's all about your self-awareness, appearance, and health. Your self-image and how you present yourself are important to you. You could act impulsively based on your self-image. Who are you, and who are you becoming?

Thursday, November 8 (Moon in Libra to Scorpio 7:19 a.m.) Venus moves into your first house. You feel vital and revitalized. You're particularly attractive to the opposite sex. Your relationship with a partner grows deep. You're sensitive and loving toward others.

Friday, November 9 (Moon in Scorpio) Whatever started yesterday related to emotional connections continues and intensifies. A relationship heats up and turns passionate. But things happen in secret. Watch out for possible deception.

Saturday, November 10 (Moon in Scorpio to Sagittarius 7:59 p.m.)   The energy from the past two days keeps flowing. Relations with the opposite sex go well. You feel physically vital. Your feelings and your thoughts are aligned.

Sunday, November 11 (Moon in Sagittarius)   The moon is in your third house of communications. You could connect with a relative or neighbor. Take what you know, and share it with others.

Monday, November 12 (Moon in Sagittarius)   You see the big picture, or at least you get a glimpse of it. You feel impulsive and inquisitive. You seek answers. Legal matters, publishing, or higher education could be on your mind.

Tuesday, November 13 (Moon in Sagittarius to Capricorn 8:01 a.m.)   The moon moves into Capricorn. Get ready for hard work. You overcome obstacles, but you must tear down the old and rebuild.

Wednesday, November 14 (Moon in Capricorn)   The moon is in your fourth house. Deal with practical matters in your home. Get ready to make repairs. Attend to any domestic issues, but maintain your emotional balance. Retreat to a quiet place and meditate.

Thursday, November 15 (Moon in Capricorn to Aquarius 6:31 p.m.)   Mars goes retrograde in your tenth house. Career issues that you thought were resolved arise. Control your anger. Watch your speed while driving, or you could end up in court or driving school.

Friday, November 16 (Moon in Aquarius)   The moon is in your fifth house of creativity. Your feelings of love in a relationship expand and take on great depth. Be emotionally honest. You tend to be protective of children. Animals play a large role.

Saturday, November 17 (Moon in Aquarius)   Your day shapes up with a focus on social activities. Take things to a new level. Find a new approach that defies the old and accepted way of doing things.

Sunday, November 18 (Moon in Aquarius to Pisces 2:15 a.m.)   Clean out the attic, the garage, or wherever you park your old stuff. If not your physical attic, straighten up your mental equivalent. Clear your desk. Use the day for reflection, expansion, and finishing projects.

Monday, November 19 (Moon in Pisces)   The moon is in your sixth house. You could feel a little down. Focus on the details of your daily work; help others where you can. Don't forget your own needs, especially in the areas of health and diet. Remember to exercise.

Tuesday, November 20 (Moon in Pisces to Aries 6:25 a.m.) Think partnership. Think cooperation. Be kind and understanding. Let things develop, especially with a partnership. Don't rush others. Help comes through friends and loved ones.

Wednesday, November 21 (Moon in Aries)   The moon is in your seventh house. Yesterday's energy related to partnerships keeps flowing. There could be some soul searching regarding a new direction. It could relate to a new partnership. Legal matters—such as a contract or even a marriage—could be involved.

Thursday, November 22 (Moon in Aries to Taurus 7:19 a.m.)   Prepare to host a big dinner today. Make use of your organizational skills. Persevere to get everything done. You're at the right place at the right time. Happy Thanksgiving!

Friday, November 23 (Moon in Taurus)   The moon is in your eighth house. On one hand, you may deal with taxes, insurance matters, or investments. On the other, the issue might relate to what you share with someone else. You feel possessive of belongings that aren't entirely yours. Things could get intense unless you back off and put everything into perspective.

Saturday, November 24 (Moon in Taurus to Gemini 6:29 a.m.)   Uranus goes direct in your sixth house, which brings a burst of new energy into your life and bodes well for your health situation. It also opens the door to unusual and idiosyncratic people who help define your individuality.

Sunday, November 25 (Moon in Gemini)   The moon is in your ninth house. You discuss or think about philosophies, religion, and mythologies. You play with ideas. There could be a foreign-born person involved, or your thoughts and interests could turn to a foreign land.

Monday, November 26 (Moon in Gemini to Cancer 6:07 a.m.)   Expect something big: a bonus, a winning lottery ticket, a royalty check, or a big raise. Negotiations go well and work in your favor. Remember: you're playing with power. Be careful not to hurt others in your enthusiasm.

Tuesday, November 27 (Moon in Cancer)   The moon is in your tenth house. You achieve a new level of prestige in your career. You're rewarded with an elevated position. You move up the ladder. In doing so, your life becomes public. You're responsive to the needs of a group of co-workers or fellow students.

Wednesday, November 28 (Moon in Cancer to Leo 8:23 a.m.)   You're at the top of your cycle as yesterday's energy expands. You can easily take the initiative and leadership role to move in a new direction. You deal with creative people, so stress originality. Trust your hunches.

245

Thursday, November 29 (Moon in Leo)   The moon is in your eleventh house. Your focus turns to working with a group of like-minded individuals as you pursue your goals. The power of the group will bolster your own position. You help others, and in turn you benefit. Your wishes and dreams come true.

Friday, November 30 (Moon in Leo to Virgo 2:45 p.m.)   After all the new energy and creative efforts this week, back off. Relax, listen to others, and spread your good news. Remain flexible with your schedule. You're optimistic and well-liked. Expect an invitation to a social gathering.

DECEMBER 2007

Saturday, December 1 (Moon in Virgo)   Mercury moves into your third house. It's all about communications, networking, writing, and getting together with friends and family. Focus on mental energy, exchanging ideas, making your point, and being understood without any strong emotions attached.

Sunday, December 2 (Moon in Virgo)   The moon is in your twelfth house. Work behind the scenes. Avoid confrontations. Take time to meditate or write in a journal. You could visit someone who's ailing in a hospital and confide in that person.

Monday, December 3 (Moon in Virgo to Libra 1:02 a.m.)   A new relationship could develop. Use your intuition to make sure that it's right for you. You could deal with a business partnership that's taking shape. You're particularly sensitive to how others feel.

Tuesday, December 4 (Moon in Libra)   The moon is in your first house of the self. The emotional energy that began yesterday continues with you becoming somewhat moody and very much aware how others feel. Rather than

246

being oversensitive about your appearance, think about the person you are becoming.

Wednesday, December 5 (Moon in Libra to Scorpio 1:32 p.m.)   Venus moves into your second house. Your financial situation improves. You get an unexpected bonus or raise. Women are helpful. Your sense of security improves, especially if it's linked with your finances.

Thursday, December 6 (Moon in Scorpio)   The moon joins Venus in your second house, carrying forward yesterday's energy and embellishing it with even more emotion. You identify emotionally with your possessions or whatever you value. Watch your spending, especially if you're shopping for a new vehicle or house.

Friday, December 7 (Moon in Scorpio)   You're passionate about your interests. Like yesterday, watch your spending. Be aware of things happening in secret. Avoid going to extremes. Forgive and forget.

Saturday, December 8 (Moon in Scorpio to Sagittarius 2:12 a.m.)   Accept whatever comes your way, but don't start anything new. Take time to reflect and plan for the future. Think about how you can expand whatever you're doing. Finish up any current projects so you're ready to move ahead on something new.

Sunday, December 9 (Moon in Sagittarius)   The moon is in your third house. You communicate with relatives and neighbors. You express yourself from the heart. A female relative could play an important role.

Monday, December 10 (Moon in Sagittarius to Capricorn 1:51 p.m.)   Think partnership; think cooperation. Don't make waves; work with others. Don't rush or show resentment toward someone who may nag. Work hard to make a relationship work. Your soul searching pays off.

Tuesday, December 11 (Moon in Capricorn)   The moon is in your fourth house. Before bed, tell yourself that you'll remember your dreams in the morning. When you wake up, write them down. It's an excellent time for dream recall. Meditate on your dreams; look for hidden messages.

Wednesday, December 12 (Moon in Capricorn)   You may feel overworked by midweek. Hang in there. Things ease up tomorrow. Help others. Attend to details; look forward to a greater sense of freedom that's coming your way. Take care of any health issues. Exercise. Watch your diet.

Thursday, December 13 (Moon in Capricorn to Aquarius 12:02 a.m.)   Freedom of thought and action is important. Release old structures. Get a new point of view. Experiment. Let others know about your new approach. People may take note of your communications skills.

Friday, December 14 (Moon in Aquarius)   The moon is in your fifth house. It's a good day for creative or procreative pursuits—sex for pleasure is an aspect of the fifth house. In love, there's great emotional depth to a relationship. You're possessive of loved ones, especially children. You nurture and protect.

Saturday, December 15 (Moon in Aquarius to Pisces 8:15 a.m.)   Something mysterious is going on. Maintain your emotional balance. Keep any secrets entrusted to you. See things as they are, not as you would like them to be. Gather information, but don't make any immediate decisions.

Sunday, December 16 (Moon in Pisces)   The moon is in your sixth house. Don't let your fears hold you back. Meet them head-on. You'll come out better for it. Stay strong in dealing with work issues. Help others, but take care of your own health.

Monday, December 17 (Moon in Pisces to Aries 1:53 p.m.)   You're at the top of your cycle. You get a fresh start. Take advantage of it. Be independent and creative; refuse to get discouraged. Stress your originality.

Tuesday, December 18 (Moon in Aries) Jupiter moves into your fourth house. It's all about expansion in the home setting. You expand your home life somehow. Maybe there's a new child on the way. Or you are going to add a new room to your house or buy a larger home. The new addition to the home could be a relative who is coming to stay with you.

Wednesday, December 19 (Moon in Aries to Taurus 4:38 p.m.) With Saturn moving into your twelfth house, you need to take some time out to refocus on your goals and reconsider who you really are. Strengthen your foundations in order to reinforce your creative base. Think in terms of a partnership.

Thursday, December 20 (Moon in Taurus) Mercury joins Jupiter in your fourth house, which means there's a lot of communications and excitement related to your home, whether you're moving to a larger home, building an addition, or adding a new member to the family.

Friday, December 21 (Moon in Taurus to Gemini 5:14 p.m.) Be versatile and changeable. Promote and explore new ideas. Your curiosity leads you into new realms. Take a risk. Experiment. Change your perspective. Be careful not to spread yourself too thin.

Saturday, December 22 (Moon in Gemini) The moon moves into your ninth house. The urge to explore and diversify that began yesterday continues into your weekend. You feel restless. You play with new ideas and look for ways to break out of the usual routine. You could prepare for a long trip.

Sunday, December 23 (Moon in Gemini to Cancer 5:19 p.m.) Secrets, mystery, intrigue, and confidential information are the order of the day. Maintain your emotional balance. See things as they are, not as you wish them to be. Avoid self-deception. Go with the flow.

Monday, December 24 (Moon in Cancer)   The moon is in Cancer, which is all about your home and family. You feel particularly nurturing, although you could be somewhat moody. Tend to loved ones; do something special for your spouse or sweetheart, and for your children.

Tuesday, December 25 (Moon in Cancer to Leo 6:53 p.m.)   Strive for universal appeal. Spiritual values surface. Look beyond the immediate. Use the day for reflection, expansion, and tying up loose ends. Accept whatever comes your way, including gifts from near and far. Merry Christmas!

Wednesday, December 26 (Moon in Leo)   The moon is in your eleventh house. You could gather together with friends or a group of like-minded people. You have deep contact with friends this holiday season. Everyone gets along well. A sense of social consciousness, sometimes overlooked, is aroused.

Thursday, December 27 (Moon in Leo to Virgo 11:45 p.m.)   You could hear about a marriage proposal or a new business partnership. Think about your direction. Where are you going and why? Use your intuition.

Friday, December 28 (Moon in Virgo)   The moon is in your twelfth house. You could deal with matters from your past or from your childhood. Work behind the scenes. Keep to yourself. Pursue a mystical or spiritual discipline.

Saturday, December 29 (Moon in Virgo)   Tend to details. Tidy up the house. Take time to write in a journal. Stick close to home. Take care of health issues. Watch your diet and exercise.

Sunday, December 30 (Moon in Virgo to Libra 8:38 a.m.)
Venus moves into your third house. Relationship with rela-

tives go well. You overcome old difficulties. A female relative may play a role. Or you could develop a romance with someone nearby. It's a good day for writing or any type of communication.

Monday, December 31 (Moon in Libra)   The moon is in your first house of the self. Make your resolutions for the year ahead. Focus on self-awareness, not just your appearance. Who are you, and who are you becoming? Your thoughts and feelings are aligned.

HAPPY NEW YEAR!

JANUARY 2008

Tuesday, January 1 (Moon in Libra to Scorpio 8:33 p.m.)   It's a number 1 day. You're at the top of your cycle as the year begins. Don't be afraid to turn in a new direction. You get a fresh start. In romance, if you're single, make room for a new love. If attached, the sparks are reignited for you and your partner.

Wednesday, January 2 (Moon in Scorpio)   The moon is in your second house. Take a look at your priorities for spending your income. Plan ahead. You equate your assets with emotional stability. Avoid making any major purchases for at least a couple days.

Thursday, January 3 (Moon in Scorpio)   Your emotions play a strong role. Expect intense emotional experiences that could relate to things happening in secret. Avoid going to extremes. Control issues surface. Other water signs, Pisces and Cancer, play a role.

Friday, January 4 (Moon in Scorpio to Sagittarius 9:14 a.m.)   It's a number 4 day. Control your impulses. Fulfill obligations. Organizational skills are highlighted. Persevere to get things done. You build foundations for a creative outlet.

Saturday, January 5 (Moon in Sagittarius)   The moon is in your third house. Keep conscious control of your emotions when communicating with others. Your thinking may be unduly influenced by matters from the past.

Sunday, January 6 (Moon in Sagittarius to Capricorn 8:43 p.m.)   It's a number 6 day. It's all about service to others. Be generous and tolerant. Focus on making others happy, but avoid scattering your energies. Be understanding; avoid confrontations.

Monday, January 7 (Moon in Capricorn)   Mercury moves into your fifth house. Expect lots of communication related to a creative project. Children could play a role; there is much to discuss with a partner or loved one. You tend to be possessive and nurturing.

Tuesday, January 8 (Moon in Capricorn)   The moon is in your fourth house. Like yesterday, you could feel emotionally possessive of loved ones. Retreat to a private place to meditate. But be sure to spend time at home with your family.

Wednesday, January 9 (Moon in Capricorn to Aquarius 6:13 a.m.)   It's a number 9 day. Finish whatever you've been working on. Visualize for the future, set your goals, and get to work. Strive for universal appeal. You're up to the challenge.

Thursday, January 10 (Moon in Aquarius)   The moon is in your fifth house. You get a fresh start on a creative project that you feel strongly about. It's something that you've been nurturing. You can tap deeply into the collective unconscious.

Friday, January 11 (Moon in Aquarius to Pisces 1:44 p.m.)   It's a number 2 day. Cooperation is highlighted. A partnership plays an important role. Use your intuition to get a sense of your day. Let things develop in their own time. Don't make waves.

Saturday, January 12 (Moon in Pisces)   The moon is in your sixth house. You could feel somewhat emotionally repressed. Don't let your fears hold you back. Confront and overcome them. Keep your resolution to exercise.

Sunday, January 13 (Moon in Pisces to Aries 7:24 p.m.)   It's a number 4 day. Your organizational skills come into play. Be methodical and thorough. You build a creative base. Emphasize quality. You can overcome any obstacles.

Monday, January 14 (Moon in Aries)   The moon is in your seventh house. The focus turns to relationships, both personal and business. The opposite sex plays an important role, but be aware of possible confrontations. It may be difficult to maintain a detached and objective perspective.

Tuesday, January 15 (Moon in Aries to Taurus 11:13 p.m.)   It's a number 6 day. Diplomacy wins the way. A domestic adjustment works out for the best. Domestic purchases are highlighted. Do a good deed. Help others wherever you can, but avoid scattering your energies.

Wednesday, January 16 (Moon in Taurus)   The moon is in your eighth house. You could attract powerful people. You take a renewed interest in a metaphysical subject.

Thursday, January 17 (Moon in Taurus)   You feel emotionally grounded. You're highly sensual; your experiences may be intense. You could deal with taxes, insurance, and investments.

Friday, January 18 (Moon in Taurus to Gemini 1:30 a.m.)   It's a number 9 day. Complete a project and get ready to start something new. Set your goals and get to work.

Saturday, January 19 (Moon in Gemini)   The moon is in your ninth house. Break away from your usual routine and get away for a day or two. Sign up for a workshop or seminar that interests you. Something related to publishing works to your favor. Pursue a new idea. Are you ready to plan a long trip?

Sunday, January 20 (Moon in Gemini to Cancer 3:06 a.m.)   It's a number 2 day. That means cooperation is highlighted. Don't rush about or show resentment. Let things develop in their own time. Avoid taking on a major project.

Monday, January 21 (Moon in Cancer)   The moon is in your tenth house. Professional concerns weigh heavily. Your life is more public. You're responsive to the needs and moods of a group and the public in general. Keep your profession and personal lives separate.

Tuesday, January 22 (Moon in Cancer to Leo 5:22 a.m.)   It's a number 4 day. That means you could face some hard work. Make use of your organizational skills. Stay focused on what you need to work on. Persevere to get things done; control your impulses to turn your attentions elsewhere.

Wednesday, January 23 (Moon in Leo)   The moon is in your eleventh house. Friends play an important role. Though you tend to try to keep everything and everyone around you in balance, step boldly to center stage and strut your stuff! Your wishes and dreams come true.

Thursday, January 24 (Moon in Leo to Virgo 9:49 a.m.)   Venus moves into your fourth house. It's a great day for romance in the home. Venus rules your sun sign. Spend time with a loved one. Patch up any differences that have arisen lately.

Friday, January 25 (Moon in Virgo)   Pluto joins Venus in your fourth house. That indicates that you will experience profound transformation related to your home life. But don't panic. It's all happening over time. It could relate to a move or a change in your marital status.

Saturday, January 26 (Moon in Virgo to Libra 5:36 p.m.)   It's a number 8 day. That means it's your power day. Be courageous. Take a chance. Expect a financial coup. You have a chance today to gain recognition and fame.

Sunday, January 27 (Moon in Libra)   The moon is in your first house. The focus is on self-awareness and general health. You're particularly sensitive to other people's feelings. It's all about the emotional self.

Monday, January 28 (Moon in Libra)   Mercury goes retrograde in your fifth house. There could be delays and confusion related to creative efforts or your children. Your attempts to nurture a creative endeavor or loved ones might be misunderstood. Don't speculate or take any unnecessary risks.

Tuesday, January 29 (Moon in Libra to Scorpio 4:35 a.m.)   It's a number 2 day. The emphasis is on working together. Use your intuition to get a sense of your day. Be kind and understanding. Partnerships play an important role.

Wednesday, January 30 (Moon in Scorpio)   Mars goes direct in your ninth house. Expect increased energy related to higher education or long-distance travel. There could be new activity related to a publishing project or anything dealing with publicity or advertising.

Thursday, January 31 (Moon in Scorpio to Sagittarius 5:08 p.m.)   It's a number 4 day. Get organized and take care of all your obligations. You build a creative base. Be methodical and thorough. Tear down the old in order to rebuild.

Friday, February 1 (Moon in Sagittarius)   The moon is in your third house. You communicate well, either verbally or in writing. Take what you know and share it with others. But keep conscious control of your emotions, especially when dealing with relatives.

Saturday, February 2 (Moon in Sagittarius)   You feel prosperous. Think abundance. Don't limit yourself. Resources are available. Follow a new path. There's strong passion in a relationship.

Sunday, February 3 (Moon in Sagittarius to Capricorn 4:52 a.m.)   It's a number 4 day. Fulfill your obligations. Your organizational skills are called upon. Keep everything in balance, including your budget. You can overcome obstacles. You build a base for your future.

Monday, February 4 (Moon in Capricorn)   The moon is in your fourth house. Family matters play a big role. You deal with the foundations of who you are. Spend time with family and loved ones; make an effort to beautify your home. Your surroundings are a reflection of who you are.

Tuesday, February 5 (Moon in Capricorn to Aquarius 2:10 p.m.)   It's a number 6 day. It's all about service to others. Be diplomatic when dealing with others who demand your time and try your patience. Be generous and tolerant. Do a good deed for someone, even if you get nothing in return.

Wednesday, February 6 (Moon in Aquarius)   There's a solar eclipse in your fifth house. That indicates that external events cause you to see a need for balance.

Thursday, February 7 (Moon in Aquarius to Pisces 8:47 p.m.)   It's a number 8 day. It's a power day. Keep your mind open to a new approach that could bring in big bucks. You're watched by people in power.

Friday, February 8 (Moon in Pisces)   The moon is in your sixth house. You could feel a bit down. Keep your resolutions about exercise and diet. Help others where you can. Visit someone who is ill.

Saturday, February 9 (Moon in Pisces)   Write down your dreams and look for hidden meanings. Ideas are ripe for development. Use your imagination. Watch for synchronicities.

Sunday, February 10 (Moon in Pisces to Aries 1:18 a.m.)   It's a number 2 day. Partnerships are highlighted. That includes both personal and professional alliances. Process everything that happened yesterday and apply it to a relationship. You could deal with something hidden, especially if your partner is a Scorpio.

Monday, February 11 (Moon in Aries)   With the moon in your seventh house, personal relations are key. Loved ones and partners are important. The opposite sex plays a prominent role. It's difficult to remain detached and objective now. Be careful that others don't manipulate your feelings.

Tuesday, February 12 (Moon in Aries to Taurus 4:35 a.m.)   It's a number 4 day. Apply yourself. Stay focused and don't wander off or avoid commitments. Clean out the old so there's room for something new. Be methodical and thorough.

Wednesday, February 13 (Moon in Taurus)   The moon is in your eighth house. You deal with shared resources; you could feel unsettled about how your partner deals with your belongings. Relations are key. An interest in metaphysics, such as life after death, plays a role.

Thursday, February 14 (Moon in Taurus to Gemini 7:20 a.m.)   It's a number 6 day. Be understanding and avoid confrontations. Be diplomatic and helpful, but avoid scattering your energies. Dance to your own tune.

Friday, February 15 (Moon in Gemini)   The moon is in your ninth house. Pursue higher education or anything dealing with the higher mind. Philosophies and worldviews attract your attention. You could plan a long journey.

Saturday, February 16 (Moon in Gemini to Cancer 10:30 a.m.)   It's a number 8 day. It's your power day. Be courageous and know that fear of failure could attract experiences that reinforce the feeling. Open up to a new approach. You attract financial success.

Sunday, February 17 (Moon in Cancer)   Venus moves into your fifth house, and Venus rules your sun sign. That's all good news. Your love life is greatly enhanced. The same could be true with any creative project, especially one that you love working on. There's great pleasure in dealing with children.

Monday, February 18 (Moon in Cancer to Leo 1:52 p.m.)   Mercury goes direct. Any confusion, miscommunication, and delays you've been experiencing recede into the past. Things move smoothly. You get your message across. Everything works better, including computers and other electronic equipment.

Tuesday, February 19 (Moon in Leo)   The moon is in your fourth house. Retreat to a private place and spend some time in meditation. See if you can recall any recent dreams that may serve to guide you. If there's time, work on a home-repair project.

Wednesday, February 20 (Moon in Leo to Virgo 7:07 p.m.)   There's a lunar eclipse in you twelfth house. Childhood issues come to the surface. Focus on dreams and past lives.

Thursday, February 21 (Moon in Virgo)   The moon is in your twelfth house. Yesterday's energy continues. You deal with secrets.

Friday, February 22 (Moon in Virgo)   There's more of the same energy as the last two days, but you dig deep for information. You tend to the details. Stick close to home, relax, and write down everything that's going on in a journal. Tend to any health concerns.

Saturday, February 23 (Moon in Virgo to Libra 2:45 a.m.)   It's a number 6 day. It's a service day. Be understanding with others and avoid confrontations. Focus on making people happy. Domestic purchases are highlighted.

Sunday, February 24 (Moon in Libra)   The moon is in your first house. You could feel somewhat moody and sensitive to the thoughts of others. Get recharged for the month ahead.

Monday, February 25 (Moon in Libra to Scorpio 1:06 a.m.)   It's a number 8 day. It's your power day. Success in finances is likely. Remember that you're playing with power, so be careful not to hurt others.

Tuesday, February 26 (Moon in Scorpio)   The moon is in your second house. You could gain a financial boost that feels like a jolt of energy. While that will make you feel more secure, you need to decide what your priorities are in handling your income. Temper your spending, even if you've just received an increase in your finances.

Wednesday, February 27 (Moon in Scorpio)   Intense emotional experiences could accompany events. You may have a tendency to go to extremes. Best to back off. Forgive and forget. Be aware of secret dealings taking place. Your sexuality and intuition are heightened.

Thursday, February 28 (Moon in Scorpio to Sagittarius 1:23 a.m.)   It's a number 2 day. The focus is on partnerships and cooperation. Use your intuition to get a sense of your day. Be supportive and patient, kind and understanding.

Friday, February 29 (Moon in Sagittarius) The moon is in your third house. You probably take care of everyday needs. Get in touch with relatives or neighbors. You'll have a message to pass on.

MARCH 2008

Saturday, March 1 (Moon in Sagittarius to Capricorn 1:33 p.m.) It's a number 3 day. Make use of your charm and wit. Your intuition is highlighted. Ease up on your routines. Hobbies are accented. Make time to listen to others, and spread your good news.

Sunday, March 2 (Moon in Capricorn) The moon is in your fourth house. Meditate, especially early in the morning. Spend time with your family and loved ones. You might deal with your parents. Make an effort to change a bad habit.

Monday, March 3 (Moon in Capricorn to Aquarius 11:25 p.m.) It's a number 5 day. Freedom of thought and action is the key phrase today. Avoid restrictions. Look for a change of scenery, possible a relocation. Variety is the spice of life. Experiment; get ready for change.

Tuesday, March 4 (Moon in Aquarius) Mars moves into your tenth house. Expect a surge of energy related to you career. Expect an elevation in prestige. It could be a comment from a boss, a raise, a bonus, or a new position with more responsibility.

Wednesday, March 5 (Moon in Aquarius) The moon is in your fifth house. Your creative abilities are emphasized. You bring great emotional depth to any creative project that you're working on. You're warm and friendly toward children and animals. You could be feeling overpossessive of loved ones.

Thursday, March 6 (Moon in Aquarius to Pisces 5:54 a.m.)   It's a number 8 day. You attract material success. Business dealings go well. Open your mind to a new approach that could bring in money.

Friday, March 7 (Moon in Pisces)   The moon is in your sixth house. You could feel sensitive and emotionally down. Help others where you can. Take care of any health issues, and get ready for a big day tomorrow. Don't let your fears hold you back.

Saturday, March 8 (Moon in Pisces to Aries 9:24 a.m.)   It's a number 1 day. You're at the top of your cycle. You get a fresh start. Explore and discover. Creativity is highlighted. Stress your originality and trust your hunches. Make room for a new love, if that's what you're looking for.

Sunday, March 9—Daylight Saving Time Begins (Moon in Aries)   The moon is in your seventh house. The focus turns to partnerships. Loved ones and partners play a major role. Any conflict will be emotional. Be careful that others don't manipulate your feelings.

Monday, March 10 (Moon in Aries to Taurus 12:15 p.m.)   It's a number 3 day. You feel optimistic. Your popularity is on the rise. Others are impressed by your charm and wit. Remain flexible and open to new ideas. Your attitude determines everything.

Tuesday, March 11 (Moon in Taurus)   The moon is in your eighth house. Things get emotionally intense, especially if you deal with shared resources or belongings. You could attract the attention of people in power. Look into any issues related to taxes, insurance, or investments.

Wednesday, March 12 (Moon in Taurus to Gemini 1:55 p.m.)   Venus moves into your sixth house. Take care of health issues. Exercise and watch your diet. Help your

261

coworkers. Your attention to their needs will be appreciated.

Thursday, March 13 (Moon in Gemini)   The moon is in your ninth house. You feel as if you need to get away from the usual routine. You could discuss new ideas and philosophies. A foreign-born person may play a role.

Friday, March 14 (Moon in Gemini to Cancer 4:38 p.m.)   Mercury joins Venus in your sixth house. You could discuss details related to your health. You could find yourself in extended communication with someone at work who needs your help.

Saturday, March 15 (Moon in Cancer)   The moon is in your tenth house. You could deal with a matter related to your reputation. Don't worry. It's all very positive. You get a boost in prestige. You're received well by others, but avoid making emotional displays in public.

Sunday, March 16 (Moon in Cancer to Leo 9:04 p.m.)   It's a number 9 day. Finish what you've started. Clear your desk and make way for the new. Look beyond the immediate, but don't start anything new. Let go of pre-conceived notions. Your sex appeal is heightened.

Monday, March 17 (Moon in Leo)   The moon is in your eleventh house. Friends play an important role, and they may help you in surprising ways. Focus on your wishes and dreams; make sure that they are an expression of who you really are.

Tuesday, March 18 (Moon in Leo)   Drama is high-lighted. Strut your stuff. You're at center stage. Dress in bold colors. Do something different with your hair or ward-robe. Focus on advertising and publicity.

Wednesday, March 19 (Moon in Leo to Virgo 3:25 a.m.)   It's a number 3 day. Get your batteries recharged. Relax and enjoy yourself. Have some fun in preparation for tomorrow when you will need to focus and keep to yourself. Spread your good news and listen to others.

Thursday, March 20 (Moon in Virgo)   The moon is in your twelfth house. Work behind the scenes. Avoid any confrontations. Use your intuition to get a sense of your day. Go deep within to look for answers.

Friday, March 21 (Moon in Virgo to Libra 11:45 a.m.)   It's a number 5 day. Get ready for adjustments that could include a possible change of jobs or a relocation. Variety is the spice of life. Let go of old structures; get a new point of view. Experiment.

Saturday, March 22 (Moon in Libra)   The moon is in your first house. You get recharged for the month ahead. Your self-awareness and appearance are important to you. You're appealing to the public. You feel physically vital; relations with the opposite sex go well.

Sunday, March 23 (Moon in Libra to Scorpio 10:07 p.m.)   It's a number 7 day. Discuss and defend your beliefs. But make sure you see things as they are. Knowledge is essential to success. Spirituality is emphasized. Keep any secrets entrusted to you to yourself.

Monday, March 24 (Moon in Scorpio)   The moon is in your second house. Expect emotional experiences related to money and your values. You have the opportunity to turn in a new direction. Take the initiative; don't follow others. Creative people play a role.

Tuesday, March 25 (Moon in Scorpio)   You could deal with a secret matter. Dig deep, research, investigate, and be aware of possible deception. Other water signs—Pisces and Cancer—figure prominently. Avoid any major purchases.

Wednesday, March 26 (Moon in Scorpio to Sagittarius 10:12 a.m.)   It's a number 1 day. You're at the top of your cycle. Be independent and creative. Take the initiative to turn in a new direction. You get a fresh start. Don't be discouraged by naysayers. Stress originality and trust your hunches.

Thursday, March 27 (Moon in Sagittarius) The moon is in your third house. Express yourself dynamically, but control your emotions. You can take what you know and share it with others, especially those with creative minds. A relative or a neighbor could play a role.

Friday, March 28 (Moon in Sagittarius to Capricorn 10:44 p.m.) It's a number 3 day. Expect an invitation from a friend or loved one. Express your affection and gratitude. Use your charm and wit; remember to remain flexible.

Saturday, March 29 (Moon in Capricorn) The moon is in your fourth house. Get organized. You deal with your home life and the very foundations of who you are and who you are becoming. Make an effort to change a bad habit. Work on your own and stay focused.

Sunday, March 30 (Moon in Capricorn) You could deal with elderly people. Your responsibilities increase. Don't take any unnecessary risks. Find a structure for what you're doing. Self-discipline is called for. Maintain your emotional equilibrium.

Monday, March 31 (Moon in Capricorn to Aquarius 9:35 a.m.) It's a number 6 day. You may need to attend to a domestic matter. Be diplomatic when dealing with others. Do a good deed for someone. Focus on making people happy.

APRIL 2008

Tuesday, April 1 (Moon in Aquarius) The moon is in your fifth house. Your sense of creativity flourishes. Any

264

creative project gets an emotional boost. In relationships, there's great emotional depth.

Wednesday, April 2 (Moon in Aquarius to Pisces 4:56 a.m.) Mercury moves into your eighth house. That means you solidify your shared resources. You and your partner talk about saving for the future. There also could be a discussion about a loan or mortgage.

Thursday April 3 (Moon in Pisces) The moon is in your sixth house. Keep your resolutions about exercise and diet. Help others. Follow your dreams. Attend to details in your daily life.

Friday, April 4 (Moon in Pisces to Aries 8:28 p.m.) It's a number 7 day. Go with the flow. Maintain your emotional balance. Express your desires, but avoid self-deception. See things as they are.

Saturday, April 5 (Moon in Aries) The moon is in your seventh house. The focus turn to partnerships, both personal and business. Loved ones play a key role. Conflicts will be emotional. Be careful that others don't manipulate your feelings.

Sunday, April 6 (Moon in Aries to Taurus 9:20 p.m.) Venus moves into your seventh house. A love partnership rules. You can accomplish a lot together.

Monday, April 7 (Moon in Taurus) The moon is in your eighth house. You attract the attention of powerful people. Be aware that your experiences could be intense. You could deal with a matter related to shared belongings, investments, or taxes. An interest in metaphysics plays a role.

Tuesday, April 8 (Moon in Taurus to Gemini 9:27 p.m.) It's a number 2 day. Cooperation is highlighted. Be supportive and patient. Use your intuition to focus on a relationship issue. Process everything that happened yesterday.

Wednesday, April 9 (Moon in Gemini)   The moon is in your ninth house. You feel a need to get away from your usual routine. Focus on new ideas, higher education, or a foreign destination. You plan to attend a workshop or seminar, or map a long trip. Pursue any plans or interests related to publishing.

Thursday, April 10 (Moon in Gemni to Cancer 10:43 p.m.)   It's a number 4 day. Get everything in order. You can overcome any bureaucratic red tape. You're in the right place at the right time. Emphasize quality. Revise and rewrite. You build a creative base.

Friday, April 11 (Moon in Cancer)   The moon is in your tenth house. The emphasis is on professional matters, or education if you're a student. You get along well with fellow workers or students, but there could be changes around you. You're in the public eye. Avoid any over-the-top emotional displays.

Saturday, April 12 (Moon in Cancer)   Stick close to home and spend time with your family. Work on a home-improvement project or beautify your home environment in some way. Your home, after all, represents the foundation of who you are. Retreat to a private place to meditate and give thanks for all that you have.

Sunday, April 13 (Moon in Cancer to Leo 2:29 a.m.)   It's a number 7 day. There's something mysterious going on around you. Something hidden or secretive comes to your attention. Dig deep for answers. Gather information, but don't make any final decisions on what you uncover until tomorrow.

Monday, April 14 (Moon in Leo)   The moon is in your eleventh house. Focus on your wishes and dreams. You may gather with a group of like-minded friends who can help you while you aid the group's goals. You take center stage with the support of those around you.

Tuesday, April 15 (Moon in Leo to Virgo 9:07 a.m.) It's a number 9 day. Strive for universal appeal. Discard preconceived notions. Visualize your future, set your goals, and get to work. Your sex appeal is heightened.

Wednesday, April 16 (Moon in Virgo) The moon is in your twelfth house. You may feel a need to withdraw and work on your own. Your actions can help you find success and also deal with rejection or failure. Relations with the opposite sex can be difficult. Keep your secrets to yourself.

Thursday, April 17 (Moon in Virgo to Libra 6:11 p.m.) It's a number 2 day. Focus on the direction you are going and your motivation for going there. Cooperation and partnerships are highlighted. Let things develop. Don't make waves.

Friday, April 18 (Moon in Libra) The moon is in your first house. The focus turns to the self, particularly your emotional self. You're sensitive to other people's feelings, and you may feel moody.

Saturday, April 19 (Moon in Libra) You feel physically vital and attractive to the opposite sex. Your sensuality is highlighted. Relationships go well. Romance is in the air. Your personal grace and magnetism play a role.

Sunday, April 20 (Moon in Libra to Scorpio 5:02 a.m.) It's a number 5 day. Freedom of thought and action rules your day. Variety is the spice of life. Approach the day with an unconventional mind-set. Release old structures; experiment today. Get a new point of view.

Monday, April 21 (Moon in Scorpio) The moon is in your second house. Expect emotional experiences related to money and your values. You feel most comfortable surrounded by familiar objects. It's not the objects themselves

267

that are important, but the memories related to them. Put off any major purchases.

Tuesday, April 22 (Moon in Scorpio to Sagittarius 5:08 p.m.) It's a number 7 day. Dig deep into a mystery. You could deal with confidential information, secrets, and intrigue. Maintain your balance. Gather information, but don't make any immediate decisions based on what you learn.

Wednesday, April 23 (Moon in Sagittarius) The moon is in your third house. You could get involved in some sort of aggressive mental activities. If you're in school, you'll do great on tests.

Thursday, April 24 (Moon in Sagittarius) You see the big picture. Keep your good humor. A publishing project pays off. You feel restless, impulsive, and inquisitive. Don't limit yourself.

Friday, April 25 (Moon in Sagittarius to Capricorn 5:48 p.m.) It's a number 1 day. You're at the top of your cycle. You get a fresh start. Stress your originality. Take the initiative to start something new, and don't be afraid to turn in a new direction. Your individuality is emphasized.

Saturday, April 26 (Moon in Capricorn) The moon is in your fourth house. Stick close to home and deal with domestic matters. Retreat to a quiet place to relax and meditate.

Sunday, April 27 (Moon in Capricorn to Aquarius 5:28 p.m.) It's a number 3 day. People appreciate your sense of optimism and your positive point of view. You express yourself well and share your creative talents. Make time to listen to others. Relax and enjoy yourself.

Monday, April 28 (Moon in Aquarius) The moon is in your fifth house. You're inspired. Your originality is highlighted. You have an infectious love of life. You feel creative and joyful. It's a great day for sex.

Tuesday, April 29 (Moon in Aquarius)   Yesterday's energy continues; you feel somewhat aloof and distant. You're still inspired, but not showing as much warmth. You are somewhat enigmatic and unpredictable. Children play a role.

Wednesday, April 30 (Moon in Aquarius to Pisces 2:11 a.m.)   Venus moves into your eighth house. You gain financially through a marriage or partnership. You express strong convictions, but you feel best working behind the scenes. Try your best to avoid any jealousies that rise.

MAY 2008

Thursday, May 1 (Moon in Pisces)   The moon is in your sixth house. Help others, but don't deny your own needs. Your personal health occupies your attention. Attend to details related to any health issue. Make a doctor or dentist appointment. Keep your resolutions about exercise and watch your diet. Don't let your fears hold you back.

Friday, May 2 (Moon in Pisces to Aries 6:51 a.m.) Mercury moves into your ninth house. You think and talk a lot about your philosophy of life. You analyze and scrutinize.

Saturday, May 3 (Moon in Aries)   The moon is in your seventh house. A legal matter comes to your attention. Loved ones and partners are important. It's difficult to remain detached and objective. Be careful that others don't manipulate your feelings.

Sunday, May 4 (Moon in Aries to Taurus 7:58 a.m.)   It's a number 8 day. It's your power day. Be courageous. You're playing with power, so be careful not to hurt others. Others in power may watch your moves.

Monday, May 5 (Moon in Taurus)   Mars moves into your eleventh house. Your relationship with a group is enhanced. Friends are energized by your presence. You appear attractive to those around you. Your wishes and dreams get a big boost.

Tuesday, May 6 (Moon in Taurus to Gemini 7:18 a.m.)   It's a number 1 day. Be independent and creative; refuse to be discouraged by naysayers. You get a fresh start. Take the lead and trust your hunches. In romance, a flirtation could turn serious.

Wednesday, May 7 (Moon in Gemini)   The moon is in your ninth house. Break with your usual routines. Plan a long trip. Sign up for a workshop or seminar. A foreign-born person plays a role, or a foreign country fits in the picture.

Thursday, May 8 (Moon in Gemini to Cancer 7:03 a.m.)   It's a number 3 day. Your attitude determines everything. Spread your good news, but listen to others. Ease up on your routine. Your vitality and natural ability to express yourself attract others. Remain flexible and open to change.

Friday, May 9 (Moon in Cancer)   Jupiter goes retrograde in your fourth house. You look around your house and find some faults. You may wish it were larger or more attractive. Or you rearrange furniture or beautify your home with a fresh coat of paint.

Saturday, May 10 (Moon in Cancer to Leo 9:11 a.m.)   It's a number 5 day. Change your perspective with an unconventional mind-set. You're versatile and changeable. But be careful not to diversify so much so that your time and energy get spread thin.

Sunday, May 11 (Moon in Leo)   The moon is in your eleventh house. You do well in a group setting. You get along well with others. You help them, and in doing so, you help yourself. You could pursue a project aimed at raising social awareness.

Monday, May 12 (Moon in Leo to Virgo 2:49 p.m.)   It's a number 7 day. You set off on a journey into the unknown. Follow your heart, but be aware of possible deception and secrets. Maintain your emotional balance. Go with the flow, but discreetly gather information. Don't act on what you find out for another day or two.

Tuesday, May 13 (Moon in Virgo)   The moon is in your twelfth house. You might feel a need to withdraw and work on your own. Unconscious attitudes can be difficult. You communicate your deepest feelings with another person. It's a great day for a mystical or spiritual discipline.

Wednesday, May 14 (Moon in Virgo to Libra 11:48 p.m.)   It's a number 8 day. It's your power day. Look for a windfall. Play the Lotto. Business discussions go well. You attract financial success. You pull a financial coup.

Thursday, May 15 (Moon in Libra)   The moon is in your first house. Your self-awareness and your appearance are important. You deal with your emotional self and the person you are becoming. You may feel moody.

Friday, May 16 (Moon in Libra)   You seek harmony and peace, the native energy of Libra. Romance is highlighted. Your personal grace and magnetism shine. You see both sides of the story.

Saturday, May 17 (Moon in Libra to Scorpio 11:00 a.m.)   It's a number 3 day. The energy of the last couple days continues. Remain flexible. Your intuition is highlighted. Your imagination is keen. Ease up on your routine. Listen to others. Your charm and wit are appreciated.

Sunday, May 18 (Moon in Scorpio)   The moon is in your second house. Put off any big purchases for a few days. Look at your priorities in spending your income. Take care of payments and collections. It's a good time for investments.

Monday, May 19 (Moon in Scorpio to Sagittarius 11:20 p.m.) It's a number 5 day. You're versatile and changeable. You have a tendency to spread out and diversify too much. Promote new ideas; follow your curiosity. Freedom of thought and action is key.

Tuesday, May 20 (Moon in Sagittarius) The moon is in your third house. You'll take care of your everyday needs. Tell others what you know, but don't get overemotional, especially when talking with relatives or neighbors.

Wednesday, May 21 (Moon in Sagittarius) See the big picture, not just the details. Travel is indicated. A matter related to publishing or the law could enter your day. Make use of your sense of humor. Spiritual values arise. Worldviews are emphasized. Advanced education could play a role.

Thursday, May 22 (Moon in Sagittarius to Capricorn 11:56 a.m.) It's a number 8 day. It's your power day. Ambition and success are highlighted. You attract financial success by dealing with problems and attending to details.

Friday, May 23 (Moon in Capricorn) The moon is in your fourth house. Yesterday's ambitious energy continues. Your success is hard earned. You may feel stressed and overburdened. Don't forget to exercise and watch your diet.

Saturday, May 24 (Moon in Capricorn to Aquarius 11:52 p.m.) Venus moves into your ninth house. You think about a long, romantic journey. You feel restless and plan an escape from the routine. Long-distance travel for pleasure is indicated. Or a flirtation with a foreign-born person could turn serious. A love of intellectual interests could play a role.

Sunday, May 25 (Moon in Aquarius)   The moon is in your fifth house. Yesterday's romantic tendencies continue. You feel creative, artistic, and romantic. There's great emotional depth in a relationship. You could feel somewhat possessive of a loved one or children in your life.

Monday, May 26 (Moon in Aquarius)   Mercury goes retrograde in your ninth house for the next three weeks. That means you can expect some delays and glitches related to a long journey or your higher education. Miscommunication causes confusion when you break away from your usual routine. A publishing project could be delayed.

Tuesday, May 27 (Moon in Aquarius to Pisces 9:39 a.m.)   It's a number 4 day. Stay focused. Control your impulses. Fulfill your obligations. Persevere to get things done. Revise and rewrite. Be methodical and thorough. There's no time for romance.

Wednesday, May 28 (Moon in Pisces)   The moon is in your sixth house. You feel somewhat overburdened. Be of service to someone who needs your help, but know when enough is enough. Take care of health issues; watch your diet.

Thursday, May 29 (Moon in Pisces to Aries 3:53 p.m.)   It's a number 6 day. Diplomacy wins the way. Be generous and tolerant. Do a good deed for someone. Focus on making people around you happy. A domestic adjustment works out for the best.

Friday, May 30 (Moon in Aries)   The moon is in your seventh house. The focus turns to relationships, business and personal ones. Initiate a new project with a partner. You could get a contract on a joint proposal. Set off on an adventure with your partner. Do something thrilling.

Saturday, May 31 (Moon in Aries to Taurus 6:19 p.m.)   It's a number 8 day. Focus on a power play. Unexpected money arrives. Buy a Lotto ticket. You have an opportunity to gain recognition, fame, and power.

JUNE 2008

Sunday, June 1 (Moon in Taurus)   The moon is in your eighth house. Experiences can turn tense and could revolve around issues related to shared possessions. You may have a desire to control your partner's resources. If that's a problem, back off. An interest in metaphysics could play a role.

Monday, June 2 (Moon in Taurus to Gemini 6:07 p.m.)   It's a number 7 day. You could launch a journey into the unknown. Secrets and intrigue play a role. You dig deep for information. Knowledge is the key to success. Avoid confusion and conflict; maintain your emotional balance. Hold off on making any major decisions based on what you've learned.

Tuesday, June 3 (Moon in Gemini)   The moon is in your ninth house. You feel a sense of wanderlust. You look beyond the immediate scene. You explore new ideas and philosophies. Sign up for a seminar or workshop; plan a trip to a distant land.

Wednesday, June 4 (Moon in Gemini to Cancer 5:17 p.m.)   It's a number 9 day. Complete a project. Clear up odds and ends. Get ready for a new cycle. Accept what comes your way, but don't start anything new.

Thursday, June 5 (Moon in Cancer)   The moon is in your tenth house. You gain prestige related to your profession. Business is highlighted. Material success and financial security play a role. You make a strong emotional commitment to your profession.

Friday, June 6 (Moon in Cancer to Leo 6:01 p.m.)   It's a number 2 day. Cooperation is key. Be kind and understanding. Family members and a partnership play important roles. Don't make waves.

Saturday, June 7 (Moon in Leo) The moon is in your eleventh house. Group activities work in your favor. You help the group, and the group helps you in return. Friends are supportive. Focus on your wishes and dreams, but make sure that your goals remain an expression of who you really are.

Sunday, June 8 (Moon in Leo to Virgo 10:02 p.m.) It's a number 4 day. The emphasis is on your organizational skills. In romance, your persistence pays off. You build a foundation for the future. Control your impulse to wander; fulfill your obligations. Be practical with money.

Monday, June 9 (Moon in Virgo) The moon is in your twelfth house. You might feel a need to work behind the scenes. A troubling matter from the past could rise up. It's a great day for a mystical or spiritual discipline. Your intuition is heightened.

Tuesday, June 10 (Moon in Virgo) Take care of details, especially related to your health. Stop fretting. Best to stick close to home and take care of loose ends. Relax and spend some time writing in a journal. You can dig deep for answers to your concerns.

Wednesday, June 11 (Moon in Virgo to Libra 5:56 a.m.) It's a number 7 day. Look beneath the surface for answers. Be aware of secret dealings and possible deception. Express your concerns, but maintain your emotional balance. Go with the flow. Knowledge is essential to success.

Thursday, June 12 (Moon in Libra) The moon is in your first house. Your batteries are recharged for the weeks ahead. You appeal to the public. Relations with the opposite sex go well. Your feelings and thoughts are aligned.

Friday, June 13 (Moon in Libra to Scorpio 4:54 p.m.)   It's a number 9 day. Finish what you started. Clear your desk for tomorrow's new cycle. Visualize the future, set your goals, and get to work. Reflect and conclude projects, but don't start anything new.

Saturday, June 14 (Moon in Scorpio)   The moon is in your second house. You could gain a financial boost that feels like a jolt of energy. Decide what your priorities are in handling your finances. Even if you experience a sudden increase of income, don't make any big purchases for a few days.

Sunday, June 15 (Moon in Scorpio)   Your energy is probably intense. Investigate, research, and be aware of possible deception. Try to avoid going to extremes. In romance, you're passionate; your sexuality is heightened.

Monday, June 16 (Moon in Scorpio to Sagittarius 5:20 a.m.)   It's a number 3 day. Remain flexible. Trust your hunches. Follow your curiosity. Stay positive. Your attitude determines everything. Make time to listen to others.

Tuesday, June 17 (Moon in Sagittarius)   You see the big picture. Spiritual values arise. Your energy flows well and everything seems to go your way. You yearn for travel or to find a new mental challenge.

Wednesday, June 18 (Moon in Sagittarius to Capricorn 5:52 p.m.)   Venus moves into your tenth house. You gain great favor in your career. You're admired in public and praised by your boss. Or you could enter a partnership in which you gain status and recognition.

Thursday, June 19 (Moon in Capricorn)   Mercury goes direct. Your communication with others will go smoothly. Misunderstandings are resolved. Everything comes into balance.

Friday, June 20 (Moon in Capricorn)   The moon is in your fourth house. Stay home and tend to domestic duties. That could involve working on a home-repair project or tending to loved ones. Spend some time by yourself in quiet meditation.

Saturday, June 21 (Moon in Capricorn to Aquarius 5:34 a.m.)   It's a number 8 day. It's your power day. Open your mind to a new approach that could bring in big bucks. You could pull a financial coup, but be careful not to hurt others.

Sunday, June 22 (Moon in Aquarius)   The moon is in your fifth house. Your sense of well-being relates to the state of affairs in a romantic relationship. You may enjoy taking a gamble, but be sure to weigh the odds carefully before you invest your assets.

Monday, June 23 (Moon in Aquarius to Pisces 3:33 p.m.)   It's a number 1 day. You're at the top of your cycle. You get a fresh start. Don't be afraid to take a risk by following a new path. Trust your hunches. Explore, discover, and create. Refuse to deal with people with closed minds.

Tuesday, June 24 (Moon in Pisces)   The moon is in your sixth house. People depend on you, and that can get to be a burden. You're restless and could consider changing jobs if the one you have doesn't feel right for you. Stop worrying. You are better off than you think.

Wednesday, June 25 (Moon in Pisces to Aries 10:50 p.m.)   It's a number 3 day. Stay positive and upbeat. Spread your good news. Diversify. Insist on getting all the information, not just bits and pieces. Listen to others.

Thursday, June 26 (Moon in Aries)   Uranus goes retrograde in your sixth house. Be aware of sudden erratic events occurring in your usually predictable daily life. It could be personal or global. At best, it could be a pleasant surprise.

Friday, June 27 (Moon in Aries)   Initiate a new project, launch a new idea, or brainstorm with associates. You're extremely persuasive, especially if you're passionate about what you're doing or selling or trying to convey. Be aware that emotions could get volatile. Remain patient.

Saturday, June 28 (Moon in Aries to Taurus 2:51 a.m.)   It's a number 6 day. Focus on making people happy. Do a good deed for someone. A domestic adjustment works out for the best. Be understanding and avoid being confrontational.

Sunday, June 29 (Moon in Taurus)   The moon is in your eighth house. You could attract powerful people. An interest in metaphysics plays a key role. Your experiences may be intense.

Monday, June 30 (Moon in Taurus to Gemini 4:04 a.m.)   It's a number 8 day. Focus on a power play. Open your mind to a new approach that could create material wealth. Business dealings go well. Financial success is highlighted. Be courageous.

JULY 2008

Tuesday, July 1 (Moon in Gemini)   Mars goes into your twelfth house. There's a lot of energy involved in secret work. Your imagination is highlighted. You do well in an artistic or creative endeavor, especially if it's related to a humanitarian activity. Work on your own.

Wednesday, July 2 (Moon in Gemini to Cancer 3:54 a.m.)   It's a number 8 day. It's your power day. You attract financial success. Buy a Lotto ticket or two. Expect a windfall. Be courageous.

278

Thursday, July 3 (Moon in Cancer)   The moon is in your tenth house. Professional matters play a central role; things work to your benefit. You gain a boost in prestige, possibly a raise. You get along well with coworkers. Your life is more in public view.

Friday, July 4 (Moon in Cancer to Leo 4:16 a.m.)   It's a number 1 day. That means you're at the top of your cycle. Be bold and forceful. Take the initiative to start something new. Don't be deterred by naysayers. Trust your hunches. Take the lead and be independent.

Saturday, July 5 (Moon in Leo)   The moon is in your eleventh house. You connect well with friends, especially with members of a group, and you benefit from your friendships. Follow your wishes and dreams; make sure that they remain an expression of who you are. You could be involved in a project that aims to improve social awareness.

Sunday, July 6 (Moon in Leo to Virgo 7:04 a.m.)   It's a number 3 day. That means you communicate well. Just enjoy connecting with people; don't worry about tomorrow. Enjoy the harmony, beauty, and pleasures of life. Your attitude determines everything.

Monday, July 7 (Moon in Virgo)   The moon is in your twelfth house. Work behind the scenes and avoid confrontations, especially with women. You could do well exploring mystical and spiritual matters. Take time for meditation.

Tuesday, July 8 (Moon in Virgo to Libra 1:32 p.m.)   It's a number 5 day. That means you're open to change and want to loosen restrictions. Take a risk and experiment. Variety is the spice of life.

Wednesday, July 9 (Moon in Libra)   The moon is in your first house. Your feelings could be extremely sensitive. You easily change your mind now. You're restless and uncertain what to do. You are responsive regarding the needs of others, so you are easily influenced by those around you.

Thursday, July 10 (Moon in Libra to Scorpio 11:35 p.m.) Mercury moves into your tenth house. You can expect that you'll be using your communication skills to the fullest in your career. That could include writing or speaking. Or travel could be called for related to your profession.

Friday, July 11 (Moon in Scorpio) The moon is in your second house. Deal with your finances. You find emotional security in your assets and material goods. It's the memories and feelings related to the belongings, not the objects themselves that are important.

Saturday, July 12 (Moon in Scorpio) Venus moves into your eleventh house. There are harmony and warmth in relationships with friends, particularly those whom you know through a group setting. A romance could develop with a particular person in the group.

Sunday, July 13 (Moon in Scorpio to Sagittarius 11:50 a.m.) It's a number 1 day. That means you're at the top of your cycle. You get a fresh start. Make sure that you take the initiative while the time is right to start a new project. In romance, make room for a new love, if that's what you want now.

Monday, July 14 (Moon in Sagittarius) The moon is in your third house. Your communications with others are subjective. Take what you know and share it with others. However, keep conscious control of your emotions when communicating with relatives and neighbors. Your thinking is unduly influenced by the past.

Tuesday, July 15 (Moon in Sagittarius) It's a number 3 day. Your charm and wit are appreciated. You're curious and inventive. Relax and get your batteries recharged. In romance, you feel loyal to your partner.

Wednesday, July 16 (Moon in Sagittarius to Capricorn 12:20 a.m.) Your responsibilities increase. You try to keep everything in balance around you. You're concerned that you may be overlooking needs in your home. Self-discipline and a firm structure to your day are important.

Thursday, July 17 (Moon in Capricorn) The moon is in your fourth house. If at all possible, stick close to home and tend to family matters. Retreat to a private place for quiet reflection on everything that's been going on. Do something to beautify your home.

Friday, July 18 (Moon in Capricorn to Aquarius 11:41 a.m.) It's a number 6 day. Service to others is emphasized. Whether you're in the home or office, you tend to nurture and care for those around you. You offer advice and support. Like yesterday, your heart is in your home and home life.

Saturday, July 19 (Moon in Aquarius) The moon is in your fifth house. You're emotionally in touch with your creative side. You're easily impressed, so make sure that you don't allow anyone to influence you on a speculative matter. Don't take any risks. Best to tend to children and loved ones. There's a lot of emotion in a romantic relationship.

Sunday, July 20 (Moon in Aquarius to Pisces 9:09 p.m.) It's a number 8 day. It's your power day. You're ambitious and goal-oriented. You can go far with your plans and achieve financial success. Take action. You can achieve recognition and fame. Avoid being negative or manipulative. Don't neglect the needs of others.

Monday, July 21 (Moon in Pisces) The moon is in your sixth house. You're busy helping others in your daily work. You offer suggestions for improvements. You're helpful and service-oriented but also restless. Take care of any health issues.

Tuesday, July 22 (Moon in Pisces) Yesterday's energy continues. You're compassionate and sensitive. You inspire others. It's all about deep healing. Follow your heart. Pay attention to your dreams and intuitive hunches. You seek universal knowledge, eternal truths, and deep spirituality.

Wednesday, July 23 (Moon in Pisces to Aries 4:23 a.m.) It's a number 2 day. Cooperation and partnerships are highlighted. You're diplomatic and capable of fixing whatever has gone wrong. As usual, you're concerned about keeping everything in balance. You excel in working with a group. You play the role of the visionary. Be honest and open.

Thursday, July 24 (Moon in Aries) The moon is in your seventh house. Yesterday's energy continues. Personal relationships, especially a partnership, play a dominant role. Your partner might be moody and sensitive. You want to be accepted for who you are, but it's difficult to remain detached and objective.

Friday, July 25 (Moon in Aries to Taurus 9:15 a.m.) It's a number 4 day. Stick to practical matters. You're seen as trustworthy and down to earth by others. Stick with this energy and avoid trying to please everyone, and you can gain recognition, success, and fame for your hard work.

Saturday, July 26 (Moon in Taurus) Mercury moves into your eleventh house. There's a lot of communication with friends, especially in a group setting. You help the group, and your friends assist you in achieving your wishes and dreams.

Sunday, July 27 (Moon in Taurus to Gemini 11:56 a.m.) It's a number 6 day. Service to others is the theme. Do a good deed for someone. Visit someone who is ill or someone in need of help. Focus on making people happy. Be sympathetic, kind, and compassionate.

Monday, July 28 (Moon in Gemini) The moon is in your ninth house. You're a dreamer and a thinker who yearns for something new, whether it's long-distance travel or taking a seminar on a subject that grabs your interest. Your beliefs are strong and sincere but changeable.

Tuesday, July 29 (Moon in Gemini to Cancer 1:12 p.m.)   It's a number 8 day. It's your power day. You have an opportunity to succeed in whatever you're pursuing. Financial success is at hand. Open your mind to a new approach that could bring in big bucks. But don't do anything that could hurt others.

Wednesday, July 30 (Moon in Cancer)   The moon is in your tenth house. You're in the public eye. You have a chance for recognition, if you're ready for it. It's a good day for sales and dealing with the public. You're responsive to the needs of those around you in the workplace as well as the public in general.

Thursday, July 31 (Moon in Cancer to Leo 2:22 p.m.)   It's a number 1 day. You take a leadership role. You get a fresh start. Stress your independence. Don't let naysayers and close-minded people influence you. Explore, discover, and create.

AUGUST 2008

Friday, August 1 (Moon in Leo)   There's a solar eclipse in your eleventh house. That means that some external events that will help you clarify a friendship or some issue concerning a group to which you belong are likely to occur.

Saturday, August 2 (Moon in Leo to Virgo 4:59 p.m.)   It's a number 9 day. Complete a project. Clear up odds and ends. Make room for something new. Apply the finishing touches, reflect on what you've accomplished, and envision how you can expand.

Sunday, August 3 (Moon in Virgo)   The moon is in your twelfth house. You can be overly self-critical and may need to bolster your confidence. Work behind the scenes and avoid conflict. Confide your deepest thoughts to a confidant.

Monday, August 4 (Moon in Virgo to Libra 10:28 p.m.)   It's a number 2 day. Use your intuition to get a sense of your day. Cooperation is highlighted. Be kind and understanding. Don't make waves; just let things develop. There could be discussions about a marriage or a partnership.

Tuesday, August 5 (Moon in Libra)   Venus moves into your twelfth house. You're introspective and in need of time alone, especially if you must recover from a frustrating romance. Your emotions are strong and controlled deep in your subconscious. Some childhood issues could surface.

Wednesday, August 6 (Moon in Libra)   The moon is in your first house. You're sensitive to other people's feelings, but you're also moody. You're concerned about your appearance.

Thursday, August 7 (Moon in Libra to Scorpio 7:27 a.m.)   It's a number 5 day. You look for a new perspective. You're versatile and changeable, but be careful not to overcommit yourself. Stay focused as best you can. Take risks; experiment. Pursue a new idea. Freedom of thought and action is key.

Friday, August 8 (Moon in Scorpio)   The moon is in your second house. You feel comfortable close to home. You identify emotionally with your belongings, particularly with the memories you associate with them. Your values are important.

Saturday, August 9 (Moon in Scorpio to Sagittarius 7:11 p.m.)   It's number 7 day. You become aware of confidential information and secret meetings. You investigate like a detective solving a mystery. Gather information, but don't act on what you learn until tomorrow.

Sunday, August 10 (Moon in Sagittarius)   Mercury moves into your twelfth house. Some of your decisions and tendencies are based on subconscious influences. Feelings rather than logic prevail. Express your thoughts to a close friend, but avoid airing your concerns in public.

Monday, August 11 (Moon in Sagittarius)   The moon is in your third house. You have an emotional need to pursue your studies of ideas and subjects that interest you. Your intellectual curiosity requires continued nurturing and growth.

Tuesday, August 12 (Moon in Sagittarius to Capricorn 7:43 a.m.)   It's a number 1 day. Be independent and creative. Get out and meet new people and have new experiences. Explore, discover, and create. In romance, make room for a new love. A flirtation turns serious.

Wednesday, August 13 (Moon in Capricorn)   The moon is in your fourth house. Stay close to home and spend time with family and loved ones. Do something to beautify your home. Reflect on everything that has been happening in your life. Focus on recalling your dreams.

Thursday, August 14 (Moon in Capricorn to Aquarius 6:57 p.m.)   It's a number 3 day. You communicate well. You're receptive to what others tell you. Enjoy the harmony, beauty, and pleasures of life. Remain flexible, curious, and inventive.

Friday, August 15 (Moon in Aquarius)   The moon is in your fifth house. You're emotionally in touch with your creative side. Be yourself and emotionally honest. There's great emotional depth in a relationship. However, you could be somewhat overpossessive of loved ones, especially children.

Saturday, August 16 (Moon in Aquarius)   There's a lunar eclipse in your fifth house. Change any bad habits that are blocking your creativity or interfering with a romantic relationship. You can break an addiction. Start from within and change your life for the better.

Sunday, August 17 (Moon in Aquarius to Pisces 3:47 a.m.)   It's a number 6 day. Service to others is the theme. Offer advice and support to those around you. Remember to be diplomatic, not aggressive or argumentative. Diplomacy wins the way. Do a good deed; make someone happy.

Monday, August 18 (Moon in Pisces)   The moon is in your sixth house. Yesterday's service-oriented energy continues. Others rely on you for help. You're the go-to person to improve, edit, or refine what others are working on. Just make sure that others don't take advantage of your willingness to help. Know when to say enough is enough.

Tuesday, August 19 (Moon in Pisces to Aries 10:11 a.m.) Mars moves into your first house. You're assertive, outgoing, and energetic, especially regarding a partnership or marriage. You'll remain that way for the next couple months. You appeal to the public; relations with the opposite sex are great.

Wednesday, August 20 (Moon in Aries)   The moon is in your seventh house. Partnerships are highlighted. You work well with others and feel secure. You may want to push someone who lags behind, but it's best not to make waves.

Thursday, August 21 (Moon in Aries to Taurus 2:38 p.m.)   It's number 1 day. Be independent and creative. Don't follow others. Just play your hunches and don't be afraid to follow a new path. Your individuality is stressed. Get out and meet new people and have new experiences.

Friday, August 22 (Moon in Taurus)   The moon is in your eighth house. Security issues arise; you feel best when you're out of debt. You may be in a position to control the assets of a partner. You tend to have a strong sense of duty

286

and obligation, so it's natural for you to look out for the interest of all parties. You could be involved in a project to help a large number of people.

Saturday, August 23 (Moon in Taurus to Gemini 5:49 p.m.)   It's a number 3 day. You communicate well. You're warm and receptive to what others say. Your attitude determines everything. Remain flexible. Pay attention to your hunches. Others are impressed by your wit and charm.

Sunday, August 24 (Moon in Gemini)   The moon is in your ninth house. You yearn for new experiences. Break with your usual routine. You're a dreamer and a thinker. Plan a long trip to a foreign land or pursue a subject that interests you, and see where it leads.

Monday, August 25 (Moon in Gemini to Cancer 8:19 p.m.)   It's a number 5 day. Yesterday's energy continues. Freedom of thought and action is key. Promote new ideas; follow your curiosity. A change in perspective works to your advantage. Approach the day with an unconventional mind-set.

Tuesday, August 26 (Moon in Cancer)   The moon is in your tenth house. Professional concerns are highlighted. You're responsive to the needs and moods of a group and of the public in general. You're warm and emotional toward fellow workers, but don't blur the boundaries between your professional and personal lives.

Wednesday, August 27 (Moon in Cancer to Leo 10:51 p.m.)   It's a number 7 day. You could delve into a mystery that involves confidential information. Knowledge is essential for success. Dig deep for answers, but maintain your emotional balance. Don't make any snap decisions on what you find out.

Thursday, August 28 (Moon in Leo)   Mercury joins Mars in your first house. You're in the public and very talkative. You express yourself well. You make connections that you hadn't realized existed. You adapt quickly to changing circumstances.

Friday, August 29 (Moon in Leo)   The moon is in your eleventh house. You work well in a group setting, especially if you're promoting a cause that helps others. You're responsive to the feelings of others. Friends play an important role. Follow your wishes and dreams.

Saturday, August 30 (Moon in Leo to Virgo 2:19 a.m.) Venus joins Mercury and Mars in your first house. Relations with the opposite sex go well. You're recharged for the month ahead and feel physically vital.

Sunday, August 31 (Moon in Virgo)   The moon is in your twelfth house. After all the high energy and romance yesterday, you feel a need to work behind the scenes. You're somewhat moody; avoid confrontations. Keep your feelings secret. Be aware that matters from the past can rise to the surface.

SEPTEMBER 2008

Monday, September 1 (Moon in Virgo to Libra 7:45 a.m.)   It's a number 9 day. Kick off the month by wrapping up a project and preparing for something new. Reflect on everything that's been taking place. Look for a way to expand your horizons, but don't start anything new.

Tuesday, September 2 (Moon in Libra)   The moon is in your first house along with Mercury, Mars, and Venus. It's a powerful time for you. Your self-awareness is keen. You deal with the person you are becoming. Your feelings and thoughts are aligned.

Wednesday, September 3 (Moon in Libra to Scorpio 4:03 p.m.)   It's a number 2 day. You can easily make use of and enhance your native ability to cooperate and work with others. You seek harmony with those around you. Tensions could flare late in the afternoon, but you have the talent to keep everything on an even keel.

Thursday, September 4 (Moon in Scorpio) The moon is in your second house. Take care of payments and collections. Deal with financial matters. Your assets are important to you. They satisfy your need for a sense of well-being.

Friday, September 5 (Moon in Scorpio) You're passionate. Your sexuality is heightened. It's a day of tense emotional experiences. Investigate a secret matter, and be aware of possible deception. Forgive and forget.

Saturday, September 6 (Moon in Scorpio to Sagittarius 3:12 a.m.) It's a number 5 day. Variety is the spice of life. Promote new ideas; follow your curiosity. You're versatile and changeable, but be careful not to spread out and diversify too much.

Sunday, September 7 (Moon in Sagittarius) Jupiter goes direct in your fourth house. Make decisions that will affect you for the coming year. That's especially true regarding matters related to your home life. You could decide to make renovations or to move. You could decide how you and your partner and loved ones can expand on your home life.

Monday, September 8 (Moon in Sagittarius to Capricorn 3:46 p.m.) It's a number 7 day. Secrets, intrigue, and confidential information play a role. Knowledge is essential to success. Gather information, but don't make any absolute decisions until tomorrow. Go with the flow. Maintain your emotional balance.

Tuesday, September 9 (Moon in Capricorn) The moon is in your fourth house. Stay close to home, if possible. Meditate and reflect on everything that has been going on. Spend time with your family and work on that home-maintenance project. Get rest and recharged for what's coming tomorrow.

Wednesday, September 10 (Moon in Capricorn) Your ambition and drive to succeed are highlighted. Your responsibilities increase. Self-discipline and structure are key. You may feel stressed and overworked. Authority figures, banks, and institutions may play a role, so do a Taurus and a Virgo.

Thursday, September 11 (Moon in Capricorn to Aquarius 3:20 a.m.) It's a number 1 day. Get out and meet new people and have new experiences. Refuse to deal with people who have closed minds. In romance, make room for a new love. A flirtation turns more serious.

Friday, September 12 (Moon in Aquarius) The moon is in your fifth house. Your creativity flourishes. You can delve deep into your subconscious for inspiration. In romance, there's great emotional depth. You're nurturing and protective of children in your life.

Saturday, September 13 (Moon in Aquarius to Pisces 12:05 p.m.) It's a number 3 day. This is your number. Enjoy the harmony, beauty, and pleasures of life. Remain flexible. Intuition is highlighted. You get your ideas across. Your popularity is on the rise.

Sunday, September 14 (Moon in Pisces) The moon is in your sixth house. Keep your resolutions about exercise; watch your diet. Attend to details related to your health. Make a doctor or dentist appointment. Your personal health occupies your attention.

Monday, September 15 (Moon in Pisces to Aries 5:39 p.m.) It's a number 5 day. Change your perspective. Approach the day with an unconventional mind-set. Let go of old structures; get a new point of view. You overcome obstacles with ease.

Tuesday, September 16 (Moon in Aries)   The moon is in your seventh house. The focus turns to relationships, business and personal ones. The opposite sex plays a prominent role. You focus on how the public relates to you. Be careful that others don't manipulate you.

Wednesday, September 17 (Moon in Aries to Taurus 8:57 p.m.)   It's a number 7 day. A confidential matter comes to your attention. Gather information, but don't make any absolute decisions until tomorrow. Sort out what is real and what is not. Go with the flow. Express your desires, but recognize your limitations. A Virgo and a Pisces play distinctive roles.

Thursday, September 18 (Moon in Taurus)   The moon is in your eighth house. Your interest in metaphysics plays a role. So do issues related to sex, death, and rebirth. Your experiences are intense, especially related to a partner. You may take an interest in controlling someone's assets.

Friday, September 19 (Moon in Taurus to Gemini 11:17 p.m.)   It's a number 9 day. Finish up a project. Straighten up your desk and get ready for something new. Visualize the future, set your goals, and get to work.

Saturday, September 20 (Moon in Gemini)   The moon is in your eighth house. Your emphasis is on creating a secure future for yourself and others. You could get a fresh start on a project that works to uplift large numbers of people. Best of luck!

Sunday, September 21 (Moon in Gemini)   You're mentally agile, but you feel restless. Check your e-mail for a special message. Publicize what you're doing. Work on a writing project, especially revising and rewriting.

Monday, September 22 (Moon in Gemini to Cancer 1:49 a.m.)   It's a number 3 day. Enjoy the harmony, beauty, and pleasures of life. Remain flexible. You communicate well. You're warm and receptive to what others say. Spread your good news.

Tuesday, September 23 (Moon in Cancer)   Venus moves into your second house. Your financial situation is going quite well. You tend to have a love of spending and buying new things. Be careful not to overspend. If you're involved in the arts, make money on your creative efforts.

Wednesday, September 24 (Moon in Cancer to Leo 5:14 a.m.)   Mercury goes retrograde in your first house. That means you can expect some delays and glitches in communication, especially related to your health, self-awareness, or personal appearance.

Thursday, September 25 (Moon in Leo)   The moon is in your eleventh house. Focus on your wishes and dreams. Examine your overall goals. Make sure these goals are still an expression of who you are. Friends and groups play an important role. You help the goals of a group, which in turn supports your interests.

Friday, September 26 (Moon in Leo to Virgo 9:53 a.m.)   It's a number 7 day. After yesterday's camaraderie, you're best being on your own. You investigate, analyze, or observe what's going on from a distance. You quickly come to a conclusion and wonder why others don't see what you see. You detect deception and recognize insincerity with ease.

Saturday, September 27 (Moon in Virgo)   The moon is in your twelfth house. Stay out of public view for now. Work behind the scenes. Difficult issues from the past might surface. Confide your thoughts and feelings to a close friend or confidant. Relations with the opposite sex can be difficult.

Sunday, September 28 (Moon in Virgo to Libra 4:06 p.m.)   It's a number 9 day. As the month comes to an end, work on wrapping up a project. Look to the future for ways to expand. Clear up odds and ends. Reflect on everything that's been going on, but don't start anything new.

Monday, September 29 (Moon in Libra) The moon is in your first house. You're sensitive to other people's feelings. You may feel moody. It's all about your emotional self. You're restless and uncertain what to do. Be aware that you can be easily influenced by others.

Tuesday, September 30 (Moon in Libra) It's a number 2 day. Partnerships and cooperation are highlighted. Use your intuition to get a sense of your day, especially as it relates to a partner. Be kind and understanding. Don't make waves or show resentment. Go with the flow.

OCTOBER 2008

Wednesday, October 1 (Moon in Libra to Scorpio 12:27 a.m.) The moon is in your second house. Your values are important. Financial matters occupy your thoughts. Deal with investments. Your assets give you a sense of security and confidence. But watch your spending.

Thursday, October 2 (Moon in Scorpio) Money issues arise again; you could get defensive about recent purchases. Investigate any secret activities. Control issues might arise. Forgive and forget. You're passionate; your sexuality is heightened now.

Friday, October 3 (Moon in Scorpio to Sagittarius 11:15 a.m.) Mars moves into your second house. You feel very strongly about your values. You're competitive in business or financial matters and feel compelled to earn as much money as you can. You're not afraid of taking a risk now.

Saturday, October 4 (Moon in Sagittarius) The moon is in your third house. You deal with the everyday world.

You want to get a message out. Accept an invitation. You could have contact with neighbors or siblings.

Sunday, October 5 (Moon in Sagittarius to Capricorn 11:49 p.m.) It's a number 5 day. Prepare for the changes coming your way. Let go of old structures; find a new point of view. Approach the day in an unconventional way. Experiment, promote new ideas, and take chances. Variety is the spice of life.

Monday, October 6 (Moon in Capricorn) The moon is in your fourth house. You deal with your home life and the foundations of who you are. Spend time at home with family and loved ones. Take the day off, if possible, or work at home. Spend some time in meditation.

Tuesday, October 7 (Moon in Capricorn) Stick with the structure. Don't experiment. Stay inside the box. Self-discipline is emphasized. Your ambition and drive to succeed are highlighted. Your responsibilities increase.

Wednesday, October 8 (Moon in Capricorn to Aquarius 12:03 p.m.) It's a number 8 day. Focus on a power play. You can go far with your plans and achieve financial success. Expect a windfall. Business discussions go well. Be courageous.

Thursday, October 9 (Moon in Aquarius) The moon is in your fifth house. There's great depth in a romantic relationship. Be emotionally honest. You're in touch with your creative side. Children play a role in your day. So do pets.

Friday, October 10 (Moon in Aquarius to Pisces 9:31 p.m.) It's a number 1 day. You get a fresh start. Stress your individuality; take the lead in a new project. Creativity is emphasized. Intuition is highlighted. Explore, discover, and create. In romance, make room for a new love, if that's what you want.

Saturday, October 11 (Moon in Pisces)   The moon is in your sixth house. It's a service-oriented day. Help others, but don't deny your own needs. Take care of any health issues. Don't let your fears hold you back.

Sunday, October 12 (Moon in Pisces)   Your imagination is highlighted. Pay attention to your dreams. Follow your hunches. Watch for synchronicities. You're sensitive and compassionate. Universal knowledge, eternal truths, and deep spirituality play a role in your day.

Monday, October 13 (Moon in Pisces to Aries 3:07 a.m.)   It's a number 4 day. Your organizational skills come into play. Stay focused; emphasize quality. Be methodical and thorough. There could be a tendency to be stubborn.

Tuesday, October 14 (Moon in Aries)   The moon is in your seventh house. A contract binding two people is on the table. Partnerships are emphasized. The opposite sex plays a prominent role. It's difficult to remain detached and objective.

Wednesday, October 15 (Moon in Aries to Taurus 5:31 a.m.)   Mercury goes direct in your first house. Communication goes smoothly, and those personal issues that surfaced fade into the past as misunderstandings are resolved. Any health concerns are clarified.

Thursday, October 16 (Moon in Taurus)   The moon is in your eighth house. Your experiences are intense and could relate to control issues about shared belongings. You could deal with taxes, insurance, or investments. Focus on your sense of stability.

Friday, October 17 (Moon in Taurus to Gemini 6:26 a.m.)   It's a number 8 day. You have a chance to gain recognition, fame, and power. Open your mind to a new approach that could bring in big bucks. Be courageous. You deal with power, so make sure that you don't hurt others.

Saturday, October 18 (Moon in Gemini)   Venus moves into your third house. Try to avoid any arguments and keep everything in balance. You get along well with family members and communicate your thoughts and feelings. Work on a writing project. You make your point with creative flair.

Sunday, October 19 (Moon in Gemini to Cancer 7:41 a.m.)   It's a number 1 day. You're at the top of your cycle. Get out and meet new people and have new experiences. You make connections that others overlook. You're determined and courageous.

Monday, October 20 (Moon in Cancer)   The moon is in your tenth house. Business and professional dealings are highlighted. Your hard work pays off. You get along well with coworkers. Your life is public, but make sure you keep your emotions under control while in the public eye.

Tuesday, October 21 (Moon in Cancer to Leo 10:36 a.m.)   It's a number 3 day. You communicate well. Like yesterday, you're warm and receptive to what others say. Enjoy the harmony, beauty, and pleasures of life. Remain flexible.

Wednesday, October 22 (Moon in Leo)   The moon is in your eleventh house. You join a group of friends or like-minded individuals in pursuit of a common goal. You help the group, and you gain from the group's energy. Follow your wishes and dreams, and make sure that they are still an expression of who you are.

Thursday, October 23 (Moon in Leo to Virgo 3:41 p.m.)   It's a number 5 day. Key words are change, variety, and freedom. Don't be limited by self-imposed restrictions. Take risks; experiment. Change your perspective.

Friday, October 24 (Moon in Virgo)   The moon is in your twelfth house. Withdraw and stay out of the public eye. Avoid confrontations, especially with the opposite sex. Your past could play a role. Unconscious attitudes can be difficult. You communicate your deepest feelings to a friend.

Saturday, October 25 (Moon in Virgo to Libra 10:48 p.m.)   It's a number 7 day. Some of yesterday's energy continues. You work best on your own today. Secrets, intrigue, and confidential information play a role. Gather information, but don't make any absolute decisions until tomorrow. Avoid confusion and conflicts.

Sunday, October 26 (Moon in Libra)   The moon is in your first house. You're sensitive to other people's feelings. You're malleable and easily influenced. Your self-awareness and appearance are important to you. You deal with the person you are becoming. Your thoughts and feelings are aligned.

Monday, October 27 (Moon in Libra)   With the moon on your ascendant, your face is in front of the public. You're recharged for the month ahead. You feel physically vital and appeal to the public. Relations with the opposite sex go well.

Tuesday, October 28 (Moon in Libra to Scorpio 7:48 a.m.)   It's a number 1 day. You get a fresh start. Stress your individuality; don't be afraid to turn in a new direction. Trust your hunches. Be independent and creative; refuse to be discouraged by naysayers. In romance, a flirtation could turn more serious.

Wednesday, October 29 (Moon in Scorpio)   The moon is in your second house. You feel best when surrounded by familiar objects. You equate your financial assets with security. Pay attention to how you are spending your income.

Thursday, October 30 (Moon in Scorpio to Sagittarius 6:41 p.m.)   It's a number 3 day. You communicate well. You're curious and inventive. Spread your good news, but listen to others. Ease up on your routine. Remain flexible.

Friday, October 31 (Moon in Sagittarius)   The moon is in your third house. Take what you know and share it with others. Stay in conscious control of your emotions when making your point, especially when dealing with relatives and neighbors. Express your deepest feelings in a journal.

NOVEMBER 2008

Saturday, November 1 (Moon in Sagittarius)   Neptune goes direct in your fifth house. Your love life takes off. There's an idealistic turn to whatever you do for pleasure. It's a great time for a creative project, especially fiction writing.

Sunday, November 2—Daylight Saving Time Ends (Moon in Sagittarius to Capricorn 6:13 a.m.)   It's a number 3 day. You get your ideas across smoothly and easily. Others appreciate your wit and charm. Foster generosity. You're warm and receptive to what others say. Relax and enjoy yourself.

Monday, November 3 (Moon in Capricorn)   The moon moves into your fourth house. You feel somewhat conflicted between your career and home life. You work hard at your profession, but you feel an urge to spend more time at home with your family. Follow that urge.

Tuesday, November 4 (Moon in Capricorn to Aquarius 7:02 p.m.)   Mercury moves into your second house. There is a lot of discussion related to your finances. You think quick, especially in terms of finances. Your values relate to material wealth rather than to intellectual ideas.

Wednesday, November 5 (Moon in Aquarius)   The moon is in your fifth house. Your creativity is enhanced. You're involved in the creative aspect of your life. You have the ability to go deep into your subconscious for inspiration. In romance, there's great emotional depth.

Thursday, November 6 (Moon in Aquarius)   Friends play an important role. Groups and social events are highlighted. Help others, but dance to your own tune. You have a great sense of freedom as you explore new ideas and look at new options. Find a new perspective.

Friday, November 7 (Moon in Aquarius to Pisces 5:44 a.m.)   It's a number 8 day. It's your power day. Focus on a power play. Financial gain is at hand. Business dealings go well. Be courageous. Fear of failure or fear that you won't measure up will attract tangible experiences that reinforce the feeling.

Saturday, November 8 (Moon in Pisces)   The moon is in your sixth house. Others rely on you for help. You're the go-to person to improve, edit, or refine what others are working on. You're compassionate and sensitive. You think deeply about whatever you're involved in. Keep your resolutions about exercise; watch your diet.

Sunday, November 9 (Moon in Pisces to Aries 12:27 p.m.)   It's a number 1 day. Stress your individuality as you get a fresh start. You creativity is emphasized. Don't be afraid to turn in a new direction. Refuse to deal with people who have closed minds.

Monday, November 10 (Moon in Aries)   The moon moves into your seventh house. You launch a new idea or project that involves a partner. You and your partner could sign a contract. You get off to a quick start. Be careful that others don't manipulate your feelings.

Tuesday, November 11 (Moon in Aries to Taurus 3:06 p.m.)   It's a number 3 day. Your attitude determines everything. You communicate well. Remain flexible. Intuition is highlighted. You're warm and receptive to what others say.

Wednesday, November 12 (Moon in Taurus)   Venus moves into your fourth house. You're loving and affectionate toward your family. You take special care in dealing with a parent. You're happy being home and handling domestic duties. Work on a project to beautify your home.

Thursday, November 13 (Moon in Taurus to Gemini 3:13 p.m.)   It's a number 5 day. Freedom of thought and action is at the center of your day. Promote new ideas; follow your curiosity. A change of scenery will do you good. Get a new perspective. You're versatile and changeable, but be careful not to spread out and diversify too much.

Friday, November 14 (Moon in Gemini)   The moon is in your ninth house. You dream of your future. You've got big ideas. They could involve a long journey to a foreign country. You're intent on breaking out of the everyday routine, but you could change your mind.

Saturday, November 15 (Moon in Gemini to Cancer 2:53 p.m.)   It's a number 7 day. You could launch a journey into the unknown. Secrets, intrigue, and confidential information could play a role. Go with the flow. Keep any secrets entrusted to you. Gather information, but don't make any quick decisions today. Avoid confusion and conflict.

Sunday, November 16 (Moon in Cancer)   Mars moves into your third house. Write in a journal. Be careful not to get too emotional when talking with relatives or neighbors.

Monday, November 17 (Moon in Cancer to Leo 4:08 p.m.)   It's a number 9 day. Finish a project and get ready for something new. Relax and reflect on everything that's been taking place, and look for ways to expand and move beyond any perceived limitations.

Tuesday, November 18 (Moon in Leo)   The moon is in your tenth house. You're at center stage in your professional life. You get a boost in prestige. You get along well with coworkers. You're more in the public, right where you're supposed to be.

Wednesday, November 19 (Moon in Leo to Virgo 8:13 p.m.)   It's a number 2 day. The emphasis turns to cooperation, working with others. Go with the flow. Use your intuition, especially concerning a partnership. But don't forget your own needs. Focus on your direction.

Thursday, November 20 (Moon in Virgo)   The moon is in your twelfth house. Stick close to home and stay out of the public view. Reflect and meditate. Matters from your past may haunt you. You can communicate your deepest feelings to another person.

Friday, November 21 (Moon in Virgo)   Like yesterday, it's best to stay close to home. Take time to write in a journal. Dig deep for information. Take care of details, especially related to your health.

Saturday, November 22 (Moon in Virgo to Libra 3:20 a.m.)   It's a number 5 day. Variety is the spice of life. Change your perspective. Approach the day with an unconventional mind-set. Release old structures; get a new point of view. You can overcome obstacles with ease.

Sunday, November 23 (Moon in Libra)   Mercury moves into your third house. Share what you know with others. However, keep conscious control of your emotions when communicating. Your thinking could be unduly influenced by the past.

Monday, November 24 (Moon in Libra to Scorpio 12:54 p.m.)   It's a number 7 day. You explore a mystery. Dig deep for information. Don't reveal a secret, especially if you've promised to remain quiet. You work best on your own. Maintain your emotional balance.

Tuesday, November 25 (Moon in Scorpio)   The moon is in your second house. You feel intensely emotional related to certain possessions. It's not the objects themselves that are so important as much as the feelings and memories you associate with them. Watch your spending. There's plenty of time before the holidays.

Wednesday, November 26 (Moon in Scorpio)   Pluto moves into your fourth house. You could undergo profound change regarding your family and where you live. But it's a slow process.

Thursday, November 27 (Moon in Scorpio to Sagittarius 12:14 a.m.)   Uranus goes direct in your sixth house. Look for sudden unexpected changes dealing with your work or coworkers. You may have been thinking your job isn't right for you, and the universe may bring one that is. Happy Thanksgiving!

Friday, November 28 (Moon in Sagittarius)   The moon is in your third house. Get your ideas across as you go about your everyday activities. You may be involved in a number of short trips. Stay in conscious control of your emotions. Matters from the past could arise in discussions with relatives.

Saturday, November 29 (Moon in Sagittarius to Capricorn 12:48 p.m.)   It's a number 3 day. Think positive; stay optimistic. Others look to you for inspiration and guidance. You can influence people with your upbeat attitude. In business dealings, diversify. Insist on all the information, not just bits and pieces.

Sunday, November 30 (Moon in Capricorn)   The moon is in your fourth house. You could initiate a romance with someone at work. You feel warmth and compassion regarding a relative. You communicate your feelings well.

DECEMBER 2008

Monday, December 1 (Moon in Capricorn)   With the moon in your fourth house, there's good energy in your home life. Stay home and work on a project to repair or beautify your house. Spend some time in quiet meditation. Recall your dreams.

Tuesday, December 2 (Moon in Capricorn to Aquarius 1:45 a.m.)   It's a number 4 day. Persevere to get things done. Your organizational skills come into play. Tear down the old in order to rebuild. Be methodical and thorough; don't get sloppy. You build foundations for your future.

Wednesday, December 3 (Moon in Aquarius)   With the moon in your fifth house, your emotions tend to overpower your intellect. Be yourself. In love, there's great emotional depth to a relationship.

Thursday, December 4 (Moon in Aquarius to Pisces 1:24 p.m.)   It's a number 6 day. Diplomacy wins the way. Focus on making people happy. Be generous and tolerant. Do a good deed for someone. Visit someone who is ill or in need of help.

Friday, December 5 (Moon in Pisces)   The moon is in your sixth house. Yesterday's energy continues. Others look to your creative touch. Help others, but don't deny your own needs. Take care of your health needs.

Saturday, December 6 (Moon in Pisces to Aries 9:45 p.m.)   It's a number 8 day. It's your power day. Business discussions go well, especially if you open your mind to a new approach. Be courageous. You attract financial success, but be careful not to hurt others.

Sunday, December 7 (Moon in Aries)   Venus moves into your fifth house. You feel vital and attractive to the opposite sex. You get along well with others, especially young people and children. Your popularity is on the rise. Pursue a creative project.

Monday, December 8 (Moon in Aries)   The moon is in your seventh house. You could negotiate or sign a contract. You take the initiative with your partner; emotions could get volatile. It's difficult to maintain an objective and detached point of view. Be careful not to let others manipulate your feelings.

Tuesday, December 9 (Moon in Aries to Taurus 1:53 a.m.) It's a number 2 day. That means partnerships are highlighted. Cooperation is the key word. Don't make waves. Don't rush or show resentment. Let things develop. Use your intuition regarding a relationship.

Wednesday, December 10 (Moon in Taurus) The moon is in your eighth house. Your experiences are intense. The issue at hand could be a joint project or possessions that you share. Try not to manipulate or control the matter. Your actions, for better or worse, could attract the attention of powerful people.

Thursday, December 11 (Moon in Taurus to Gemini 2:34 a.m.) It's a number 4 day. Take care of your obligations. Persevere to get things done. Control your impulses to wander. Be methodical and thorough. Tear down in order to rebuild. Be practical with money.

Friday, December 12 (Moon in Gemini) As Mercury moves into your fourth house, you feel emotionally attached to your home environment. The domestic scene rules. Redecorate a room. You feel close to your parents. Domestic purchases are highlighted today and tomorrow.

Saturday, December 13 (Moon in Gemini to Cancer 1:41 a.m.) It's a number 6 day. Diplomacy wins the way. Be sympathetic, kind, and compassionate. Do a good deed for someone. Attend to someone who is ill or in need of your help. A domestic adjustment works out for the best.

Sunday, December 14 (Moon in Cancer) The moon is in your tenth house, and even though it's Sunday, you focus on a professional matter. You've got homework or you could visit coworkers at a holiday gathering. You're warm and receptive. Your prestige is enhanced.

Monday, December 15 (Moon in Cancer to Leo 1:23 a.m.) It's a number 8 day. Back to work on a power day. Business deals swing your way. You're in the driver's seat. You feel the power. Be especially careful not to run over others as you strive for your financial goals.

Tuesday, December 16 (Moon in Leo) With the moon in your eleventh house, friends play a significant role. They embolden you to pursue your wishes and dreams. You do exceedingly well working with a group, especially if you're involved in a project that emphasizes raising social consciousness.

Wednesday, December 17 (Moon in Leo to Virgo 3:36 a.m.) It's a number 1 day. You're at the top of your cycle. It's a new beginning. Your intuition is highlighted. You make connections that others overlook. Get out and meet new people. You attract creative individuals. Explore and discover.

Thursday, December 18 (Moon in Virgo) The moon is in your twelfth house. Withdraw and work behind the scenes. Don't worry about getting out in public. You could deal with some issues from your past. A long talk with a close friend or confidant helps resolve a matter.

Friday, December 19 (Moon in Virgo to Libra 9:23 a.m.) It's a number 3 day. Your attitude determines everything. Spread your good news. Ease up on routines. Your popularity is on the rise. Your imagination is keen. Remain flexible.

Saturday, December 20 (Moon in Libra) With the moon in your first house, the focus is on self-awareness. You're sensitive to the needs of others and therefore influenced easily. You may feel moody. It's all about your emotional self.

Sunday, December 21 (Moon in Libra to Scorpio 6:37 p.m.) It's a number 5 day. Promote new ideas; follow

305

your curiosity. Freedom of thought and action is key. A change of scenery lifts your spirits. You're versatile and changeable. But be careful not to spread out and diversify too much.

Monday, December 22 (Moon in Scorpio)   The moon is in your second house. Handle finances. Pay your bills and collect what's owed to you. Investments pay off. But watch your spending.

Tuesday, December 23 (Moon in Scorpio)   Your experiences are emotional. You feel best when you're surrounded by your possessions. Investigate, research, and be aware of possible deception.

Wednesday, December 24 (Moon in Scorpio to Sagittarius 6:14 a.m.)   It's a number 8 day. It's your power day. You can go far with your plans and achieve financial success. You play with power, so be careful not to hurt others.

Thursday, December 25 (Moon in Sagittarius)   The moon is in your third house. You communicate well with relatives and neighbors. Spiritual values surface. You get your message across, but don't overdo it. Merry Christmas!

Friday, December 26 (Moon in Sagittarius to Capricorn 6:57 p.m.)   It's a number 1 day. You find yourself back at the top of your cycle. You get a fresh start. Make room for a new love. Get out and do something that you've never done before. You're determined and courageous.

Saturday, December 27 (Moon in Capricorn)   Mars moves into your fourth house. Dig in and work on a home-repair project. There's a lot of energy directed toward the domestic scene. Parents could play a role.

Sunday, December 28 (Moon in Capricorn)   Your ambition and drive to succeed are highlighted. Your responsibilities in the home increase. Your parents again could enter the picture. Maintain your emotional balance. A Taurus and a Virgo play a prominent role.

Monday, December 29 (Moon in Capricorn to Aquarius 7:44 a.m.)   It's a number 4 day. Get caught up on your work before the upcoming holiday. Tear down the old in order to build the new. You can overcome bureaucratic red tape. There could be a tendency to be stubborn, but you can overcome obstacles.

Tuesday, December 30 (Moon in Aquarius)   The moon is in your fifth house. Your emotions tend to overpower your intellect. You're in touch with your creative side. You could be somewhat possessive of loved ones, especially children. In romance, you feel a deep connection.

Wednesday, December 31 (Moon in Aquarius)   Saturn turns retrograde in your twelfth house. Your New Year's plans could get disrupted. Be aware that someone in your party could drink excessively. Don't allow that person to drive.

HAPPY NEW YEAR!

SYDNEY OMARR

Born on August 5, 1926, in Philadelphia, Pennsylvania, Sydney Omarr was the only person ever given full-time duty in the U.S. Army as an astrologer. He is regarded as the most erudite astrologer of our time and the best known, through his syndicated column and his radio and television programs (he was Merv Griffin's "resident astrologer"). Omarr has been called the most "knowledgeable astrologer since Evangeline Adams." His forecasts of Nixon's downfall, the end of World War II in mid-August of 1945, the assassination of John F. Kennedy, Roosevelt's election to a fourth term and his death in office . . . these and many others are on the record and quoted enough to be considered "legendary."

ABOUT THE SERIES

This is one of a series of twelve *Sydney Omarr® Day-by-Day Astrological Guides* for the signs of 2008. For questions and comments about the book, go to www.tjmacgregor.com.